Linear Audo - Volume 2

Authors:

Kendall Castor-Perry

Bob Cordell

EUVL

Gary Galo

Marcel van de Gevel

Samuel Groner

Rudolf Moers

Nelson Pass

Guido Tent

Stuart Yaniger

Opportunity is missed by most people because it comes dressed in overalls and looks like work.
Thomas Edison

Linear Audio is published by Linear Audio of Hoensbroek, The Netherlands.
Published in September 2011.
Second edition September 2013.

Design, Prepress: Fred Zurel, F&N Eigen Beheer - www.eigenbeheer.nl
Production: F&N Eigen Beheer, Castricum, The Netherlands
ISBN: 978198294829

www.linearaudio.net

Digital Audio: Progress, Stagnation and Regression

Gary Galo

Since the beginning of sound recording history the goal in capturing and reproducing a musical event has been to come as close as possible to the sound of the original performance. One of the advantages of being an audio engineer in a large music school is that I hear live, unamplified music on a daily basis. The background of students practicing in the corridors of practice rooms near my office, and the abundance of concerts and recitals on our busy calendar, afford a unique opportunity, and a continual reminder of the sound of the "real thing." Our school of around 550 students has a symphony orchestra, a wind ensemble, two concert bands, two jazz bands, and several choirs, including Crane Chorus, a 200-voice ensemble that performs a major choral work each spring in collaboration with the Crane Symphony Orchestra, and whose history dates back to the group's founding in 1931. The list of distinguished guest conductors who have appeared with the group over the decades includes Robert Shaw, Nadia Boulanger, Leopold Stokowski, Stanley Chapple, Michael Tilson Thomas and Aaron Copland.

The spring 2011 performance was a very special one. Helmuth Rilling, one of the foremost Bach conductors of our time, led an uncut performance of that composer's *Mass in B-minor* after a week of rehearsals, during most of which I sat in the audience, score in hand (ducking back stage on occasion, to see how the sound captured by my recording equipment compared to what I was hearing in the hall). After the final rehearsal, students lined up to have Maestro Rilling autograph their scores. I had something else in mind. I brought a Denon LP dating from 1974 of Rilling performing Bach organ works on the organ of the Gedächtniskirche in Stuttgart. Rilling has made hundreds of recordings during his long career, both as conductor and organist, but this one occupies an interesting place in sound recording history, being one of the first digitally-mastered LP records. Denon had developed the first practical 8-channel digital recorder in 1972, the model DN-023-R, and used that system to produce a number of records during the years that followed.

Denon's early digital recorder, pictured in the LP's accompanying booklet, was literally a truck-load of equipment, including a digital processor, a monitor, and a 4-head, 2-inch video tape recorder for storage of the digital data. It was technically primitive by today's standards. Although it had a 47.25kHz sampling rate, higher than what would be adopted for the Compact Disc eight years later,

its resolution was only 14 bits. When I handed the LP to Maestro Rilling, I asked if he remembered it. He replied "Yes. It was a long time ago." Indeed, and during the intervening 37 years the progress made in digital audio technology has been remarkable.

Re-hearing parts of that record, and another digitally-recorded Denon LP of Janáček's *Sinfonietta* and *Taras Bulba* performed by the Czech Philharmonic Orchestra conducted by Zdeněk Košler made in 1977, is a reminder of the considerable shortcomings of digital audio technology during those formative years. The virtues of digital audio are certainly evident, especially the rock-solid stability of pitch and low background noise, the latter aided by Denon's velvet LP surfaces. But, along with that comes a bright, edgy treble region that was especially unflattering to orchestral strings, a truncation of hall ambience, and an overall sonic picture that, for all of its apparent "clarity," seems cold and analytical. The Janáček recording was a joint venture with Supraphon, and it's interesting to note that the Czechoslovakian record label cut their LPs from the analog tapes run simultaneously at the original sessions.

The next major advance would be the Soundstream digital recording system, used for the first Telarc digitally-mastered LP in 1978 – Frederick Fennell and the Cleveland Symphonic Winds performing, among other works, Holst's First Suite in E-flat for Military Band, with the "bass drum heard 'round the world" at the beginning of the last movement. Soundstream's designer, the late Thomas Stockham, initially made a compromise different from the one chosen by Denon. Stockham opted for 16 bits of resolution, but settled for a lower sampling rate of 37.5kHz. By the time the Soundstream system was used for the first Telarc digital sessions, the sampling frequency had been increased to 50kHz. With a sampling rate higher than what would be adopted for the Compact Disc a few years later, 16 bits of resolution at a time when anything higher than 14 bits was still considered impractical by many designers, and the use of dither, the Soundstream recorder was several years ahead of the competition.

The Fennell recording became an instant audiophile hit, along with two subsequent sonic spectaculars of music by Stravinsky, *The Firebird* Suite with Robert Shaw and the Atlanta Symphony and *Le Sacre du Printemps* with Lorin Maazel and the Cleveland Orchestra. Although many audiophiles complained loud and clear about the shortcomings of the Telarc digital recordings, the Soundstream recorder represented a considerable advance over Denon's 14-bit system. As far as the potential of digital recording was concerned the Denon recordings represented a glass that was half empty. With the Soundstream recorder, as it had evolved by 1978, the glass was now half full. The excellent SACD transfers of those early Telarc recordings show just how far ahead of his time Thomas Stockham really was. Purely from a sonic standpoint, I have little interest in re-hearing any other digital recordings from the 1970s, yet those early Soundstream efforts, as preserved in the superb SACD format, still warrant listening now and then.

Surely no technology has ever been "perfect" the first time around, and many advances in the field

of audio over the past 125 years are no exception. In 1912 Thomas Edison, realizing that the days of the cylinder were numbered, introduced his own proprietary disc record and phonograph, which he called the Diamond Disc. Edison's advertisements proudly proclaimed "the final perfection" of the disc phonograph, and noted opera singers under contract to Edison travelled around the country to participate in Edison's famous "tone tests." An Edison recording of a singer would alternate with the same singer performing live. Listeners were allegedly unable to hear any difference between the live sound and the Edison "Re-Creation." From where we sit today Edison's Diamond Disc records, however advanced they were by the standards of 1912, bear little resemblance to the sound of live music.

Electrical recording, arguably the single most significant advance in the entire history of sound recording, became a commercial reality in 1925 after ten years of work in the laboratory, but it was hardly "perfect" the first time. Though wider in frequency response, and free of the horn resonances that plagued acoustical recording, Western Electric's first condenser microphone and disc cutter had chatter and resonance problems of their own, introducing new types of distortion not heard on acoustically-recorded discs. Fortunately progress in minimizing these problems was rapid, and by mid-1926 several decades of acoustical recordings had been rendered technically obsolete. Early long-playing records, though free of the 3-to-5 minute time limitation of the 78-rpm side, and quieter due to the use of vinyl rather than shellac-based compounds, had narrower frequency response than 78s, often sounding quite dull in the treble region compared to the discs they were replacing. Yet within a few years of their introduction in 1948, the era of "high fidelity" was upon us, and only a handful of music lovers were nostalgic for the 78-rpm record. Indeed, the conductor Fritz Reiner once remarked that, around 1950, records began to sound like music.

Digital audio has been slower in gaining acceptance in the audiophile community. When the Compact Disc was introduced in 1982, consumers finally had the potential of hearing a copy of the digital studio master in their living rooms, and this remained true as long as digital masters were made at the same 44.1kHz/16-bit standard as the finished CD product (most were, Soundstream's 50kHz sampling rate, and British Decca's 48kHz/18-bit system being exceptions). Yet many audiophiles, myself included, found the first CDs and players wanting at best, and excruciatingly bad at their worst. Far from rendering several decades of LP records technically obsolete, many audiophiles would continue to find analog recording more musically natural and satisfying for many years to come.

Although the advantages of recording at higher sampling and bit rates were certainly known, at least from a theoretical standpoint, in the late 1970s, progress in the field of digital audio would be dependent on advances in digital signal processing which, in turn, would require increasing levels of integration and miniaturization at the chip level. Once processed, digital audio data must be stored and the technology available throughout the 1980s had limitations. The Compact Disc pushed the limits of available technology when it was introduced and, indeed, came perilously close to being launched as a 14-bit format.

By around 1990 digital conversion technology – both A/D and D/A – had advanced considerably. I still use a number of CDs from that decade, especially the Mercury Living Presence reissues produced by Wilma Cozart Fine and a number of the RCA Victor Living Stereo discs, as reference material for equipment evaluations. But, as digital recording at higher sampling rates and bit rates became possible, high-resolution masters had to be converted to the CD standard, and the consumer could no longer hear a clone of the digital master in their listening rooms.

The DVD, with a single-layer capacity of 4.7GB, paved the way for high-resolution digital audio for consumers. The DVD-Audio format, introduced in 2000, supports 192kHz sampling rates in 2-channel stereo and 96kHz sampling rates in 5.1 surround, all with 24 bits of resolution. The Super Audio Compact Disc (SACD), the carrier for the Direct-Stream Digital (DSD) recording process, followed in 2002, and was introduced by Sony with great fanfare at the Audio Engineering Society convention in New York City that year. Since the introduction of these formats, high-resolution recording and editing systems, including the Sonoma DSD Recorder/Editor and the Pyramix/Merging Technologies DXD (Digital eXtended Definition) Workstation, have provided ultra-high-performance recording, editing and mastering for these formats. Digital audio has come a long, long way since Denon's DN-023-R digital recording system was used to master Maestro Rilling's 1974 LP of Bach organ works. Today's high-resolution digital technology can produce recordings of unprecedented accuracy and realism, and also offers the capability of converting classic analog recordings to the digital domain with fidelity to the original that was unheard of during the first two decades of digital audio.

There are still music lovers who prefer the sound of vinyl, and continue to support the niche market for audiophiles LPs, many of which are excellent. I've been collecting disc records for almost 50 years, and I still take pleasure in building and refining equipment to play not only LPs, but the 3000-plus 78-rpm recordings in my collection. But, as much as I enjoy playing analog recordings, and getting the best possible sound from them, I firmly believe that digital audio has evolved to the point where there's no longer any cause for complaint. In recent years I have made high-resolution digital transfers of many high-quality analog tapes, including some that I recorded many years ago, along with some recorded by others. Having had the opportunity to compare LP records cut from these tapes to my recent digital transfers, there's no question in my mind that the digital transfers are more faithful to the original tapes than the LPs. Indeed, digital audio is now so good that it's tempting to proclaim "the final perfection" of sound recording, as Edison did back in 1912. I know better, of course, and twenty years from now, if my hearing is still intact, I may very well have a different view of the digital audio technology that existed in 2011. That said, when I listen to the best SACDs and DVD-Audio discs in my collection, I find myself wondering just how much better it really can, or needs to, be.

All of this should cause consumers of recorded music to rejoice, but it hasn't. Sadly, the average consumer has shown little interest in high-resolution digital audio, and ever decreasing interest in the

Compact Disc. Sony hoped that the SACD would eventually replace the conventional CD, but this was not to be. By the 2007 AES convention there was no trace of Direct Stream Digital or the SACD in Sony's booth, its inventor having ceased support for the format. With only a handful of exceptions, it's now difficult to find anyone promoting high-resolution digital audio at AES conventions. Furthermore, the possession of recordings as physical artifacts seems to be rapidly disappearing, and concern for sound quality is at an all-time low. Downloads are becoming the preferred method for purchasing new recordings, in compressed formats for MP3 players, iPods and the like, despite their mediocre sound quality. For those of us who have spent our lives as serious record collectors, this is a lamentable situation. I view a great recording as more than just a file on a hard drive. It's a physical entity with liner notes, artwork and, hopefully, a medium that captures a performance worthy of preservation in the best possible sound.

The audio and recording industry has, naturally, reflected the wishes of the marketplace. Only a handful of audiophile labels continue to issue SACDs (in many cases, the same audiophile labels that continue to produce high-quality LPs), and hardly any are making DVD-Audio discs. SACD and DVD-Audio, far from being embraced by the consumer, have become fringe audiophile formats appealing to a very small percentage of the music-buying public. There are those, including some of the promoters of Pure Audio Blu-ray, who would say that the "format war" between DVD-Audio and SACD killed both formats. This is nonsense, in my view. Within a year of Sony's introduction of the SACD there were universal players that would handle all of the existing 120mm digital audio formats. Since DVD-Audio and SACD both use a DVD as the physical medium, we were spared another Beta vs VHS battle, which involved physically-incompatible media. SACD and DVD-Audio failed in the marketplace due to a lack of interest in high quality sound.

With no advances in digital audio standards over the past 10 years, one could say that digital audio technology has entered a period of stagnation. We should be so lucky. As I stated earlier, the current state of high-resolution digital audio is so good that, were it to remain at this level for the foreseeable future, I could be a very happy listener. No, rather than stagnation, we are in a period of regression. Consumer preference for compressed, quickly-downloadable audio formats has done more than merely bringing progress in digital audio to a halt – it has taken the reproduction of music backwards. By the mid-1990s most of the problems inherent in early digital recording and the first generation of CDs – harsh treble, truncation of hall ambience, poor soundstage reproduction, cold and analytical sound, etc. – had been greatly minimized. The development of high-resolution formats has made those problems a thing of the past. But compressed formats have brought all of those problems back. Sadly, an entire generation of young people has grown up listening to those formats, with no exposure to high-quality sound reproduction. Without realizing it, the youngest generation of music listeners has very low expectations regarding audio, because they've never been exposed to anything better. This does not bode well for the future of audio or the already-troubled recording industry.

Can the Pure Audio Blu-ray format save the day? Strictly in terms of sound quality, the format offers no sonic improvement over the SACD, and its only advantage over DVD-Audio is 192kHz sampling rates in surround (DVD-Audio supports 192kHz sampling rates in stereo, but is "limited" to 96kHz in surround). But, this autonomous audio format developed for the Blu-ray disc does offer a couple of other advantages over SACD and DVD-Audio. One is the lack of special hardware requirements, which neither SACD nor DVD-Audio could claim. Any Blu-ray player can play Pure Audio discs, as well as conventional CDs – you don't need to purchase a special or "universal" player. Unlike DVD-Audio discs that contain multiple programs, Pure Audio Blu-ray discs don't require the users to turn on their televisions to select the program they wish to play. I resent having to turn on my television to play an audio-only disc and have always found this aspect of DVD-Audio to be a decided annoyance. The developers of the Pure Audio Blu-ray format – msm-studios in Munich – defined the functions of the color buttons found on all Blu-ray player remote controls for selection of stereo or the various surround programs. Those definitions have now been endorsed as a standard by the Audio Engineering Society.

The major record companies are sitting on a treasure trove of superb analog tapes, in all genres of music, most of which have not been transferred to high-resolution digital formats. BMG transferred a large quantity of the RCA Victor Living Stereo material to SACD, many of which were sonically excellent. Universal also did a handful of fine SACD transfers of the Mercury Living Presence catalog. But, both companies got burned by poor sales, so those projects were terminated. The Pure Audio Blu-ray format presents an opportunity to try again, but this will only happen if money can be made on such projects. This will require a major change in the listening habits of consumers. Serious music listening is not something that can accompany jogging or mowing the lawn. It requires sitting in an optimally-placed chair, in a room with equipment of reasonable quality, and simply *listening*. It does require setting aside time to do so, but for those of us who find life without music unimaginable the rewards are enormous. Pure Audio Blu-ray has the potential to introduce an entire generation of listeners to the possibilities of high-quality audio. Though I'm not optimistic, I would welcome being proven wrong!

Both Menno Vanderveen and Marcel van de Gevel commented on Bruno Putzey's article
The F-word - or, why there is no such thing as too much feedback;

Cyril Bateman and Samuel Groner commented to Ed Simon on Resistor non-linearity –
there's more to Ω than meets the eye;

Brad Wood and Burkhard Vogel commented to Ovidiu Popa's article On the Noise performance of
Low Noise Input Stages.

Read these and all other Letters and the author's reply on-line at www.linearaudio.net

*Due to unforeseen circumstances, the second part of Scott Wurcer's low noise mike preamplifier design
will appear in Volume 3.*

The Ultra-linear Power Amplifier - Expressions and symbols used in this article

'Working point': this is the combination of anode, cathode and grid voltages that define the operational voltages and currents of the tube. Also called 'bias point' or 'quiescent point'.

'Control grid base': the possible range of $V_{g1,k}$ between $V_{g1,k}=0$ and the cutoff-point for $I_a=0$.

Expressions and symbols related to the anode:

Anode static transconductance	:	$S = \dfrac{\Delta I_a}{\Delta V_{g1,k}}$	(constant V_{ak} and $V_{g2,k}$)
For small signals	:	$S = \dfrac{i_a}{v_{g1,k}}$	(constant V_{ak} and $V_{g2,k}$)
Anode AC <u>internal</u> resistance	:	$r_i = \dfrac{\Delta V_{ak}}{\Delta I_a}$	(constant $V_{g1,k}$ and $V_{g2,k}$)
For small signals	:	$r_i = \dfrac{v_{ak}}{i_a}$	(constant $V_{g1,k}$ and $V_{g2,k}$)
Anode amplification factor	:	$\mu = \left\|\dfrac{\Delta V_{ak}}{\Delta V_{g1,k}}\right\|$	(constant I_a and $V_{g2,k}$)
For small signals	:	$\mu = \left\|\dfrac{v_{ak}}{v_{g1,k}}\right\|$	(constant I_a and $V_{g2,k}$)
Anode penetration factor	:	$D_a = \mu^{-1} = \dfrac{1}{\mu}$	

Expressions and symbols related to the screen grid:

Screen grid static transconductance:		$S_2 = \dfrac{\Delta I_{g2}}{\Delta V_{g1,k}}$	(constant V_{ak} and $V_{g2,k}$)
For small signals	:	$S_2 = \dfrac{i_{g2}}{v_{g1,k}}$	(constant V_{ak} and $V_{g2,k}$)
Screen grid AC <u>internal</u> resistance	:	$r_{i2} = \dfrac{\Delta V_{g2,k}}{\Delta I_{g2}}$	(constant $V_{g1,k}$ and V_{ak})
For small signals	:	$r_{i2} = \dfrac{v_{g2,k}}{i_{g2}}$	(constant $V_{g1,k}$ and V_{ak})
Screen grid amplification factor	:	$\mu_{g2,g1} = \left\|\dfrac{\Delta V_{g2,k}}{\Delta V_{g1,k}}\right\|$	(constant I_{g2} and V_{ak})
For small signals	:	$\mu_{g2,g1} = \left\|\dfrac{v_{g2,k}}{v_{g1,k}}\right\|$	(constant I_{g2} and V_{ak})
Screen grid penetration factor	:	$D_{g2} = \mu_{g2,g1}^{-1} = \dfrac{1}{\mu_{g2,g1}}$	

Further expressions and symbols:

Barkhausen anode formula	:	$\mu = S \cdot r_i$
Barkhausen screen grid formula	:	$\mu_{g2,g1} = S_2 \cdot r_{i2}$
Pentode in triode mode	:	$\mu_{pentode\ as\ triode} = \mu_{g2,g1}$
Anode AC <u>external</u> resistance	:	r_a (external AC load at the anode)

The Ultra-Linear Power Amplifier
An adventure between triode and pentode

Rudolf Moers

1 Introduction

In 1951, David Hafler and Herbert Keroes introduced a pentode power amplifier, in which a tap of the primary transformer winding was connected to the screen grid of the power pentode [2]. They called this the Ultra-Linear power amplifier. This power amplifier shows the advantages of a triode, low anode AC internal resistance and low distortion, as well as the advantages of a pentode, large delivered anode AC power and good efficiency. The narrative given by David Hafler and Herbert Keroes is good and substantiated in practice; this is very important.

What I personally missed in their narration is a theoretical explanation of the operation of the ultra-linear circuit. I have several electronics books including the well known seven parts of the electron tube book range, written by scientists of the Philips Gloeilampenfabrieken Company at Eindhoven in the Netherlands. I also have all the electronics books of the company school written by A.J. Sietsma. In none of these books did I find a theoretical explanation of the operation of the ultra-linear circuit. I do not suggest that such an explanation does not exist; I just have not been able to find it. Therefore I went on an adventure between triode and pentode myself. In this adventure, theory will be checked against practice.

Opgave 5

Gegeven:

$R_i = 50 \text{ k}\Omega$; $S = 12\frac{1}{2} \text{ mA/V}$;
$\mu_{g2g1} = 15$; $S_2 = 2,5 \text{ mA/V}$;
$n_1 : n_2 : n_3 = 40 : 1 : 15$; $R_{lsp} = 7,5 \Omega$.

Gevraagd:

1. Bereken $\dfrac{v_a}{v_i}$ indien men de eindtrap niet tegenkoppelt (d.w.z. g_2 ligt dan aan punt A).

2. Bereken $\dfrac{v_a}{v_i}$ indien men de eindtrap wel tegenkoppelt (zoals in het gegeven schema).

3. Welke soort tegenkoppeling treedt er hier op?
   Opmerking: zie blz. 343, opgave 18.

Figure 1. Homework exercise from the great book from 1959 by A.J. Sietsma [3].

When doing research for my book [1], I was pleasantly surprised to find the homework exercise of **figure 1**. Unfortunately, it is in Dutch but you should be able to understand the circuit.

Philips never published information concerning ultra-linear power gain because they never produced such an amplifier. I contacted Sietsma about the why and how of this homework exercise, but he is too old to be able to answer. His son told me that his father used to make up all homework exercises himself. He probably wanted to check the knowledge of his students concerning "screen grid negative feedback" which is the technical name for the marketing name Ultra-Linear.

It was this homework exercise which motivated me to do a close investigation of the ultra-linear power amplifier. Thanks to Sietsma I developed my own network analysis of the circuit, which he probably also did, although it was never published. Using my own network analysis method I solved this exercise in 2006, and achieved the same results as Sietsma. During the European Triode Festival (ETF) 2010, I presented a paper on this subject and for an extended narration I recommend reference [1].

2   An adventure between triode and pentode

You seldom encounter a single ended ultra-linear power amplifier. In principle, it is very well possible to construct one, but I do not know whether these power amplifiers perform satisfactorily. However, the single ended ultra-linear power amplifier is very suitable to explain the Ultra-Linear concept. We will see later that a *separate* explanation of the push pull ultra-linear power amplifier in classes A, B and AB with their calculations of powers and efficiencies is not required. This seems too good to be true, but I will show it to be so. In **figure 2** we have the single ended topology with anode AC external resistance r_a. The related anode characteristics $I_a = f(V_{ak})$ with the $V_{g1,k}$-curve which lies halfway inside the control grid base are also given (see sidebar for explanation of terms and symbols). This is the most favorable working point because we are then in the middle of the upper and lower bends of the anode static/dynamic transconductance $I_a = f(V_{g1,k})$. We must avoid these bends because of the distortions they cause. The <u>triode connection</u> gives $V_{g2,k} = V_{ak} \neq$ constant and the <u>pentode connection</u> gives $V_{g2,k} = V_b =$ constant. The reason that both anode characteristics are not linear is also visible with the related Child-Langmuir equations above in the anode characteristics of figure 2.

With the <u>triode connection,</u> we see a faint concave curvature. With the <u>pentode connection,</u> we see a steep convex curvature and after the knee it changes into an almost horizontal flat line. Anticipating what will come later, an x-coordinate is shown along the primary winding of the output transformer. The transformer terminal connected to V_b is the point where $x = 0$. Because V_b is a short circuit for AC currents, we can say that $x = 0 =$ grounded. The terminal of the transformer connected to the anode is where $x = 1$. Scale x is divided linearly along the primary transformer winding.

What would we do, if we would want a linear anode characteristic in the form $I_a = k_{ultralinear} \cdot V_{ak}$?

If the triode and pentode anode characteristics are *concave* and *convex* respectively, we can then imagine that between *concave* and *convex* there is a *linear compromise*. Screen grid g_2 connected to the anode makes the anode characteristic *concave* and connected to V_b makes the anode characteristic *convex*.

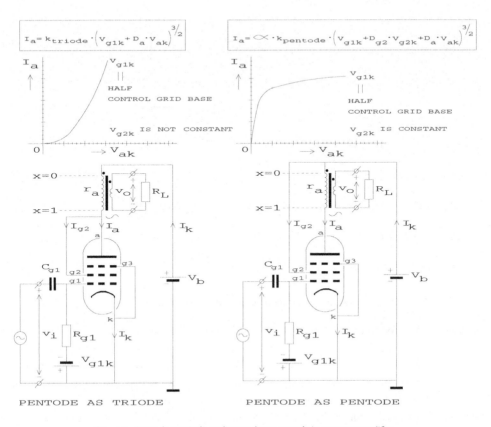

Figure 2. Pentode as triode and pentode as pentode in a power amplifier.

Thus, it is obvious that the connection of screen grid g_2 to the primary transformer winding, somewhere in between the anode and V_b, will give a more linear anode characteristic and that is shown in **figure 3**.

The impedance between the screen grid primary transformer tap x and V_b is called $x \cdot r_a$ and the impedance between this tap and the anode is called $(1-x) \cdot r_a$. Because V_b is a short circuit for AC currents, we can say that screen grid cathode AC voltage $v_{g2,k}$ is a tap of anode cathode AC voltage v_{ak}. The screen grid cathode DC voltage $V_{g2,k}$ still applies to the screen grid, but from here on, screen grid cathode AC voltage $v_{g2,k}$ is superimposed. $(V_{g2,k} + v_{g2,k})$ changes dynamically and because of this, the attractive force on the electrons in the electron cloud around the cathode changes dynamically. The screen grid behaves slightly adversely as does the anode with triodes, but with a less attractive force than in a real triodes.
You can also see this in the pentode equation: $i_a = S \cdot \left(v_{g1,k} + \dfrac{v_{g2,k}}{\mu_{g2,g1}} + \dfrac{v_{ak}}{\mu} \right)$ see reference [1]

13

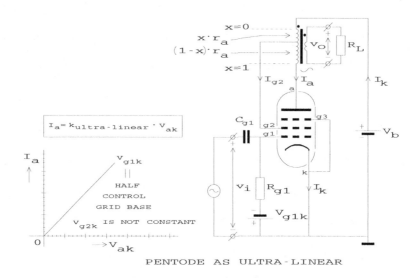

PENTODE AS ULTRA-LINEAR

Figure 3. Pentode as ultra-linear power amplifier.

Because μ is large for pentodes, the factor v_{ak}/μ can be neglected. In addition, as long as the screen grid is decoupled by a C_{g2} or by an external voltage source $V_{g2,k}$, then $v_{g2,k} = 0$ and due to this factor, $v_{g2,k}/\mu_{g2,g1} = 0$. However, $v_{g2,k} \neq 0$ and $\mu_{g2,g1}$ is not large thus factor $v_{g2,k}/\mu_{g2,g1}$ can no longer be neglected and gives a significant contribution to anode AC current i_a. Output signals v_{ak} and $v_{g2,k}$ are opposite in phase to the input signal $v_{g1,k} = v_i$ and counteract anode AC current i_a. This is a classic case of *voltage negative feedback*. Figure 3 also shows the linear anode characteristic $I_a = f(V_{ak})$ and again with the $V_{g1,k}$-curve which lies halfway inside the control grid base. Once again, this is the most favorable working point because here we are in between the upper and lower bends of the anode static/dynamic transconductance $I_a = f(V_{g1,k})$. Thus, the constant $k_{ultralinear}$ is a real constant, and independent of $V_{g2,k}$ and V_{ak}. When we neglect the primary transformer copper resistance ($R_p = 0$), we can say $V_b = V_{ak} = V_{g2,k}$. We will see later that $v_{g2,k}$ is almost equal to $x \cdot v_{ak}$. This equation seems obvious, but is not fully correct, although in practice it can be applied without large errors. I will come back to this issue later.

The next question is, at which screen grid tap or for which value of x do we get a linear anode characteristic? **Figure 4** shows the answer: for $x = 0.4$.

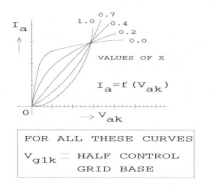

Figure 4. Dynamic ultra-linear anode characteristic $I_a = f(V_{ak})$ with x as parameter.

The value **x = 0.4** is an "average opinion" of the manufacturers of output transformers and electron tubes. Some of them use **x = 0.33** as an "average opinion". Actually, x is different for each type of electron tube, sometimes on each specimen of one type. So what is the ideal value of tap x for a certain application? You must be pragmatic in this situation, because what if the ideal value would be $x = 0.38$? Should we then get a specific output transformer for this value? Or can we make do with an output transformer with several taps to choose $x = 0.30$, $x = 0.35$ or $x = 0.40$? All these taps do not contribute to the transformer bandwidth and other quality aspects. Maybe you should just choose $x = 0.4$ and accept that you don't have an ideal linearity for each pentode specimen.

In section 5 of this article we will do a nice practical determination of x for a specific pentode specimen.

3 Power and efficiency

Figure 4 shows that we have a pentode behaving as a pentode for $x = 0.0$ and a pentode behaving as a triode for $x = 1.0$.

This corresponds with the x-values shown in figures 2 and 3. Additionally, all $V_{g1,k}$-curves lie halfway inside the control grid base. How would it look for other $V_{g1,k}$-curves? That can be seen in **figure 5**. With a reasonable triode, see figure 5.a, curve $V_{g1,k} = 0$ goes through the origin of the anode characteristic. With a reasonable pentode, see figure 5.c, curve $V_{g1,k} = 0$ lies almost at the top of the anode characteristic. *Purely hypothetical*, imagine the screen grid tap is adjustable with a slider on the primary winding of a variable output transformer. When the slider moves from $x = 0$ to $x = 1$, the anode characteristic goes from pentode to triode, see figures 5.c and 5.a respectively. When the slider moves back to $x = 0.4$, you can see the situation of figure 5.b. Here, the $V_{g1,k}$-curve which lies halfway inside the control grid base, goes through the origin of the anode characteristic and curve $V_{g1,k} = 0$ lies well above the origin. Even with an ideal triode, curve $V_{g1,k} = 0$ never lies above the origin. This gives great expectation and promise when we apply full-power drive to control grid g_1.

Driving the control grid beyond $V_{g1,k} = 0$ is not desirable due to control grid current which must be avoided. We have the lowest drive level with v_{ap} (anode peak AC voltage) with the triode, because we are limited by curve $V_{g1,k} = 0$. We have the highest drive level with v_{ap} with the pentode, despite the limit of the knee which lies not far from the I_a-axis. With ultra-linear, the drive level with v_{ap} is significantly more than with the triode and is just slightly less with the pentode. The limit for ultra-linear is caused by the *constriction* of the $V_{g1,k}$-curves.

In the ideal case of ultra-linear mode, the $V_{g1,k}$-curves between 0 and halfway in the control grid base will end at the I_a-axis, and the $V_{g1,k}$-curves between halfway in the control grid base and the complete control grid base will end on the V_{ak}-axis. Furthermore, curve $V_{g1,k} = \frac{1}{2} \cdot V_{g1,k0}$ will go straight through the origin of the anode characteristic. However, ideal pentodes do not exist; but we can recognize the following relationship: $v_{ap,triode} \ll v_{ap,ultra\text{-}linear} < v_{ap,pentode}$

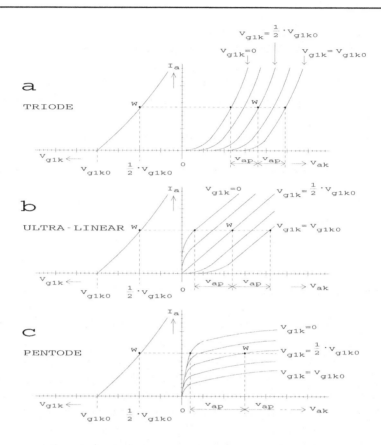

Figure 5. Comparison of the dynamic transconductance and dynamic anode characteristics for triode, ultra-linear and pentode mode.

Figure 6 from [6] shows the practical anode characteristics $I_a = f(V_{ak})$ of a KT88 pentode in triode, ultra-linear with $x = 0.4$ (40 % tap) and pentode mode. The lower right in figure 6 shows how the manufacturer specifies the ultra-linear anode characteristics $I_a = f(V_{ak})$ in practice. In this case, the $V_{g1,k}$-curves lie between 0 V and −60 V. With some interpolation, the center curve $V_{g1,k} = -30$ V goes rather nicely through the origin. Curve $V_{g1,k} = 0$ V starts parallel on the I_a-axis and curves slightly horizontal at the top of the anode characteristic. Curve $V_{g1,k} = -60$ V lies almost flat against the V_{ak}-axis. The constrictions of all $V_{g1,k}$-curves to the origin are not shown correctly. This part of the anode characteristic is probably different for each specimen, and moreover we must avoid drive levels in that v_{ap} range. Let us make a comparison between the distances of the curves $V_{g1,k} = 0$ and the I_a-axis for triode, ultra-linear and pentode mode **(table 1)**:

Note: The vertical position of the $V_{g1,k}$-curves in $I_a = f(V_{ak})$ depend on the magnitude of $Vg_{2,k}$. For ultra-linear and for pentode this is similar.

Triode	$Vg2,k = V_{ak}$; $Ia = 100$mA	$Vg1,k = 0$ to Ia-axis:	75V
Ultra-Linear	$Vg2,k = 276$ V; $Ia = 100$mA	$Vg1,k = 0$ to Ia-axis:	30V
Pentode	$Vg2,k = 300$ V; $Ia = 100$mA	$Vg1,k = 0$ to Ia-axis:	20V

Table 1. Voltage distance between Vg1,k = 0 and the Ia-axis.

Svetlana KT88
High Performance Audio
Beam Power Tetrode

Typical Operation Class A₁ (single tube)

DC plate voltage	400	V
Grid no.2 DC (screen) voltage	225	V
Grid no.1 DC (control) voltage	-16.5	V
Peak AF grid no.1 (control) voltage	16.5	V
Zero-signal plate current	87	mA
Max signal plate current	105	mA
Zero signal grid no.2 (screen) current	4	mAdc
Max signal grid no.2 (screen) current	18	mA
Transconductance	11.5	mA/Volt
Signal output	19	W

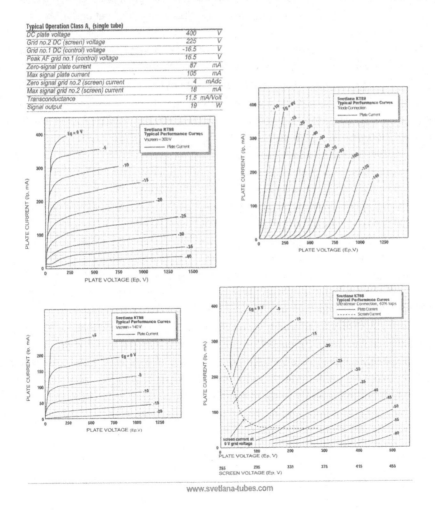

www.svetlana-tubes.com

Figure 6. KT88 Beam Power Tetrode in triode, ultra-linear (x = 0.4 = 40%) and pentode mode.

Figure 7 shows the theoretical ideal versions of the practical figures 5 and 6. Anode AC peak voltage v_{ap} and anode AC peak current i_{ap}, which determine the delivered anode power, are smaller in triode mode than in ultra-linear mode. However, in pentode mode, anode AC peak voltage v_{ap} and anode AC peak current i_{ap} are equal to those in ultra-linear mode. This means that the *delivered anode power in ultra-linear mode is equal to the delivered anode power pentode mode*. This is very desirable. Furthermore, we can see that the *$V_{g1,k}$-curves in ultra-linear mode have the same linearity as the $V_{g1,k}$-curves in triode mode*. This too is very desirable.

Figures 7.b and 7.c show two "fictive rotation points":
When we rotate all the $V_{g1,k}$-curves of figure 7.b clockwise 45° we get figure 7.c.
When we rotate all the $V_{g1,k}$-curves of figure 7.c counterclockwise 45° we get figure 7.b.

Once again, anode AC peak voltage v_{ap} and anode AC peak current i_{ap} are the same in ultra-linear mode and in pentode mode. Both modes have the same delivered anode power.
This means that we do not need to derive separate equations for ultra-linear mode; we can just take the results from the pentode case. This is applicable for single ended or push pull in classes A, B and AB, but only in theory, of course. How should we handle this in practice? We can not use the situation of figure 7, but we *can* use the situation of figure 6.
Earlier we saw that: $\mathbf{v_{ap,triode} \ll v_{ap,ultra\text{-}linear} < v_{ap,pentode}}$
In reality, the mentioned "constriction" in ultra-linear mode is larger than the "knee area" of the pentode mode. We must not use these areas, to avoid non-linear distortions. Thus, if you want to calculate the delivered anode power in ultra-linear mode, first calculate the delivered anode power in pentode mode and decrease it by a certain factor. But how much should it be decreased?

It seems to me that an estimate of between 20 % and 30 % should be subtracted from the delivered anode power in pentode mode. Now where does your author get this insight?
In reference [4], some design examples are shown with the following results for output power:
Two EL34 with VDV6040PP transformer: $p_{triode} = $ 13 W, $p_{ultra\text{-}linear} = 33$ W and $p_{pentode} = 40$ W
Four EL34 with VDV3070PP transformer: $p_{triode} = $ 30 W, $p_{ultra\text{-}linear} = 70$ W and $p_{pentode} = 80$ W
Thus, the estimate of between 20 % and 30 % decrease seems reasonable. In addition, the delivered power in ultra-linear mode is quite sufficient for listening to in your living room. It is obvious that the efficiency of ultra-linear mode lies between the efficiencies of triode and pentode mode. In the practical section 7 of this article we will see that the power behavior and the efficiency of ultra-linear mode come closer to pentode mode than to triode mode.

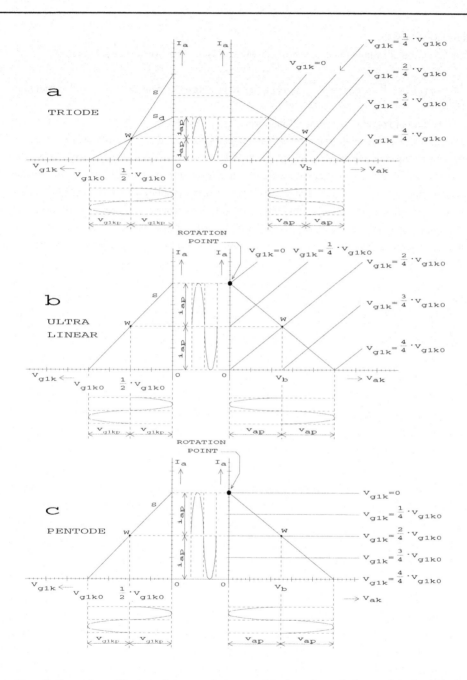

Figure 7. Comparison of the dynamic transconductance and the dynamic anode characteristics for an ideal triode, an ideal ultra-linear configuration and an ideal pentode.

4 Network analysis

Consider again the ultra-linear circuit of figure 3. My goal is to show you anode AC gain

$A_a = \dfrac{v_{ak}}{v_{g1,k}} = f(x)$, circuit AC gain $A = \dfrac{v_o}{v_i} = f(x)$ and circuit output AC resistance $r_{out} = f(x)$ as function

of the screen grid tap position x on the primary transformer winding.

Before we apply a network analysis for the ultra-linear power amplifier, a review of the pentode characteristics and pentode quantities is necessary. Especially so because current manufacturers of pentodes deliver poor and inconsistent datasheets. One quantity has several names worldwide: conductance, transconductance, mutual conductance, slope, steilheid (Dutch) and steilheit (German) with symbol g, g_m and S. Another one is anode AC internal resistance which can be called r_i or plate resistance r_p or R_p or anode resistance r_a. It's important to have these definitions clear to understand the following narrative. I have listed the various expressions and symbols I use in this article in the sidebar.

Figures 8 and 9 show how the various pentode quantities can be determined from the pentode characteristics. There's noting new here; you can find the same information in many vintage electronics books.

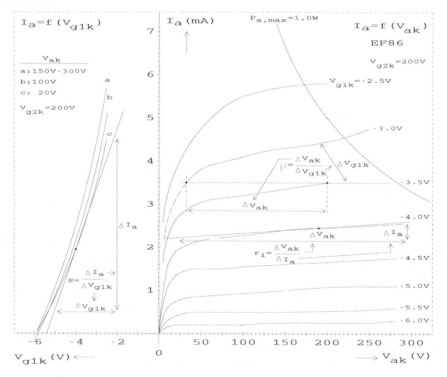

Figure 8. Determination of the anode quantities.

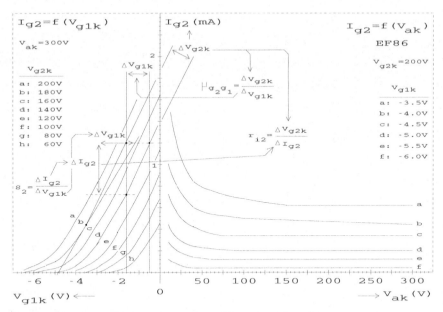

Figure 9. Determination of the screen grid quantities.

Figure 10 shows anode current I_a and screen grid current I_{g2} in one characteristic. We see that the cut-off points of both transconductance curves are positioned equally on the $V_{g1,k}$-axis at a certain $V_{g2,k}$. So both control grid bases are equal: $\Delta V_{g1,k \text{ for } S} = \Delta V_{g1,k \text{ for } S2}$

This gives $V_{g1,k} = \dfrac{\Delta I_a}{S} = \dfrac{\Delta I_{g2}}{S_2}$ and the relationship between anode current and screen grid current

is: $I_{g2} = \dfrac{S_2}{S} \cdot I_a$ and $i_{g2} = \dfrac{S_2}{S} \cdot i_a$

We have already seen pentode equation:

$$i_a = S \cdot \left(v_{g1,k} + \frac{v_{g2,k}}{\mu_{g2,g1}} + \frac{v_{ak}}{\mu} \right)$$

But now we can see a second one:

$$i_{g2} = S_2 \cdot \left(v_{g1,k} + \frac{v_{g2,k}}{\mu_{g2,g1}} + \frac{v_{ak}}{\mu} \right)$$

You can now see the beginning of this section as an introduction for the next part of the narration and to recognize equations and symbols. From now on, in the rest of this section much will "fall from the sky" and normally I do not like that, but I do not want to bore you with equation derivation. In reference [1] all following mathematics are derived in small and easy steps. A piece of cake really, but now I will show you only the direction of the network analyses.

21

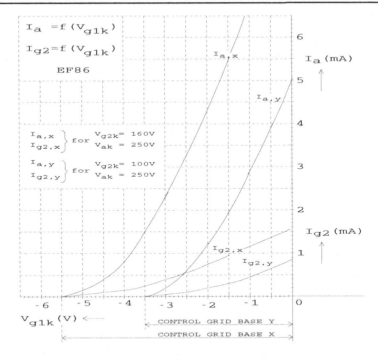

Figure 10. Anode DC current and screen grid DC current in a single steepness graph.

With help of both pentode equations and some mathematical tricks it is possible to obtain a *current source equivalent circuit* and *a voltage source equivalent circuit* for the pentode.
When we apply these equivalent circuits with an output transformer with screen grid tap, we then obtain the *current source equivalent circuit* and *a voltage source equivalent circuit* for the *pentode as ultra-linear power amplifier*.
These equivalent circuits have as original the circuit of figure 3, and are shown in **figure 11**.

We neglect the copper resistances of the transformer windings. Furthermore, we consider that transformer efficiency $\eta_{transformer}$ = 100%. Kirchhoff's first law is still $i_k = i_a + i_{g2}$ for AC and load resistor R_L is purely resistive. Using some mesh-network rules we can derive the important equation:

$$\frac{v_{ak}}{r_a} = -\left(i_a + x \cdot i_{g2}\right) = -i_{total}$$

Important note: total AC current i_{total} is _not the same_ as cathode AC current i_k!

Anode AC current i_a and a fraction **x** of the of screen grid AC current i_{g2} deliver the primary power to anode AC external resistance r_a. This is really an algebraic approach. The approach from figure 11 is as follows:
i_a and i_{g2} together are active in the primary part $x \cdot r_a$ and i_a alone is active in primary part $(1 - x) \cdot r_a$.
What we do algebraically is to define a total AC current i_{total} which flows through the total anode AC external resistance r_a and which does not 'see' the tap to the screen grid.

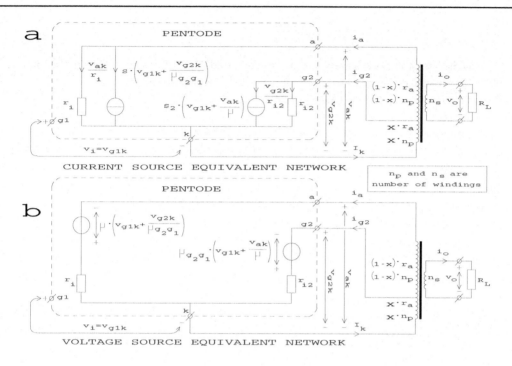

Figure 11. Current source equivalent circuit (a) and voltage source equivalent circuit (b) of the ultra-linear power amplifier.

Anode AC current i_a and screen grid AC current i_{g2}, which, in reality, see partially different AC resistances, are replaced by $i_{total} = (i_a + x \cdot i_{g2})$ which flows through <u>one</u> AC resistance. *However, r_a without screen grid tap and i_{total} are both fictional. Admittedly, our imagination is put to the test.*
In section 8, I will show you that these assertions are actually allowed.

Further it would be nice if $x = \dfrac{v_{g2,k}}{v_{ak}}$ but in that case the current through $x \cdot r_a$ must be the same as

the current through $(1-x) \cdot r_a$. Unfortunately that is not the situation, but in practice $x = 0.4$ and $i_{g2} \approx 0.2 \times i_a$.

Thus $\dfrac{v_{ak}}{r_a} = -(i_a + x \cdot i_{g2})$ becomes $\dfrac{v_{ak}}{r_a} = -(i_a + 0.4 \times 0.2 \times i_a) = 1.08 \times i_a = -i_{total} \approx i_a$.

Thus, statement $x = \dfrac{v_{g2,k}}{v_{ak}}$ is allowed.

Now we have all mathematical tools to derive anode AC gain $A_a = \dfrac{v_{ak}}{v_{g1,k}} = f(x),$, circuit AC gain

$A = \dfrac{v_o}{v_i} = f(x)$ and circuit output AC resistance $r_{out} = f(x)$.

In 1959, Sietsma probably achieved the same results as I did in 2006. Unfortunately, he did not publish it, and I had to derive it independently; just a matter of brave calculations.
In section 6 I will prove the following equations:

Anode AC gain:

$$A_a = \frac{v_{ak}}{v_{g1,k}} = -\frac{(S + x \cdot S_2) \cdot r_a}{1 + \left(\dfrac{x}{\mu_{g2,g1}} + \dfrac{1}{\mu} \right) \cdot (S + x \cdot S_2) \cdot r_a}$$

Circuit AC gain:

$$A = \frac{v_o}{v_i} = -\frac{n_s}{n_p} \cdot \frac{(S + x \cdot S_2) \cdot r_a}{1 + \left(\dfrac{x}{\mu_{g2,g1}} + \dfrac{1}{\mu} \right) \cdot (S + x \cdot S_2) \cdot r_a}$$

Circuit AC output resistance:

$$r_{out} = \left(\frac{n_s}{n_p} \right)^2 \cdot \frac{1}{(S + x \cdot S_2) \cdot \left(\dfrac{x}{\mu_{g2,g1}} + \dfrac{1}{\mu} \right)}$$

The quantities shown in these equations have already been explained and are constant at a certain working point. The only variable quantity is screen grid primary transformer tap x. When you apply $x = 0$ and $x = 1$ in these equations, you get the anode AC gain, circuit AC gain and circuit AC output resistance for pentode and triode respectively. Again, in reference [1] these are derived in small and very easy steps.

5   Practical determination of the screen grid tap

It would be nice if figure 4 could be made visible on an oscilloscope screen. During the European Triode Festival 2007, Yves Monmagnon demonstrated his Tube Curve Tracer. Later I saw some results of this equipment on the internet, see reference [7], but at that time I was not aware of the ETF event. Many years before, while attending secondary technical school, I learned how to display transistor characteristics on an oscilloscope screen, but making voltage sources for control grid, screen grid and anode which can increase from 0 V to an adjustable maximum voltage of more than |400| V seems to me not easy. Before I had seen photos of Yves's presentation in 2007, I had already developed another method, see **figure 12**.

Supply voltage V_b is a short circuit for AC current, and the amplitudes of anode cathode AC voltage V_{ak} and screen grid cathode AC voltage $V_{g2,k}$ start from point $V_{ak} = V_b$ on the V_{ak}-axis of figure 12.
On curve $x_{TR} = 1.00$ for the triode, $V_{g2,k} = V_{ak}$ is always valid. To get $V_{ak} = 175$ V in point TR at an anode DC current of $I_a = 14$ mA, we must get $V_{g2,k} = 175$. By coincidence that is also V_{ak}.

On curve $x_{PE} = 0.00$ for the pentode, $V_{g2,k} = V_b = 300$V is always valid. To get $V_{ak} = 175$ V in point PE at an anode DC current of $I_a = 72$ mA, we must get $V_{g2,k} = 300$ V. By coincidence that is also V_b.
The curves $V_{g1,k} = \frac{1}{2}$ control grid base for the triode and the pentode cross at working point W

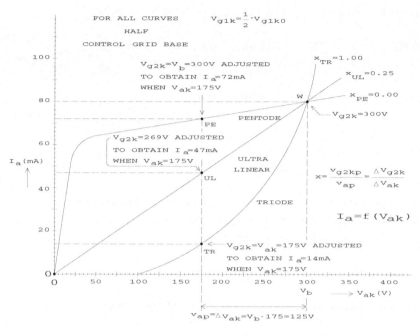

Figure 12. Explanation of the method to determine the screen grid tap x.

at $I_{aw} = 80$ mA and $V_{akw} = 300$ V. We can now draw a straight line, ultra-linear, between working point W and the origin. We call this line x_{UL}.

From point x_{UL} at $V_{ak} = 175$ V, we can read $I_a = 47$ mA. Now we must offer a certain voltage of $V_{g2,k}$ to get $I_a = 47$ mA at $V_{ak} = 175$ V. In this case $V_{g2,k} = 269$ V.

The characteristics for triode and pentode of figure 12 are measured with the test circuit of **figure 13**.

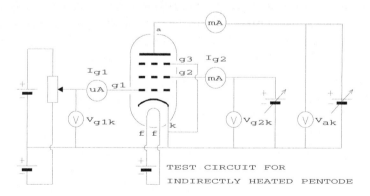

Figure 13. Test circuit for research into the static pentode characteristic.

We can now determine screen grid primary transformer taps x_{TR}, x_{UL} and x_{PE}.

At point PE:
$$V_{g2.kp} = \Delta V_{g2,k} = V_b - 300\,V = \;\;0\,V$$
$$V_{ap} = \Delta V_{ak} = V_b - 175\,V = 125\,V \rightarrow \;\; x_{PE} = \frac{V_{g2,kp}}{V_{ap}} = \frac{\Delta V_{g2,k}}{\Delta V_{ak}} = \frac{0V}{125V} = 0.00$$

At point UL:
$$V_{g2.kp} = \Delta V_{g2,k} = V_b - 269\,V = \;\;31\,V$$
$$V_{ap} = \Delta V_{ak} = V_b - 175\,V = 125\,V \rightarrow \;\; x_{UL} = \frac{V_{g2,kp}}{V_{ap}} = \frac{\Delta V_{g2,k}}{\Delta V_{ak}} = \frac{31V}{125V} = 0.25$$

At point TR:
$$V_{g2.kp} = \Delta V_{g2,k} = V_b - 175\,V = 125\,V$$
$$V_{ap} = \Delta V_{ak} = V_b - 175\,V = 125\,V \rightarrow \;\; x_{TR} = \frac{V_{g2,kp}}{V_{ap}} = \frac{\Delta V_{g2,k}}{\Delta V_{ak}} = \frac{125V}{125V} = 1.00$$

If the explanation of this method is not 100 % clear, it will be soon because we now apply this method in a practical case. **Figure 14** shows the anode characteristics for five different values of screen grid primary transformer tap x of specimen KT88 no.1.

Line 1 is measured in advance with the pentode in triode mode: $x = 1.00$.

Line 2 is drawn afterwards "freehand", but we do not know yet that the corresponding $x = 0.42$.

Line 3 is drawn afterwards with a straight ruler, but we do not know yet that the corresponding $x = 0.25$.
Line 4 is drawn afterwards "freehand", but we do not know yet that the corresponding $x = 0.13$.

Line 5 is measured in advance with the pentode in pentode mode: $x = 0.00$.

From all lines we can read I_a for each V_{ak}. We must now search for the necessary value of $V_{g2,k}$ at each point on these lines. Therefore, we need the test circuit of figure 13 which I have used to measure the lines 1 and 5. At a certain anode DC current I_a and at an adjusted anode cathode DC voltage V_{ak}, the value of screen grid cathode DC voltage $V_{g2,k}$ which I have measured, must be subtracted from $V_b = 300\,V$. Also V_{ak} must be subtracted from $V_b = 300\,V$. This gives you $\Delta V_{g2,k}$ and ΔV_{ak} respectively.

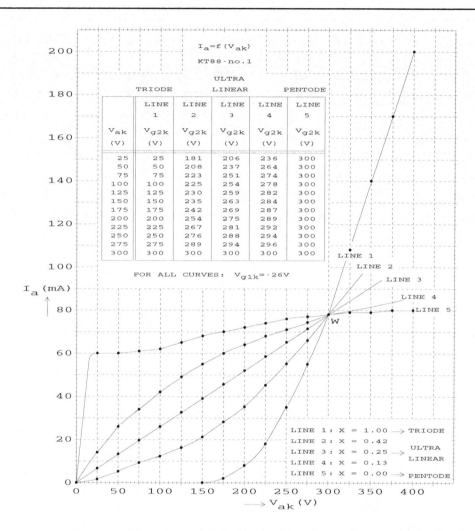

Figure 14. Anode characteristic of KT88 no.1 for different values of screen grid primary transformer tap x. The corresponding values of V_{g2k} at each measured point is shown in the table.

The next five tables show the method of figures 12 and 14 explained in practice and deliver the evidence that for all measured values (the dots on the lines), the screen grid primary transformer tap x is the same for the corresponding line. We also measure the screen grid DC current I_{g2} for later use.

V_{ak} (V) adjusted	I_a (mA) read on I_a-axis	I_{g2} (mA) measured	$V_{g2,k}$ (V) adjusted to read I_a	ΔV_{ak} (V) [300V – V_{ak}]	$\Delta V_{g2,k}$ (V) [300V – $V_{g2,k}$]	$x = \dfrac{\Delta V_{g2,k}}{\Delta V_{ak}}$
0	0	0	0	300	300	1
25	0	0	25	275	275	1
50	0	0	50	250	250	1
75	0	0	75	225	225	1
100	0	0	100	200	200	1
125	0	0	125	175	175	1
150	0	0	150	150	150	1
175	2,6	0,1	175	125	125	1
200	8,5	0,7	200	100	100	1
225	19,2	1,6	225	75	75	1
250	35,6	2,9	250	50	50	1
275	55	4,6	275	25	25	1
300	79	7	300	0	0	unknown
325	110	9,2	325			
350	140	12,1	350	Not further than point W		
375	170	16,5	375			
400	200	21	400			

Table 2. Measured values for line 1, fig 14. The adjustment of $V_{g2,k}$ happens automatically of course, because the screen grid is connected to the anode. The screen grid primary transformer tap $x = 1.00$ but that will surprise nobody, so this is the pentode in triode mode.

V_{ak} (V) adjusted	I_a (mA) read on I_a-axis	I_{g2} (mA) measured	$V_{g2,k}$ (V) adjusted to read I_a	ΔV_{ak} (V) [300V – V_{ak}]	$\Delta V_{g2,k}$ (V) [300V – $V_{g2,k}$]	$x = \dfrac{\Delta V_{g2,k}}{\Delta V_{ak}}$
0	0	0	unknown	300	unknown	unknown
25	2	0,9	181	275	119	0,43
50	5	5,5	208	250	92	0,37
75	9	8,9	223	225	77	0,34
100	12	7,6	225	200	75	0,38
125	17	5,9	230	175	70	0,40
150	22	4,2	235	150	65	0,43
175	28	3,6	242	125	58	0,46
200	36	4	254	100	46	0,46
225	46	4,7	267	75	33	0,44
250	55	5,3	276	50	24	0,48
275	66	6,2	289	25	11	0,44
300	78	7	300	0	0	unknown

Table 3. Measured values of line 2, fig 14. The average value of all screen grid primary transformer taps $x_{average} = 0.42$.

V_{ak} (V) adjusted	I_a (mA) read on I_a-axis	I_{g2} (mA) measured	$V_{g2,k}$ (V) adjusted to read I_a	ΔV_{ak} (V) [300V − V_{ak}]	$\Delta V_{g2,k}$ (V) [300V − $V_{g2,k}$]	$x = \dfrac{\Delta V_{g2,k}}{\Delta V_{ak}}$
0	0	0	unknown	300	unknown	unknown
25	6,5	3,8	206	275	94	0,34
50	13	12,5	237	250	63	0,25
75	19,5	16	251	225	49	0,22
100	26	13	254	200	46	0,23
125	32,5	10,4	259	175	41	0,23
150	39	8	263	150	37	0,25
175	45,5	7	269	125	31	0,25
200	52	6,5	275	100	25	0,25
225	58,5	6,5	281	75	19	0,25
250	65	6,5	288	50	12	0,24
275	71,5	6,5	294	25	6	0,24
300	78	7,1	300	0	0	unknown

Table 4. Measured values of line 3, fig 14. The average value of all screen grid primary transformer taps $x_{average}$ = 0.25. For this specimen KT88 no.1 we have pure ultra-linear at x = 0.25.

V_{ak} (V) adjusted	I_a (mA) read on I_a-axis	I_{g2} (mA) measured	$V_{g2,k}$ (V) adjusted to read I_a	ΔV_{ak} (V) [300V − V_{ak}]	$\Delta V_{g2,k}$ (V) [300V − $V_{g2,k}$]	$x = \dfrac{\Delta V_{g2,k}}{\Delta V_{ak}}$
0	0	0	unknown	300	unknown	unknown
25	15	9,5	236	275	64	0,23
50	26	19,7	264	250	36	0,14
75	34	20,6	274	225	26	0,12
100	41	17,7	278	200	22	0,11
125	49	14,2	282	175	18	0,10
150	55	11,2	284	150	16	0,11
175	60	9,4	287	125	13	0,10
200	64	8,1	289	100	11	0,11
225	68	7,6	292	75	8	0,11
250	71	7,1	294	50	6	0,12
275	74	7	296	25	4	0,16
300	78	7	300	0	0	unknown

Table 5. Measured values of line 4, fig 14. The average value of all screen grid primary transformer taps $x_{average}$ = 0.13.

V_{ak} (V) adjusted	I_a (mA) read on I_a-axis	I_{g2} (mA) measured	$V_{g2,k}$ (V) adjusted to read I_a	ΔV_{ak} (V) [300V – V_{ak}]	$\Delta V_{g2,k}$ (V) [300V – $V_{g2,k}$]	$x = \dfrac{\Delta V_{g2,k}}{\Delta V_{ak}}$
0	1	54	300	300	0	0
25	60	30	300	275	0	0
50	60	30	300	250	0	0
75	61	28	300	225	0	0
100	63	22	300	200	0	0
125	65	19	300	175	0	0
150	68	14	300	150	0	0
175	70	12	300	125	0	0
200	72	9,5	300	100	0	0
225	74	8,5	300	75	0	0
250	75	7,8	300	50	0	0
275	76	7,2	300	25	0	0
300	77	7	300	0	0	unknown
325	78	6,5	300			
350	79	6,3	300	Not further than point W		
375	80	6	300			
400	80	6	300			

Table 6. Measured values of line 5, fig 14. The adjustment of $V_{g2,k}$ happens automatically of course, because the screen grid is connected to Vb. The screen grid primary transformer tap x = 0.00 but that will surprise nobody; this is pentode mode.

With this method you can determine screen grid primary transformer tap x for each specimen pentode and from each curvature in $I_a = f(V_{ak})$. In practice, we are only interested in the ultra-linear application.

Lines 2 and 4 in fig 14, drawn "freehand", are just an illustration to show how the value of x can lie between triode and ultra-linear and between ultra-linear and pentode.

I have also recorded screen grid DC current I_{g2} during this measurement because it is interesting to see the influence of screen grid primary transformer tap x on I_{g2}, see **figure 15** for the results.
Line 1 shows triode behavior. Screen grid DC current I_{g2} increases the same as anode DC current I_a. Less steeply of course, because screen grid static transconductance S_2 is smaller than anode static transconductance S.

Line 5 shows pentode behavior. Because $I_k = I_a + I_{g2} \approx$ constant, the curvature of screen grid DC current I_{g2} is mirrored with respect to anode DC current I_a. The strange "step" of specimen KT88-no.1 in the area where 25 V < V_{ak} < 50 V, which is typical for Beam Power Tetrodes, can be found in both currents mentioned. We already know the curvature of I_{g2}, see figure 9.

Lines 2, 3 and 4 are very different. We first see "fast" triode behavior at low values of V_{ak} because now the positive screen grid is seen as the "anode" by the electrons of the electron cloud around the cathode. Hence, I_{g2} is increasing. Thereafter pentode behavior is more dominant. The result is a maximum value of I_{g2} at approximately V_{ak} = 75 V.

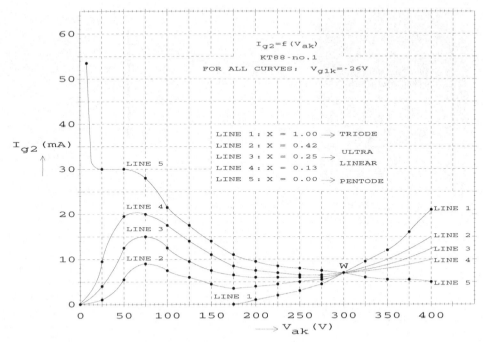

Figure 15. Characteristic of Ig2 = f (Vak) for different values of screen grid tap x.

6   Practical anode AC gain and circuit AC output resistance as function of the screen grid tap

In the network analysis of section 4, we have seen the influence of the screen grid primary transformer tap x on the anode AC gain, circuit AC gain and the circuit AC output resistance: $A_a = f(x)$, $A = f(x)$, and $r_{out} = f(x)$. Now it is time to find out what happens in a real circuit. **Figure 16** shows the test circuit. What immediately is apparent is the output transformer with the 10 taps. Once, before I had ever heard about the ultra-linear power amplifier, I did an investigation about the maximum delivered anode power of a 300B triode versus the normalized anode AC external resistance r_a/r_i. When you know that for a 300B in normal operation $r_i = 700\ \Omega$, then it does not seems strange that the taps of the primary transformer winding (r_a) of figure 16 are a multiples of 700 Ω. Although that anode power investigation was quite interesting, it is beyond the scope of this article. See chapter 4 of reference [1] for that investigation.

For those of you who want to do the same experiments I did, you can order this test output transformer from the Dutch transformer manufacturer AE-europe. The type number is 27844 and its maximum DC current is 200 mA. Do not expect enough bandwidth and other audio qualities, but it is useful for power investigations at medium audio frequencies.

I again used pentode specimen KT88-no.1 at the following working point: $V_{ak,w} = 300$ V, $I_{a,w} = 80$ mA, $V_{g1,kw} = -26$ V, $V_{g2,kw} \approx 300$ V and $I_{g2,w} \approx 8$ mA

31

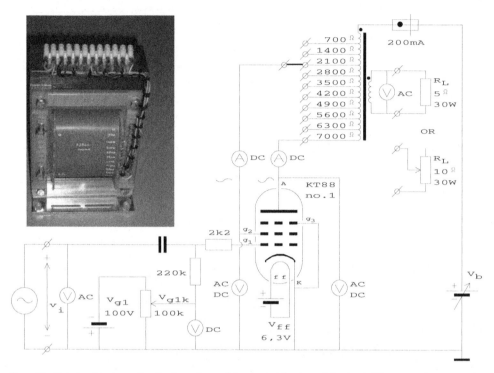

Figure 16. Test circuit to determine the dependence of the anode AC gain and the circuit AC output resistance on the screen grid tap x.

Note that if working point W changes slightly with other values of screen grid primary transformer tap x, we must change $V_{g1,kw}$ slightly to achieve the nominal setting. There is a voltage drop across the primary transformer winding of $(I_a + I_{g2}) \cdot (1 - x) \cdot R_p$ which depends on the screen grid primary transformer tap x. It varies and is approximately 10 V. At each value of x, the working point is adjusted as necessary.

Looking at the test circuit of figure 16 we would expect the following values of x at each tap:

$$x = \frac{0\,\Omega}{7000\,\Omega} = 0.0 \; ; \; x = \frac{700\,\Omega}{7000\,\Omega} = 0.1 \; ; \; x = \frac{1400\,\Omega}{7000\,\Omega} = 0.2 \; ; \; x = \frac{2100}{7000} = 0.3 \; ; \; \ldots \; x = \frac{7000\,\Omega}{7000\,\Omega} = 1.0$$

We define $x_{measured} = \dfrac{\Delta V_{g2,k}}{\Delta V_{ak}} = \dfrac{v_{g2,k}}{v_{ak}}$ and measurements will determine whether $x = x_{measured}$.

How linearly are the taps divided over the primary transformer winding? What is the influence of I_{g2} and i_{g2} on the function of the tap? What is the influence of screen grid AC internal resistance r_{i2} on x? We must realize that this test transformer is not designed and produced for ultra-linear applications, but it is available so let us try. Hence the introduction of quantity $x_{measured}$:

$V_{g2,k} = x \cdot V_{ak}$ → $V_{g2,k} = x_{measured} \cdot V_{ak}$

We start with anode AC gain $A_a = f(x_{measured})$.

You will observe that the output voltages and powers are rather low. Please do not judge that too harshly. In the other applications with KT88 pentodes, the supply voltage can be 400 V instead of 300 V. Realize that the delivered output power is proportional with (V_b^2/r_a).

OK, here we go: anode AC external resistance $r_a = 7000\ \Omega$. Fraction $R_i = V_{ak}/I_{aw} = 300\ \text{V}/80\ \text{mA} = 3750\ \Omega$. That give us the fraction $r_a/R_i = 7000/3750 = 1.87$ and reference [1] shows that this value is very unfavorable to achieve large output power. But I promise you; all will eventually be well concerning the output power; please be patient.

We also need equation $A_a = \dfrac{V_{ak}}{V_{g1,k}} = -\dfrac{(S + x \cdot S_2) \cdot r_a}{1 + \left(\dfrac{x}{\mu_{g2,g1}} + \dfrac{1}{\mu}\right) \cdot (S + x \cdot S_2) \cdot r_a}$ and for x we substitute in $x_{measured}$.

We can get the following quantities from the datasheets of the KT88:
$S = 11.5\ \text{mA/V}$ and $r_i = 12\ \text{k}\Omega$ and $\mu_{g2,g1} = 8$. Unfortunately, S_2 is not given, but that is (not) to be expected from the current manufacturers of electron tubes. In the previous measurements, we have seen that at $V_{ak} = 300\ \text{V}$, $I_a \approx 10 \cdot I_{g2}$. So I make the assumption that $S = 10 \cdot S_2$ and that gives us $S_2 = 1.15\ \text{mA/V}$. We now have all the necessary quantities to substitute in the equation together with $x_{measured}$. We start with $v_{g1,k} = 3.72\ \text{V}_{RMS} = 5.25\ \text{V}_p$, to avoid v_{ap} clipping at $x = x_{measured} = 0.0$.

Output power $p_a = \dfrac{v_{ak,RMS}^2}{r_a}$ and $p_{R_L} = \dfrac{v_{R_L,RMS}^2}{r_a}$ will be very poor, but as promised will be well in the end.

The results of the measurements and calculations are shown in **table 7** and as expected, $x \neq x_{measured}$, because the taps are not perfectly linearly divided over the primary transformer winding. We will see later that with an actual toroidal-core transformer, $x = x_{measured}$.

x	$V_{g1,k}$ (VRMS)	$V_{g2,k}$ (VRMS)	V_{ak} (VRMS)	$x_{measured} = \dfrac{V_{g2,k}}{V_{ak}}$	p_a (W)	V_{RL} (VRMS)	P_{RL} (W)	$\|A_a\| = \dfrac{V_{ak}}{V_{g1,k}}$	$\|A_a\|$ with formula
0.0	3.72	0.0	158.0	0.00	3.60	4.01	3.20	42.4	50.6
0.1	3.72	19.2	60.8	0.32	0.53	1.51	0.45	16.3	16.8
0.2	3.72	21.3	47.7	0.45	0.33	1.22	0.29	12.8	13.3
0.3	3.72	22.3	40.7	0.55	0.24	1.01	0.20	10.9	11.3
0.4	3.72	23.2	36.1	0.64	0.19	0.92	0.16	9.7	10.1
0.5	3.72	23.6	33.4	0.71	0.16	0.83	0.14	9.0	9.3
0.6	3.72	23.9	30.9	0.77	0.14	0.78	0.12	8.3	8.7
0.7	3.72	23.2	28.9	0.84	0.12	0.73	0.11	7.8	8.1
0.8	3.72	24.2	27.3	0.89	0.11	0.69	0.10	7.3	7.7
0.9	3.72	24.6	26.1	0.94	0.10	0.65	0.09	7.0	7.3
1.0	3.72	25.0	25.0	1.00	0.09	0.62	0.08	6.6	7.0

Table 7. The results of measurements and calculations based on figure 16.

Figure 17 shows plots of the table 7 results of the ninth and tenth column as a function of the fifth column, or in other words the functions $A_{a,measured} = f(x_{measured})$ and $A_{a,calculated} = f(x_{measured})$ respectively. The agreement between theory and practice is good. Only at low values of $x_{measured}$ there are some differences.

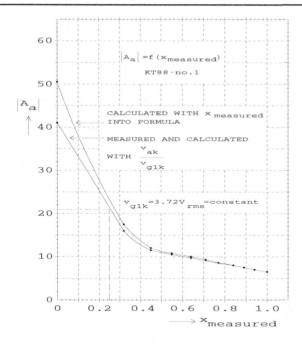

Figure 17. $p_a = f(x_{measured})$ for a constant $v_{g1,k}$, calculated and measured.

This test transformer has no taps at $0.00 < x < 0.10$ and $0.00 < x_{measured} < 0.32$. In the other ranges we see that the decrease in $|A_a|$ almost perfectly tracks the increase in x and $x_{measured}$. The larger x and $x_{measured}$, the greater the screen grid negative feedback and the decrease in $|A_a|$. A low anode gain delivers low values of v_{ak} and v_{RL} and thus, a low p_a and p_{RL}, see columns 6 and 8 of table 7. However, no one can stop us to leave the value $v_{g1,k} = 3.72$ V as it is for each value of x. The larger the value of x the more we move toward triode and the less the upper bend in transconductance characteristic $I_a = f(V_{g1,k})$. Hence, the control grid base increases and can be used with a larger value of $v_{g1,k}$.

Figure 18 shows $p_a = f(x_{measured})$ for $v_{g1,k} = 3.72$ V, the second column of table 7, and shows $p_a = f(x_{measured})$ with adjusted $v_{g1,k}$ which is as large as possible without causing non-linear distortion visible on the oscilloscope. The anode power then lies between 2.5 W and 5.5 W and that will provide reasonable sound levels. More power can be obtained by increasing $V_{akw} = V_b$ and I_{aw}, but I will not do that here. Of course, we must choose fraction r_a/R_i optimally, see reference [1]. As promised, those power numbers will all turn out to be fine.

The dashed lines in fig 17 show the gain for $x_{measured} = 0.25$ and that is the ultra-linear mode for this specimen KT88-no.1. See also line 3 of figure 14 and the seventh column of table 4.

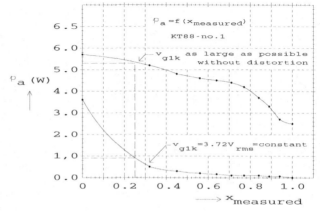

Figure 18. $p_a = f(x_{measured})$ for a constant $v_{g1,k}$ and for an adjusted $v_{g1,k}$.

We now continue with the circuit AC output resistance as a function of the actual screen grid primary transformer tap x, or $r_{out} = f(x_{measured})$.

In theory, we can apply Thevenin's $r_{out} = \left|\dfrac{v_{open}}{i_{shortcircuit}}\right|$ but in practice this is dangerous.

Shorting i_{RL} is permissible for a short time, but $V_{RL,open}$ is dangerous. When a secondary load on the output transformer is removed suddenly, an inductive high voltage may appear which can destroy the power tube. (This is the reason you should never disconnect the loudspeakers from the outputs of your electron tube amplifier when it is not switched off). We will determine r_{out} according to **figure 19**.

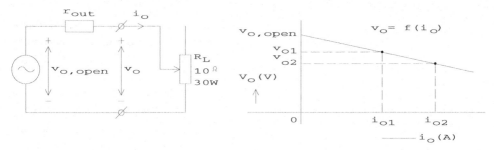

Figure 19. Voltage source model to determine circuit AC output resistance r_{out}.

The voltage source is the secondary side of the output transformer and we want to know the value of r_{out}. Use a wire-wound adjustable resistor of 10Ω/30W as the load resistor R_L and set the slider at mid-position; now $R_L = 5\ \Omega$.

From figure 19 we can derive :

$$v_{o,open} = i_{o1} \cdot r_{out} + v_{o1}$$
$$v_{o,open} = i_{o2} \cdot r_{out} + v_{o2}$$

We now use the following equations:

$$i_{o1} \cdot r_{out} + v_{o1} = i_{o2} \cdot r_{out} + v_{o2} \quad \Leftrightarrow$$
$$(v_{o2} - v_{o1}) = (i_{o1} - i_{o2}) \cdot r_{out} \quad \Leftrightarrow$$
$$r_{out} = \frac{(v_{o2} - v_{o1})}{(i_1 - i_2)} \quad \Leftrightarrow$$
$$r_{out} = \frac{\Delta v_o}{\Delta i_o}$$

By adjusting the slider slightly clockwise or counterclockwise, we can create Δv_o and Δi_o and apply this for each value of x and $x_{measured}$. At larger values of x and $x_{measured}$, when the gain is low and thus the values of v_o and i_o are also low, we can increase $v_i = v_{g1,k}$ to achieve larger values of v_o and i_o.
If $v_o \approx 5\ V$ then $i_o \approx 1\ A$ because $R_L = 5\ \Omega$. These values are very easily measured with a voltmeter and a current probe. For each value of x and $x_{measured}$ we can make a table for v_{o1}, v_{o2}, i_{o1}, i_{o2} and r_{out}.

We also need equation $\quad r_{out} = \left(\dfrac{n_s}{n_p}\right)^2 \cdot \dfrac{1}{(S + x \cdot S_2) \cdot \left(\dfrac{x}{\mu_{g2,g1}} + \dfrac{1}{\mu}\right)}\quad$ and substitute $x_{average}$ for x.

The values of S, S_2, μ and $\mu_{g2,g1}$ have already been determined. The square of the transformer winding ratio is of course $(n_s/n_p)^2$. When you look at the design impedances of the test transformer you get the square of the winding ratio as $5\Omega/7000\Omega = 1/1400$. To get the *actual* values, it is better to look at the measured values of v_{RL} at the primary side and v_{ak} at the secondary side, in table 7. When you calculate this fraction for each x and $x_{measured}$ you get $v_{RL}/v_{ak} = 0.025$ so the square of the winding ratio is $(v_{RL}/v_{ak})^2 = 1/1600$. All the 'ingredients' of this equation are now known and we will apply this eleven times as we step x from 0.0 to 1.0 in 0.1 increments. We will put all results of $r_{out\text{-}calculated}$ and $r_{out\text{-}measured}$ in the same table as the measured values and then draw the graphs as shown in **figure 20**.

The difference between $r_{out\text{-}calculated}$ and $r_{out\text{-}measured}$ for each $x_{measured}$ is approximately 0.75 Ω, which is caused by the primary and secondary copper resistances of the test transformer and the wire/contact resistances of the test circuit. In the ultra-linear mode, for $x_{measured} = 0.25$, we find an output impedance of $r_{out\text{-}calculated} = 3.3\,\Omega$ (dashed lines). Knowing the importance of r_{out} on the damping factor, audiophiles can be expected to hear the difference in sound character due to the differences in r_{out} caused by different $x_{measured}$ values.

At last, we can conclude that the network analysis of section 4 matches reality!

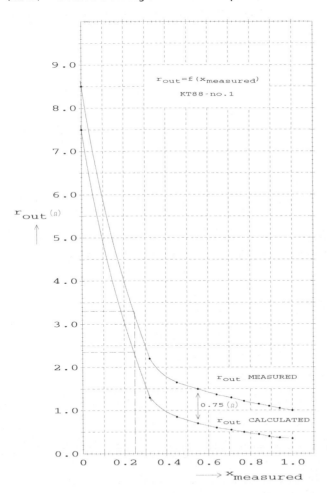

Figure 20. $r_{out} = f(x_{measured})$, *calculated and measured.*

7 Practical comparison of a triode, ultra-linear and pentode power amplifier

In this section we will compare the output power and efficiency, the frequency behavior and the non-linear distortion of an existing electron tube amplifier which we can make to work as a triode, ultra-linear or pentode amplifier by changing some jumpers. The schematic, from reference [4], is shown in **figure 21**.

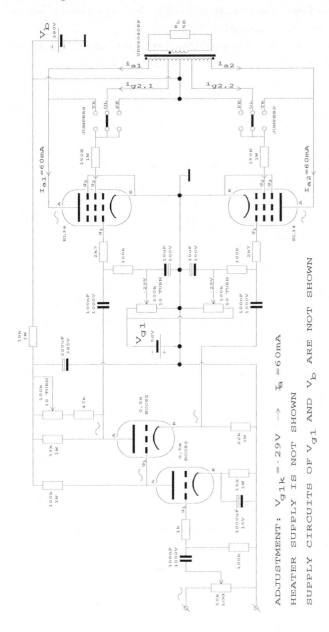

Figure 21. Circuit of one mono block of my first amplifier, the design is from reference [4].

First I will start with the comparison of output power and efficiency.

For each mentioned configuration the working point is set to $I_{aw} = 60$ mA at $v_{g1,kp} = 0$ V.

In reference [4] 13 W is promised for the triode, 33 W for ultra-linear and 40 W for pentode. Tests after construction showed some distortion at those levels so I decreased these powers to 12 W for triode, 23 W for ultra-linear and 25 W for pentode. With these values there were no non-linear distortions visible on the oscilloscope screen and these powers are very large for use in a living room. Despite the "easy EL34" and the "standard circuit", the sound quality is fantastic.

Figure 22 shows output power and efficiency as function of the control grid cathode AC peak voltage $v_{g1,kp}$ for the mono block of figure 21. The vertical axes show, on a common scale:

Input power	-	P_{in}
Anode dissipation	-	P_a
Delivered anode power	-	p_a
Anode efficiency	-	η_{anode}

The reason that P_{in} increases slowly is because I_a increases from 60 mA to 72 mA, to 80 mA and to 86 mA in the configurations triode, ultra-linear and pentode respectively. The working point moves from class A to class AB. The differences in output power between the triode and ultra-linear modes are relatively large. The differences in output power between the ultra-linear and pentode configurations are very small, as I have noted before.

Furthermore, you can see the differences in control grid base for the triode, ultra-linear and pentode configurations. The value of maximum $v_{g1,kp}$ to obtain maximum delivered anode power p_a is different. In order to be able to use the same preamp again in all cases, I used a "select-jumper" in series with the slider of the volume potentiometer. With three different values of resistors in series with the slider I could select three different input voltage levels.

Next, I continue with the comparison of the frequency behavior.

Figures 23 through 25 show the amplitude-frequency characteristic and the phase-frequency characteristic for triode, ultra-linear and pentode configuration respectively. During the measurements, the input of the amplifier was terminated by a resistor of 600 Ω and the input signal offered was 775 mV$_{RMS}$ = 0 dB, thus 1 mW input power.

The AC output voltage was measured across the load resistor of 5 Ω and thus, the output power can be calculated by the equations shown below. The powers which are then obtained are less than the powers of figure 22 because the input signal is now limited to 775 mV$_{RMS}$ = 0 dB, 1 mW input power. When you increase the input level to 1.6 V$_{RMS}$, the power levels of figure 22 can be reached easily. When we want these maximum power levels at 0 dB at the input, the voltage gain of the preamplifier and the phase shifter must be increased.

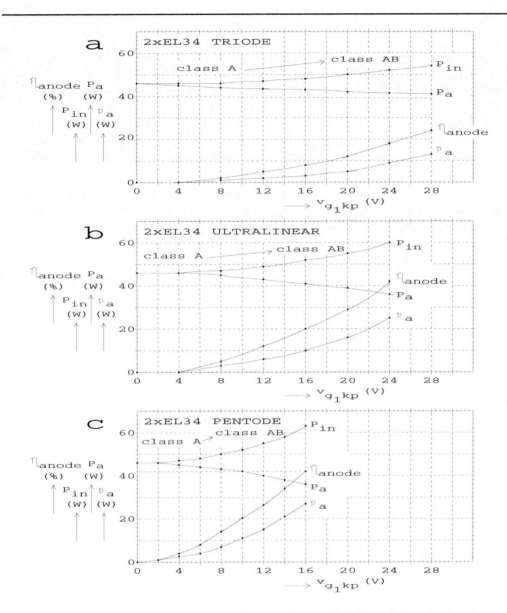

Figure 22. The output power, dissipation and the efficiency of the mono block of figure 22. Top to bottom: triode, ultra-linear and pentode mode.

Power gain : $A_p = 10 \cdot^{10} \log \dfrac{P_{out}}{P_{in}} = 10 \cdot^{10} \log \dfrac{\left(\dfrac{v^2 R_L}{R_L}\right)}{0.001}$

Voltage gain: $A_v = 20 \cdot^{10} \log \dfrac{v_{out}}{v_{in}} = 20 \cdot^{10} \log \dfrac{v_{R_L}}{0.775}$

Comparison of figures 23 through 25 shows that the crossover points at the lower end of the audio spectrum are almost the same for triode, ultra-linear and pentode mode. At the upper end of the audio spectrum, the crossover points are significantly different. The bandwidth increases from triode, via ultra-linear to pentode. We could believe that the larger $C_{a,g1}$ and the *Miller-effect* would have a large negative effect for triodes, but triodes have a low-value anode AC internal resistance r_i. Pentodes have a very low $C_{a,g1}$, but their anode AC internal resistances r_i are very high. The balance with the quantities $C_{a,g1}$ plus Miller-effect versus r_i tips towards triodes. Regarding the ultra-linear configuration, the bandwidth lies between those of triodes and pentodes. Furthermore, expect no slopes of 6 dB/octave or 20 dB/decade because this complete amplifier circuit with its several stages is a "patchwork" of separate amplitude-frequency characteristics and phase-frequency characteristics.

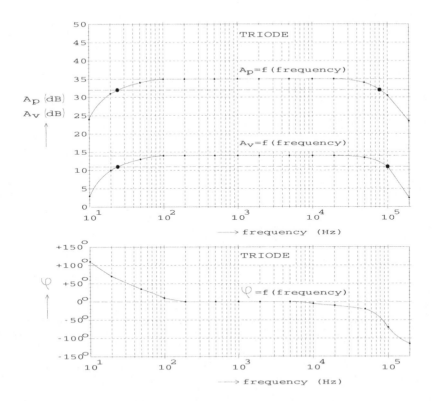

Figure 23. Measured frequency response of the mono block of figure 21 in <u>triode</u> configuration.

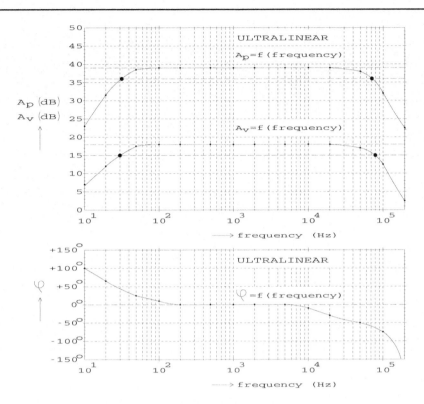

Figure 24. Measured frequency response of the amplifier of figure 21 in ultra-linear configuration.

We see that in figures 23 through 25 the power bandwidth is slightly smaller than the voltage band-width; this can be understood from the following calculations:

$$A_p = 10 \cdot {}^{10}\log\left(\frac{P_{5\Omega}}{P_{600\Omega}}\right) = 10 \times {}^{10}\log\left(\frac{v_{R_L}^2/5}{0.001}\right) = 10 \times {}^{10}\log\left(\frac{v_{R_L}^2}{0.005}\right) = 10 \times {}^{10}\log\left(\frac{v_{R_L}}{\sqrt{0.005}}\right)^2 = 20 \times {}^{10}\log\left(\frac{v_{R_L}}{0.0707}\right)$$

$$A_p = 20 \times {}^{10}\log\left(\frac{v_{R_L}}{0.707 \times 0.1}\right) = 20 \times {}^{10}\log\left(\frac{v_{R_L}}{0.707} \times 10\right) = 20 \times {}^{10}\log\left(\frac{v_{R_L}}{0.707}\right) + 20 \times {}^{10}\log 10 \qquad \Leftrightarrow$$

The power gain factor is: $\quad A_p = 20 \cdot {}^{10}\log\dfrac{v_{R_L}}{0.707} + 20$

The voltage gain factor is: $\quad A_v = 20 \cdot {}^{10}\log\dfrac{v_{R_L}}{0.775}$

Imagine 10 V_{RMS} is measured across load resistance R_L of the pentode amplifier, see figure 25.

$$A_p = 20 \cdot {}^{10}\log\frac{v_{R_L}}{0.707} + 20 = 20 \times {}^{10}\log\frac{10}{0.707} + 20 = 20 \times {}^{10}\log 14.1 + 20 = 23 + 20 \quad \Leftrightarrow \quad \mathbf{A_p = 43\ dB}$$

$$A_v = 20 \cdot {}^{10}\log\frac{v_{R_L}}{0.775} = 20 \times {}^{10}\log\frac{10}{0.775} = 20 \times {}^{10}\log 12.9 \qquad\qquad \Leftrightarrow \quad \mathbf{A_v = 22\ dB}$$

41

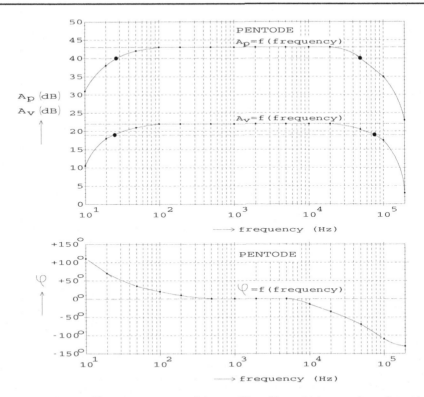

Figure 25. Measured frequency response of the amplifier of figure 21 in <u>pentode</u> configuration.

The difference between A_p and A_v is 21 dB and you can see that in figure 25. The slopes are different because *log14.1* of A_p is not equal to *log12.9* of A_v.

Lastly, I will compare non-linear distortions, see figure 26.
- If we accept just visible distortions on the oscilloscope, we can take the maximum power shown as delivered by the anode, p_a, multiplied by the transformer efficiency of about 93 %.

Configuration TRIODE:
- The triode amplifier generates mainly even harmonics (2nd) and that meets theory.
- A push pull power amplifier should eliminate the even harmonics, but not in the actual case of this amplifier. This is because although the anode DC currents are equal, the power tubes (and their parameters) are not identical.
- The figures for the distortion are not so bad, but opinions about this differ.
- This triode amplifier sounds very good, even at full-power drive. Of course, this is my personal opinion.

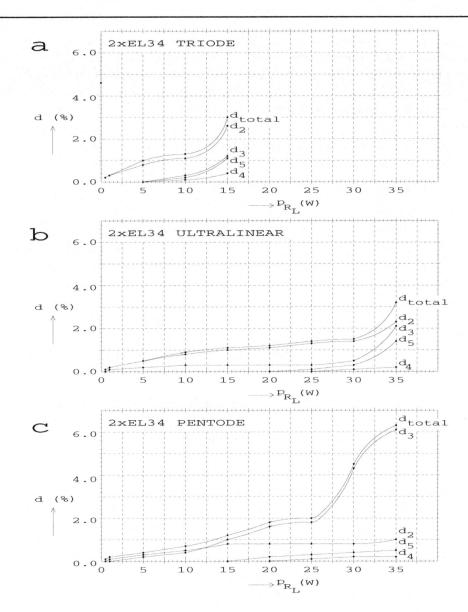

Figure 26. The harmonic distortions d_2, d_3, d_4, d_5 and d_{total} (= THD) as function of output power p_{RL} of the circuit of figure 21 in the configurations triode, ultra-linear and pentode.

Configuration ULTRA-LINEAR:

- The ultra-linear amplifier has almost the same figures for distortion as the triode configuration. This is with a delivered anode power of 35 W, double the power of the triode configuration. Personally, I find this a very good result, but your opinion is possibly different.

- The maximum power is almost the same as that of the pentode configuration, but with half the distortion figures of the pentode configuration.
- Up to 30 W delivered anode power, this configuration leans slightly toward the triode configuration due to the even harmonics (2nd). Above this 30 W, the configuration leans more to the pentode configuration with its strongly increasing 3rd and 5th harmonics. Due to this, d_{total} increases strongly
- 20 W anode power gives a lot of sound volume and with 1 % distortion this is quite good.
- This ultra-linear amplifier sounds very good, also even at full-power drive. Of course, this is again, my personal opinion.

Configuration PENTODE:
- The pentode amplifier is known for its odd harmonics (3rd) and these are not (partially) cancelled by the push-pull configuration. The 2nd harmonic is half that of the ultra-linear configuration and is cancelled better by the push pull configuration. This is a pentode property. It seems that the pentode characteristics of these specimens of the EL34 tube are more equal than those of the triode characteristics of these same specimens.
- The pentode has too much distortion at maximum delivered anode power, but 25 W with d_{total} = 2 % is not bad.
- My listening opinion says that at full-power drive this pentode amplifier does not sound very good, but at 25 W output power, your author cannot hear any disturbances.

8   Contribution of the anode AC current and screen grid AC current to ultra-linear power

In the network analyses of section 4 we have seen equation: $\dfrac{v_{ak}}{r_a} = -\left(i_a + x \cdot i_{g2}\right) = i_{total}$

As explained previously, i_{total} is a fictive AC current flowing through the anode AC external resistance r_a <u>without</u> screen grid primary transformer tap x. It delivers the same power as the real existing anode AC current i_a and the real existing screen grid AC current i_{g2} in their relationship $\left(i_a + x \cdot i_{g2}\right)$. They deliver power to anode AC external resistance r_a <u>with</u> a screen grid primary transformer tap x.
We will now study these real existing anode AC current i_a and the real existing screen grid AC current i_{g2} in their relationship $\left(i_a + x \cdot i_{g2}\right)$. Therefore, we use the test amplifier of the previous section (fig 21) where we select the ultra-linear mode. We use two current probes to achieve an oscilloscope picture for the currents. The results are shown in **figure 27**.

When you connect these current probes to both a DC and an AC voltmeter, you then can measure the currents I_{a1}, I_{a2}, $I_{g2,1}$, $I_{g2,2}$, i_{a1}, i_{a2}, $i_{g2,1}$ and $i_{g2,2}$ respectively. These currents are also mentioned in the schematic of figure 21. We will do the calculations with the AC currents. For the VDV6040PP output transformer, r_{aa} = 6000 Ω and x = 0.40. **Table 8** shows $x = x_{measured}$. In contrast to the test transformer, this one has a real screen grid primary transformer tap.

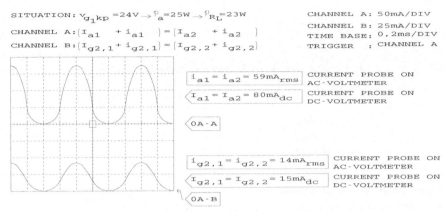

SITUATION: $v_{g_1kp} = 24V \rightarrow P_a = 25W \rightarrow P_{RL} = 23W$

CHANNEL A: $(I_{a1} + i_{a1}) = (I_{a2} + i_{a2})$
CHANNEL B: $(I_{g2,1} + i_{g2,1}) = (I_{g2,2} + i_{g2,2})$

CHANNEL A: 50mA/DIV
CHANNEL B: 25mA/DIV
TIME BASE: 0,2ms/DIV
TRIGGER   : CHANNEL A

$i_{a1} = i_{a2} = 59mA_{rms}$ — CURRENT PROBE ON AC-VOLTMETER

$I_{a1} = I_{a2} = 80mA_{dc}$ — CURRENT PROBE ON DC-VOLTMETER

$\langle$ 0A-A

$i_{g2,1} = i_{g2,2} = 14mA_{rms}$ — CURRENT PROBE ON AC-VOLTMETER

$I_{g2,1} = I_{g2,2} = 15mA_{dc}$ — CURRENT PROBE ON DC-VOLTMETER

$\langle$ 0A-B

Figure 27. Anode currents and screen grid currents for the ultra-linear power amplifier

v_{ak} (V_{RMS})	$v_{g2,k}$ (V_{RMS})	$x_{measured} = \dfrac{v_{g2,k}}{v_{ak}}$	given x of power transformer VDV6040PP
31,1	12,5	0,402	0,4
100,0	40,1	0,401	0,4
193,6	78,0	0,403	0,4

Table 8. Actual anode- and screen grid voltages and $x_{measured}$ for nominal $x=0.4$

The measured values are also shown in figure 27 where $v_{ak} = 193.6$ V and $v_{g2,k} = 78.0$ V:

- $i_{a1} = i_{a2} = i_a = 59$ mARMS
- $I_{a1} = I_{a2} = I_a = 80$ mADC
- $i_{g2,1} = i_{g2,2} = i_{g2} = 14$ mARMS
- $I_{g2,1} = I_{g2,2} = I_{g2} = 15$ mADC

If we substitute these measured values of i_a and i_{g2} in the equation for i_{total} we get the measured fictive AC current:

$$i_{total} = i_{a,measured} + x \cdot i_{g2,measured} = 59 + 0.4 \times 14 = 59 + 5.6 \Leftrightarrow$$
$$i_{total} = 64.6 \text{ mA}_{RMS}$$

We can also read anode power p_a for full-power drive ultra-linear from figure 22: $p_a = 25$ W

For each power pentode this is: $p_{a-EL34} = 12.5W$

Also

$$P_{a-EL34} = i_{total}^2 \cdot r_a \quad \text{and} \quad r_a = \tfrac{1}{2} \cdot r_{aa} = \tfrac{1}{2} \times 6000\Omega = 3000\Omega$$

Substitute all:

$$12.5 = i_{total}^2 \times 3000 \quad \Leftrightarrow$$

$$i_{total} = \sqrt{\frac{12.5}{3000}} = \sqrt{4.1667 \times 10^{-3}} = 0.0645 \ A_{RMS} \quad \Leftrightarrow$$

$$i_{total} = 64.5 \text{ mA}_{RMS}$$

Calculated differently : $p_{a-EL34} = \dfrac{v_{ak}^2}{r_a}$

Substitute $\quad\quad\quad 12.5 = \dfrac{v_{ak}^2}{3000} \Leftrightarrow v_{ak} = \sqrt{12.5 \times 3000} = \sqrt{37500} = 193.6 V_{RMS}$

Apply equation $\quad : \; i_{total} = i_{a,measured} + x \cdot i_{g2,measured} = \dfrac{v_{ak}}{r_a}$

Substitute $\quad\quad\quad : \; i_{total} = \dfrac{193.6 V_{RMS}}{3000\Omega} = 0.0645 A_{RMS}$

$i_{total} = \boldsymbol{64.5}\ \text{mA}_{\text{RMS}}$

I'm sure you will allow me to neglect the difference of 0.1 mA$_{\text{RMS}}$.
The effect of this fictive i_{total} is an anode power of 12.5 W for one power pentode.
The effect of $(i_{a,measured} + 0.4\, x\, 1_{g2,\,measured})$ is also an anode power of 12.5 W for one power pentode.

Thus, a piece of network analysis has been proven: *quod érat demonstrándum*

References

[1] *Fundamental Amplifier Techniques with Electron Tubes*; 1ˢᵗ edition 2010; Rudolf Moers; Published by Elektor International Media BV; ISBN 978-0-905705-93-4

[2] *An Ultra-Linear Amplifier*; David Hafler and Herbert I. Keroes; article in Audio Engineering; November 1951

[3] *Radio Technique part 1*; 2ⁿᵈ edition 1959; A.J. Sietsma; Published by H. Stam, Haarlem

[4] *Modern High-End Valve Amplifiers based on toroidal output transformers*; 1ˢᵗ edition; Menno van der Veen; Published by Elektor International Media BV; ISBN 0-905705-63-7

[5] *Lehrbuch der Elektronenröhren und ihrer technischen anwendungen*; 8ᵗʰ edition 1928; Dr. H. Barkhausen; Published by S. Hirzel Verlag Leipzig

[6] *www.svetlana-tubes.com*

[7] *www.triodefestival.net* ➤ ETF2007 ➤ Tube Curves Tracer

The C70 KT-88 Vacuum Tube Stereo Amplifier

Bob Cordell

1. Introduction

Those who know me may be surprised to see an article on a vacuum tube amplifier written by me. Several years ago I needed a vacuum tube amplifier to compare with solid state designs for use in listening and measurement workshops that a few friends and I were presenting at the Rocky Mountain Audio Fest. I had built numerous tube amplifiers in the late '60's, so I decided to build one for this purpose using some updated technology and design approaches. I re-designed a 35 wpc amplifier that

Figure 1: The C70 Power Amplifier.

I had built in 1968, keeping little more than the chassis, output transformers, power transformer and power supply choke. This amplifier is the result of that effort.

Vacuum tube amplifiers are alive and well in the high-end audiophile community. Indeed, several people asked me if I had any material on vacuum tube amplifiers in my new book, "Designing Audio Power Amplifiers" [1]. Unfortunately, there was just no room at the time, and some will be distressed to know that I devoted 4 chapters to class D amplifiers instead.

In many ways the amplifier described here is a classic design, using KT88s in a class AB pentode arrangement. Why not ultra-linear? The transformers from the old amplifier I used did not have ultra-linear taps on them – simple as that. The amplifier is pictured in **Figure 1**.

This amplifier differs from many classic designs in some ways as well. The topology comprises two differential amplifier stages in tandem and avoids the use of an explicit phase splitter stage – the differential pairs implicitly provide the phase splitter function. Solid state current sources are used to supply the tail currents to these long-tailed pairs (LTPs). Providing the tail current source for the input stage from the -35V supply allows the input stage grids to be biased at 0V while having a high-impedance current source for the tail.

MOSFET power transistors are used to implement two pass regulators for supply of the screen, driver and input stage rail voltages. The output voltages for these regulators slowly track the main power

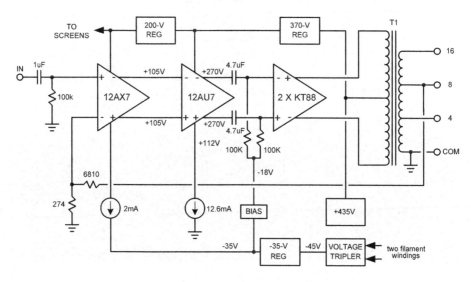

Figure 2: Simplified block diagram of the amplifier showing its differential signal path.

supply voltage, so technically they are more akin to capacitance multipliers. Regulated screen supplies in a Pentode design are especially advantageous, but rarely found in practice. Fixed bias is used in the output stage.

The design is "over-tubed", employing the large KT88s to produce only 35 watts using a 7200-ohm output transformer with a 435V power supply. In essence, the KT88s are loafing. This, in combination with the 7200-ohm output transformer's larger turns ratio (30:1), provides a higher output current capability than one would normally obtain. Tighter bass and better bass extension are among the advantages of this approach. The higher plate dissipation of the KT88 also allows a somewhat higher class AB1 output stage bias setting that reduces distortion.

Figure 2 is a block diagram showing the arrangement of the amplifier. The signal path is fully differential from input to output, and does not employ an explicit phase splitter. Instead, the 12AX7 (V1) input differential pair provides implicit phase inversion by having the input applied to one side and the negative feedback applied to the other side of its input. The use of a high impedance transistor current source (Q1) for the tail of the pair provides exceptional common mode rejection and phase splitting action, even out to high frequencies. The current source is connected to a –35V supply. There is no capacitor in the feedback shunt return path of the amplifier, and instead a DC balance adjustment is incorporated in the input stage cathode circuit. It is adjusted to achieve equal driver plate voltages in the presence of minor vacuum tube offset voltages.

The driver employs a 12AU7 differential amplifier (V2), which is direct coupled from the input differential pair. It employs a transistor tail current source (Q2) referenced to ground. This provides good common mode rejection and further enhances the balance and symmetry of the phase-split signals provided by the input stage.

There is only one coupling capacitor (per differential side) within the amplifier's feedback loop. It is in the forward path, coupling the differential driver outputs to the KT-88 grids. The presence of only a single capacitive coupling within the feedback loop greatly enhances low frequency stability, tightness and extension. The coupling capacitors are a relatively large 4.7 uF. Both AC balance and DC balance adjustments are provided for the KT-88 output stage.

The power supply provides 435 volts from an over-sized power transformer (actually a Sixties-vintage television power transformer), silicon rectifiers and 600 uF of capacitance with a choke in a pi configuration. The power supply is heavily bypassed and snubbed with smaller-value capacitors. A MOSFET voltage regulator implemented with Q3 provides 370V to the driver stage, while a second MOSFET voltage regulator (Q4) provides 200V to the input stage and the screens of the output tubes. A pair of filament windings connected in series provides -45V via a voltage tripler. This voltage is regulated to -35V for use by the input stage current source and the fixed bias circuit for the output stage.

The important features of the C70 are summarized as follows:
- 35 Watts per channel
- KT-88 output tubes, Class-AB pentode, fixed bias
- 435V power supply with 600 uF capacitance and choke
- Regulated screen, input stage, driver and fixed-bias supplies
- Fully balanced differential design with no explicit phase splitter
- Transistor current sources for the long-tailed pairs
- No electrolytic capacitors in the signal path
- Only one coupling capacitor stage within the feedback loop
- Extensive input, output and power supply RFI immunity enhancements
- 4 Hz to 45 kHz, +0/- 1 dB
- Medium feedback design (24dB) with damping factor of 23

The key components, the output transformers, are from the 1960's and are no longer available. However, the design can be made to work some modern output transformers with appropriate changes to the feedback compensation. In fact, a modern transformer that is compatible has been identified and will be discussed later. It is available from Dynakit® Vacuum Tube Audio Products.

2. Input and driver circuits
Figure 3 shows the input and driver circuits, consisting of two differential amplifier stages implemented with 12AX7 and 12AU7 devices.

The input pair is biased with a tail current of 2 mA provided by Q1 and the driver pair is biased with a tail current of 12.6 mA provided by Q2. Resistors R10 and R22 absorb some of the voltage drop and power dissipation to enable the use of TO-92 and TO-126 transistors for the current sources. The voltage reference for the input current source is an 8.2V Zener diode, while that for the driver current source is the +10V regulated power supply. Notice that the input stage tail is powered from a -35V power supply. The cathodes of the driver stage float at about 110V so as to permit DC coupling from the input pair to the driver pair.

Each half of the V1 input pair operates at a plate current of 1 mA with a transconductance of about 1700 uS. Plate resistance of V1 is about 60k on each side. Each half of the V2 driver pair operates at a plate current of 6.3 mA and a transconductance of about 2600 uS. Plate resistance of each half of V2 is about 7.5k. The low-frequency differential gain of the input stage is about 45, while that of the driver stage is about 12.

R4 and C2 form an input low pass filter at about 160 kHz. Negative feedback is established by R15 in series from the 8-ohm tap of the output transformer feeding into the shunt resistance R14. Many classic amplifiers take the feedback from the 16-ohm tap, but the distortions of output transformers

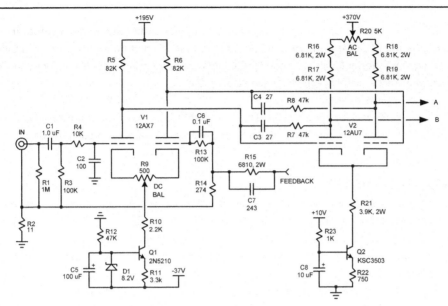

Figure 3: The DC-coupled differential input and driver stages of the amplifier

are such that lower distortion and more uniform frequency response result when the feedback is taken from the tap actually used to drive the load. R2 is employed to break ground loops at the input.

Potentiometer R9 provides adjustment of the DC balance of the input stage. It is adjusted to make the plates of V2A and V2B be at equal potentials. Potentiometer R20 is the AC balance adjustment for the output stage. In the absence of a more detailed adjustment procedure using a distortion analyzer, it is adjusted so that the AC signals at the plates of V2A and V2B are of equal amplitude.

The frequency compensation used with this amplifier is called differential Miller compensation. It is implemented by series R-C networks connected from grid to plate on V2. The advantage to this compensation as compared to conventional shunt compensation is that it encloses the driver in a local feedback loop that reduces driver distortion and driver output impedance. This is not unlike the way that Miller compensation is used in solid-state amplifiers. As compared with conventional shunt compensation at the plates of V1, the value of the Miller capacitors will be smaller by a factor of roughly G2+1 (where G2 is the voltage gain of the driver stage). Similarly, the value of the series resistors will be larger by about that same factor. C3/C4 and R7/R8 provide a pole-zero compensation frequency characteristic, while C7 provides some lead compensation in the feedback path.

The details of the negative feedback compensation in any vacuum tube amplifier depend on the characteristics of the output transformer, since it has a strong influence on the open-loop gain and phase of the amplifier. The transformers in this amplifier came from an amplifier that the author built in the 1960's and are of unknown origin and are certainly no longer available. For this reason, the

feedback compensation used in this amplifier might not work with some modern output trans-formers. Altering negative feedback compensation to fit a different transformer can be a tricky process requiring substantial skill and good test equipment. Some general guidelines for frequency compensation of a VT amplifier are discussed below.

Overall negative feedback in the audio band is about 24 dB. Closed-loop gain of the amplifier to the 8-ohm tap is about 25. An input level of 670 mV rms produces 35 watts into an 8-ohm load.

3. Fixed bias vs. cathode bias

Many classic VT amplifiers use cathode bias in their class AB output stages. Cathode bias connects the pair of output tube cathodes to ground through a resistor that is bypassed. Sometimes separate by-passed cathode bias resistors are used. The control grids are referenced to ground and the voltage drop across the cathode bias resistor provides the necessary negative grid-cathode bias. This works fine in the quiescent state but causes the negative grid bias to increase as output power increases. This results in program-dependent bias. Moreover, the increase in bias with signal is given a time constant by the cathode bypass capacitor, usually an electrolytic. After a high-power interval, the bias may remain high briefly, under-biasing the amplifier for the subsequent softer interval, possibly resulting in class B operation with its attendant crossover distortion. Finally, cathode bias wastes HT voltage, as the useable amount of HT voltage is the actual HT voltage less the amount of the cath-ode bias.

Fixed bias eliminates the shortcomings of cathode bias, but incurs the increased cost of a separate negative voltage supply. Fixed bias also provides the opportunity for a DC bias balance pot to com-pensate for minor tube differences (even present in matched pairs).

4. Over-tubed amplifier design

Over-tubed amplifier design encompasses two things. First the primary impedance of the output transformer is greater than one normally uses for the given amount of power output. In other words, the turns ratio is larger. Secondly, larger output tubes, capable of conducting more current than nor-mal for the given rated output power are used. The combined effect of these two practices makes for an amplifier that is capable of much higher current delivery than normal. In a sense, this is analo-gous to high-current solid state amplifiers. This is not unlike an automobile with a higher gear ratio in the drive train, resulting in higher torque capability. At the same time, the over-tubed amplifier re-quires a higher-voltage power supply to achieve a given output power. This is akin to the engine in the car needing to be capable of higher RPMs. The over-tubed amplifier is also capable of delivering enough current to overcome some reduced transformer inductance as mild saturation occurs, al-lowing for more bass to be delivered through a given-sized-core transformer.

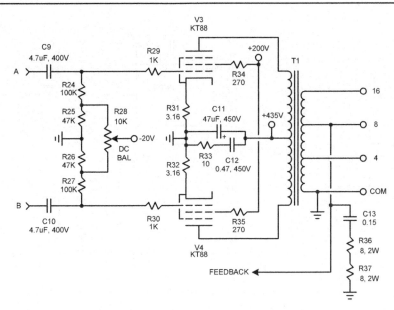

Figure 4: The KT-88 output stage operating in pentode mode.

5. Power output stage

The output stage is shown in **Figure 4.** It comprises a pair of KT-88 output tubes operating in Class AB1 pentode mode with fixed bias of about -18V. Grid drive is about 40V p-p at full output. R31 and R32 are for measuring cathode current. The output transformer has a 7200-ohm primary, higher than that normally employed with KT-88 output tubes. The higher turns ratio (30:1 to the 8-ohm tap) provides a lower output impedance and greater current drive capability at the expense of reduced power capability into an 8-ohm load for a given supply voltage.

The amplifier output circuit includes a series R-C Zobel network. This is common for solid state amplifiers, but is not often seen in vacuum tube amplifiers. This improves high-frequency stability and immunity to RFI. Potentiometer R28 controls DC balance. The fixed bias voltage is controlled by R67 in **Figure 7**. Bias is set to about 63 mA per output tube. This corresponds to about 200 mV across each of the 3.16-ohm cathode resistors. Plate dissipation for each KT88 is thus about 27W.

6. Quiescent power dissipation

One reason why tube amplifiers may sound better is their relative absence of crossover distortion. Although any class AB design will in principle generate crossover distortion, the higher relative quiescent bias current combined with the softer cutoff characteristic of vacuum tubes will mitigate it. Consider the ratio of quiescent output stage power dissipation to rated power for this vacuum tube amplifier to that for typical BJT and MOSFET power amplifiers. At 63mA per tube and a 435-V HT

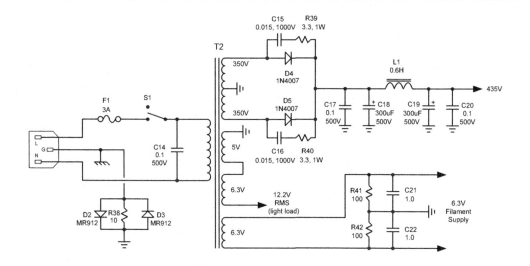

Figure 5: The main power supply delivers 435V and includes substantial reservoir capacitance and filtering.

supply, this amplifier dissipates 54W at idle and is rated at 35W, for a quiescent-to-rated power ratio of 154%. In contrast, a 35W BJT amplifier biased at 115mA (RE=0.22) with 38V rails dissipates 9W for a ratio of 26%. A 35W MOSFET power amplifier biased at 150mA with 42V rails dissipates 13W for a ratio of 37%. The typical vacuum tube amplifier is operating closer to class A than the typical solid state amplifier. In this amplifier, this can be verified by looking at the voltage across the cathode resistors as a function of power level with an oscilloscope. The cathode currents will remain sinusoidal to a larger power level.

7. Main power supply

The main high-voltage power supply is shown in **Figure 5**. This was built with an old television power transformer that included several secondary filament windings.

Diodes D2 and D3 and R38 connect the mains ground to the chassis ground in such a way that ground loops are broken, but where any potential difference is limited to one diode drop.

The high voltage supply is a conventional full-wave design employing a center-tapped secondary. The power transformer delivers 350-0-350 VAC at the idle load current of 330 mA. C15, C16, R39 and R40 provide snubbing for the silicon rectifiers. The main supply includes a 0.6H choke that is surrounded by 300 uF on each side. The loaded output voltage of the supply is about 435V with ripple of about 50mV p-p. The choke can be replaced by a 15-ohm resistor with ripple increasing to 1.2V p-p with a negligible effect on amplifier hum due to the use of regulated HT supplies for everything except the output stage plate supply.

Two filament windings are connected in series to provide about 12.2 V rms for use by low-voltage power supplies described later. These two filament windings are lightly loaded, so they produce a bit more than the rated 6.3V + 5V. C21 and C22 provide additional RFI filtering for the filament supply.

8. Screen and low-voltage supply

The plate voltages for the input stage and driver are quasi-regulated, as is the screen voltage for the output stage. The voltages will slowly track changes in the mains voltage, and the arrangement is somewhat of a cross between a regulator and a capacitance multiplier. These supplies are very quiet and free of ripple and EMI. The HT regulator circuit employs IRFP240 power MOSFET devices as pass transistors and is shown in **Figure 6**. The power MOSFETs dissipate some power and are mounted to the aluminum chassis of the power amplifier for heat sinking. The V_{DSS} rating of 200V for these devices is a bit marginal and MOSFETs with a higher V_{DSS} would be desirable.

The two necessary voltages, +370V and +200V, are established by resistive voltage dividers feeding the gates of the MOSFET pass transistors. These voltages are filtered, but largely un-regulated, in that they are intended to track changes in the available main power supply voltage. If I had it to do again, I would fixed-regulate these supplies (at greater cost) so that output stage bias would be less affected by line voltage changes causing screen grid voltage changes.

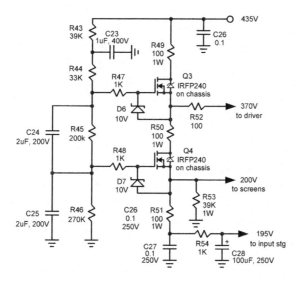

Figure 6: MOSFET pass regulators provide clean input stage, driver stage and screen voltages at low impedances.

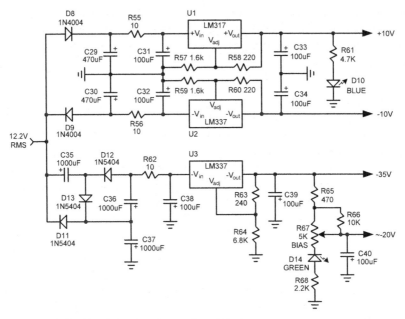

Figure 7: Regulated low-voltage supply provides -35V for input stage current source and output stage fixed bias.

Gate stopper resistors R47 and R48 provide stability against parasitic oscillations, while Zeners D6 and D7 protect the gates from voltage swings that could harm them. Resistors R49 and R50 also help assure high-frequency stability.

Resistor R53 guarantees a minimum amount of current flow in the pass regulators in the absence of load while the vacuum tubes are warming up. R54 and C28 provide some additional filtering for the input stage plate supply. It is important to minimize the influence of mains voltage transients on the input and driver supplies because in most vacuum tube amplifiers such changes can be propagated to the grids of the output tubes, disturbing their bias.

9. Fixed bias and +/-10-volt supplies

The fixed bias supply for the output stage grids is shown in **Figure 7**. This circuit applies 12.2V rms from the main power transformer to a 3-diode voltage tripler to provide about –47 volts DC. This is then regulated by an LM337 to a constant –35 volts. This voltage is then applied to an adjustable voltage divider to provide the approximate –18 volts used for the fixed bias. R67 is the bias adjusting potentiometer. The –35-volt supply is also used for the input stage tail current source. One can optionally use separate pot arrangements to be sure that both channels are operating at the same bias current.

Plus and minus 10-volt power supplies are also provided in the amplifier. This circuitry is also shown in Figure 7. It is a simple half-wave-rectified power supply whose output is regulated by LM317 and LM337 IC regulators. The +10-volt supply is used as a reference for the driver tail current source and for the Blue power-on LED. The –10-volt supply is not used. These supplies were included for possible use by auxiliary circuits.

10. The output transformer
The output transformer is the heart and soul of a vacuum tube amplifier. A very simplified model of the output transformer I used is shown in **Figure 8**. It is a good quality unit of modest size from the 1960's.

The primary inductance can introduce a low-frequency roll-off. Imperfect magnetic coupling between the primary and secondary results in what is called leakage inductance [2], which is effectively in series with the primary. It can be determined by measuring the inductance of the primary when the secondary is shorted. Leakage inductance can introduce high-frequency roll-off and excess phase lag. It can be reduced by interleaving the transformer windings to improve magnetic coupling. Interleaving can be done among segments of a given winding and/or among different windings. Without interleaving, the two halves of a center-tapped primary will not necessarily have the same transmission characteristics to the secondary, for example.

The effective primary capacitance results from the proximity of different portions of the windings. It includes the reflected secondary winding capacitances scaled by the inverse square of the turns ratio. Primary capacitance causes high-frequency roll-off. It is generally increased by interleaving of the windings. In reality, the leakage inductances and primary capacitances are distributed along with the winding resistances, and can actually result in some transmission-line-like behavior.

Using a different output transformer can affect amplifier stability in a number of ways. First of all, a transformer with a different turns ratio can alter the open-loop gain. This can have a big effect since transformer primary impedances typically range from 8000 ohms down to 2000 ohms, and the turns ratio goes as the square root of the rated impedance. Theoretically this could result in a 6 dB range

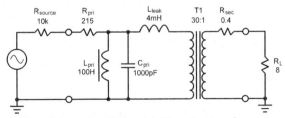

Figure 8: A very simplified model of the output transformer.

of open-loop gain. However, in a given amplifier the reasonable range of useable output transformer impedances might be from 4000 ohms to 8000 ohms (as in this design), resulting in a turns ratio range of less than 1.4:1, corresponding to a 3 dB range in open loop gain at most.

The effective primary capacitance can have a significant influence on the high-frequency portion of the open-loop gain characteristic. This capacitance forms a pole with the net impedance at the primary, consisting of the output tube plate impedance and the impedance of the load reflected by the square of the turns ratio. In this amplifier, with a 30:1 turns ratio, an 8-ohm load, and a 10k plate to plate output tube resistance, the effective primary impedance is about 4200 ohms. With a 1000pF primary capacitance, the pole lies at 4.2k and 1000pF, or 38kHz. If the transformer is replaced with one whose primary capacitance is only 500pF, this pole will rise to 76kHz, increasing the HF open-loop gain and possibly causing instability. In principle, this could be compensated by adding a 600pF capacitor across the primary, but the capacitor would have to have a voltage rating of 1000V or more. The effective primary capacitance is strongly influenced by the amount of interleaving in the transformer windings.

11. Frequency compensation

Compensating a vacuum tube amplifier can be a difficult and frustrating process, due to the presence of the output transformer in the loop. They are distributed LCR devices with a complex frequency response and numerous opportunities for resonances. Here I share a few pragmatic guidelines.

The first step in compensation should be to characterize the output transformer. Here we assume that the feedback will be taken from the 8-ohm tap and that the transformer will be loaded at the 8-ohm tap with an 8-ohm load. Feed one-half of the primary with a sinusoid through a 10k resistor and load the 8-ohm tap with an 8-ohm resistor. Measure the output at the 8-ohm tap. The 10k resistor approximates the plate resistance of a pentode, and is not critical. The load impedance seen across one-half of the primary will be 7200 ohms/4 = 1800 ohms for the transformer used in the C70.

We do not want to see any frequency response peaks that rise much above the 0-dB frequency response reference at 1 kHz. We also do not want to see any frequency response dips. In general, we like to see a well-behaved approximation to a 6 dB/octave roll-off caused by the effective primary capacitance of the transformer working against the net impedance seen at the primary. A second pole will often define the higher-frequency roll-off. Take note of where the higher-frequency roll-off of the transformer begins. This may be in the neighborhood of 200 kHz. Choose your amplifier gain crossover frequency to lie about an octave below this frequency. The gain crossover frequency for the C70 amplifier lies below 100 kHz.

As a check, repeat this test using the other half of the primary. You might be surprised at how big the difference is for some output transformers. The difference will tend to be smaller for transformers

with better interleaving of the primaries. You will also often see differences in the DC winding resistance from either end of the primary to the center tap. You may also want to look for differences in the measured frequency response at the 16-ohm and 4-ohm taps while the transformer is still loaded at the 8-ohm tap.

Sometimes the frequency response of the output transformer can be tamed and smoothed a bit by incorporating a heavier-than-normal Zobel network at the output. Try loading the 8-ohm tap with a Zobel network sufficiently heavy to eliminate any peaks in the transformer frequency response. A good starting point is a network with about 16 ohms resistance and a capacitor that is large enough to attenuate any peaks. Do not use a capacitor that is larger than necessary, nor a resistor that is smaller than necessary, as power dissipation in the resistor must be considered and overly heavy loading at high frequencies will increase HF distortion.

Measure the mid-band loop gain of the amplifier at 1 kHz. This is done by disconnecting the feedback network from the output transformer and feeding it from an audio oscillator while measuring the signal amplitude at the output tap from which the feedback is normally taken. Choose the compensation Miller capacitance so that the loop gain will fall to unity at the chosen gain crossover frequency as if the transformer response were flat. Verify the chosen roll-off by measuring loop gain at 20kHz. In this case it should be 14 dB for a 100kHz gain crossover frequency.

The resistance in series with the compensation capacitance provides a zero that partially compensates for the initial phase lag and gain roll-off of the output transformer. Choose its starting value to provide a zero in the vicinity of the -3-dB response of the transformer as measured above.

Close the loop and check the frequency response of the amplifier. Hopefully it will not oscillate. It may show a significant gain peak in the frequency range near the chosen gain crossover frequency, perhaps as much as 6 dB. Adjust the resistor to find the value that results in the smallest peak, hopefully 3 dB or less. If you cannot get the peak down to 3 dB, you should consider choosing a lower gain crossover frequency and start over.

Now add the lead capacitor in the feedback loop. Start with a small value that forms a corner with the feedback resistor in the vicinity of the second pole of the transformer frequency response. This should decrease the peak in the frequency response. Increase the value of the lead capacitor until there is no peak, and perhaps as much as 3 dB of attenuation at the chosen gain crossover frequency. Don't use a capacitor that is larger than necessary. The response should show a reasonably smooth roll-off as frequency is increased with no local peaks, up to frequencies more than an octave above the gain crossover frequency.

Check the gain margin by shunting the feedback resistor with one of equal value. Also shunt the lead capacitor by one of equal value. If the amplifier does not oscillate, you have at least 6 dB of gain mar-

gin. It is also useful to check the response to a 10-kHz square wave under these conditions to see how close to oscillation the ringing is.

Check the square wave response with the input filter capacitor C2 disconnected. There should be minimal ringing and perhaps only a small amount of overshoot, maybe 10%. The initial overshoot peak and one much smaller one after that is acceptable. There should be no sign of a small-amplitude higher-frequency ringing superimposed on this waveform. The compensation elements above can be adjusted to improve the square wave response, but always go back and check the closed-loop frequency response and gain margin to make sure that they have not be unduly compromised.

This process sounds straightforward, but it can take a lot of time, experimentation and iteration. Moreover, it is only one pragmatic way to arrive at satisfactory frequency compensation for the amplifier.

12. Low-frequency negative feedback

Most vacuum tube amplifiers suffer from potential low-frequency instability due to the use of inter-stage coupling capacitors and the phase shift that they add to the overall feedback loop. This can lead to motor-boating. Just as with frequency compensation in amplifiers at high frequencies, the amount of negative feedback at low frequencies is limited by stability issues in these vacuum tube amplifiers. This inevitably leads to decreasing amounts of negative feedback at low frequencies, exacerbating low-frequency distortion. A vacuum tube amplifier whose LF response falls 3 dB at 10 Hz probably has only 6 dB of negative feedback at 20 Hz. The very low LF cutoff of the C70 is made possible by the use of only one coupling capacitor in the loop. This means that the amount of negative feedback available at 20 Hz is still nearly its full amount, leading to much lower distortion at low frequencies. As a side benefit, the amplifier frequency response extends to unusually low frequencies.

13. Performance

Figure 9 shows the frequency response of the amplifier. Frequency response is 3 Hz to 45 kHz +0/-1 dB. The –3dB frequencies are 1.8Hz and 75kHz. The low-frequency response is exceptional, being down only 1 dB at 3Hz. This extended low-frequency response is made possible by the design topology that requires only one coupling capacitor in the feedback loop. The high-frequency response is limited by the output transformer's primary capacitance and leakage inductance along with the necessary feedback frequency compensation when using this output transformer.

The A-weighted noise is about 112 dB below full output and -97 dB with respect to 2.83V output (1W, 8 ohms). Hum is 100uV at the output, which, referred to 2.83V, is 89 dB down. It is predominantly 60Hz.

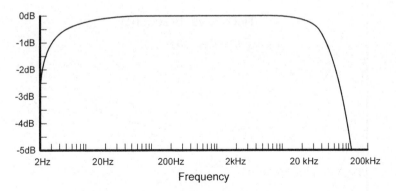

Figure 9: Frequency response of the amplifier extends to unusually low frequencies.

Figure 10 shows THD+N vs. power into an 8-ohm load at 50 Hz, 1 kHz and 20 kHz. Output power at 1% THD+N at 1 kHz into an 8-ohm load is about 35 watts. **Figure 11** shows THD+N vs. frequency at 1 watt, 8 watts and 28 watts into an 8-ohm load. Distortion is below 0.05% from 20Hz to 20kHz at 1 watt output. At 8 watts, THD+N is below 0.2% from 25Hz to 20kHz. As a reference, THD+N at 1 watt for the legendary McIntosh 275 is shown with the dashed curve [3]. The '275 is the gold-standard of classic vacuum tube audio power amplifiers. Putting aside the fact that the '275 is rated at twice the power, this amplifier compares very favorably to the '275 in distortion performance.

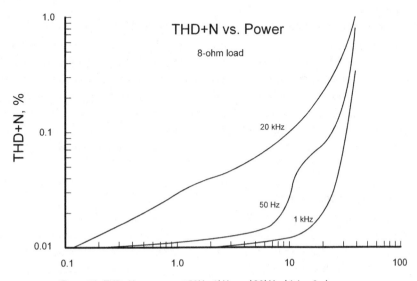

Figure 10: THD+N vs. power at 50Hz, 1kHz and 20kHz driving 8 ohms.

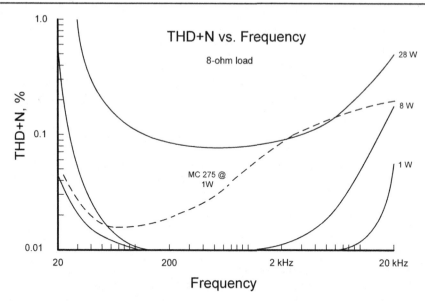

Figure 11: THD+N vs. Frequency at 1W, 8W and 28W driving 8 ohms. Note comparison with McIntosh MC275 at 1W [3].

Notice the substantial increase in THD+N at 8w and 28w as frequency decreases below 50Hz. This is evidence of output transformer core saturation. Larger output transformers would have improved the THD+N substantially at 20 Hz.

14. Listening tests

As one who has been designing solid-state amplifiers since the 1970's I must say that this VT amplifier sounded very good. Indeed, it sounded much better than it had a right to sound based on its measured power and distortion performance. This is often said of vacuum tube amplifiers. The C70 was demonstrated at a "bottle-head" meeting and met with praise. It was auditioned at the 2006 RMAF and HE2007 audio shows where it was used in listening and measurement workshops. There it was compared against a 200+ wpc solid-state amplifier and was also very well-received. To my ears, the C70 is solid across the full audio band and not the least bit sloppy or mushy like some VT amplifiers. The bass is surprisingly authoritative, but not at the expense of the midrange and highs.

15. Adjusting the output stage bias

In general, too little output stage bias will result in crossover distortion, and increased bias will reduce distortion. However, too much bias may cause excessive plate dissipation and actually reduce maximum output power. Once DC and AC balance have been optimized at a reasonable bias current setting, one can adjust the bias and observe distortion and maximum output power versus bias current. Distortion at low frequencies should also be checked as a function of bias. DC balance and AC bal-

ance should be trimmed after making any changes to the bias current. This amplifier has been adjusted for an output stage bias of 63mA per tube. Always let the amplifier warm up for at least one-half hour before making any adjustments.

Rated plate dissipation for the KT88 is 42W. With the existing bias of 63mA and a plate supply of 435V, plate dissipation at idle is 27W. This is fairly conservative and yet allows a healthy idle bias for low distortion. This is another advantage of the over-tubed design.

16. Adjusting DC balance

If the two output tubes do not operate at the same bias current, the difference in current can act to increase distortion and output transformer core saturation effects. It is always important to employ matched pairs of output tubes, but modest differences can occur between even matched pairs. This means that the two tubes in a pair will not operate at the same current even if their grid voltages are the same. DC balance should be adjusted so that the voltage drop across each of the cathode resistors is the same. VT amplifiers that do not have a DC balance adjustment will often be operating suboptimally.

17. Adjusting the AC balance

The AC balance adjustment takes care of driver signal balance and differences in output tube transconductance. Once again, a "matched pair" of output tubes cannot be assumed to be perfectly matched. Moreover, even when operated at the same bias current, the two tubes in a pair may not have exactly the same transconductance.

AC balance strongly influences second harmonic distortion. Although it is sometimes said that vacuum tube amplifiers produce more second harmonic distortion, the symmetrical design of push-pull vacuum tube amplifiers suggests that second harmonic distortion should actually be fairly low. Tube amplifiers that do not benefit from DC and AC balance adjustments are likely to suffer from increased amounts of second harmonic distortion. For those who like second harmonic distortion, the AC balance pot provides an opportunity to adjust it to taste.

AC balance is best adjusted using a distortion analyzer. The amplifier should be operated at 1/3 power at 1 kHz and the AC balance should be adjusted for minimal distortion. I have seen proper adjustment of AC balance reduce distortion by a factor of two in otherwise balanced amplifiers using matched output pairs. The optimum position will sometimes be a bit different for different frequencies, and the choice of frequency at which to set the optimum is a compromise.

18. An alternative output transformer

As mentioned earlier, this amplifier was built with output transformers from the 1960's that are un-fortunately no longer available. However, I have tested the amplifier with a transformer that is in cur-rent manufacture and is readily obtainable. It is the A-470 from Dynakit Corporation. They sell it as a drop-in equivalent of the 35-watt transformer used in the original Dynaco ST-70. Dynaco has long had a great reputation for its output transformers, traceable back to the Acrosound output transformers developed by David Hafler. These modern versions are wound to the same specifications and meas-ure very well. They are specified as having a 4300-ohm primary, which is quite a bit different from the transformers I used. However, measured performance of the amplifier is very close to the original, and bass response is a bit better at higher power levels because the A-470 transformers have a bit more iron. Listening tests that I conducted after the amplifier was fitted with the A-470 output transform-ers confirmed the high sound quality of these transformers. Optimal compensation for these trans-formers is slightly different, with C3/C4 at 22pF and R7/R8 at 100k. The A-470 transformers are available from:

Dynakit Inc.
55 Walman Ave
Clifton, NJ 07011
www.dynakitparts.com
dynakitparts@aol.com
(973) 340-1695

The Dynakit PA-060 power transformer, also designed for the Dynaco ST-70, is probably a compati-ble choice for the C70, but I have not evaluated it.

19. Conclusion

The topology and design techniques discussed here should be useful to those who wish to design and build modern vacuum tube amplifiers. Moreover, this amplifier demonstrates the level of per-formance that can be achieved in a classic push-pull power amplifier. For more audio information visit my site at www.cordellaudio.com.

References

[1] Bob Cordell, "Designing Audio Power Amplifiers", McGraw-Hill, 2010, ISBN 978-0-07-164024-4.
[2] Pierre Touzelet, "On The Leakage Inductance in Audio Transformers", Linear Audio, vol. 0, Sep-tember 2010.
[3] Stereophile, McIntosh MC275 power amplifier review, September 2010.

Look, Ma, No Distortion! The Class i output stage

Kendall Castor-Perry

Introduction

This paper introduces a systematic approach to very low distortion push-pull output stage design for audio power amplifiers. Work on this has been going on (well, on and off, to tell the truth) since February 2nd, 1981, according to my notebooks. The results presented here focus on algebraic analysis and simulation. But a great deal was learned from producing working hardware especially in the initial years.

Push-me, pull-you: the core problems presented by push-pull output stages

Firstly, conventional push-pull output stages (the current-delivering, unity-gain back-ends of the vast majority of linear amplifier topologies at any power level) aren't very linear. What does that mean? It means that under load (i.e. when significant current of either polarity flows at the output terminal), an error voltage is created between input and output. This error voltage isn't generally related linearly to either the output voltage or the output current, and represents a significant source of non-linearity and of the consequent distortion to signals. Cordell's excellent recent book [5] has a comprehensive and contemporary study.

So, one goal is to create a high output-current circuit that delivers high linearity before the soothing balm of global negative feedback (NFB) is applied. Poor linearity in the output stage is typically the driving factor for the choice of how much NFB to use. Now, I'm not a "feedback denier", but I like to see it used to make an excellent amplifier excellenter in some way, not to make a marginal amplifier meet a quantitative specification that may or may not have any impact on the sound quality. So I like to begin with an analysis of circuit behaviour that shows where the performance comes from, and quantifies its sensitivity to circuit parameters. This analytical rigour isn't found often enough in audio amplifier engineering discourse.

The linearity issue relates to imperfect handover between the pushing and pulling halves of the circuit. At some point, this handover turns into a rout, and the current flowing in one of the halves falls to zero. This cessation of correct operation causes dynamic difficulties when the stage needs to 'get

going' again as the direction of demanded current changes. Significant distortion and HF stability issues ensue, and it's generally considered a Bad Thing if the current in one half of a push-pull output stage falls to zero. So the second issue we must contend with is the 'switching distortion' problem. This is the bundle of effects generated by the cessation of current flow in one half of the push-pull stage.

Linearity and switching effects are bracketed together under the broadly used term "crossover distortion", though several mechanisms cause the difficulties. Margan concentrates on the subtle consequences of switching distortion [1]. It's a goal of this present work to eliminate entirely the performance-limiting behaviour that arises from these mechanisms.

Note that setting a finite quiescent current *doesn't* ensure that the current in one half of the push-pull stage won't fall to zero if you pull enough current out of the other side. In all 'classical' Class AB output stages, the current in one half is certain to fall to zero if you pull enough current out of the other side.

The uneasy truce between the pushing and pulling halves also results in uncertainties in circuit bias currents. The temperature dependencies of multiple devices of varying technologies and power levels make for a thermal stability challenge. Thank goodness that the affluent consumers that purchase high quality audio amplifiers operate them in centrally-heated (or cooled) living environments. High current amplifiers that need to run over the entire industrial (or even military) temperature range, need a more rigorous and disciplined approach to setting and maintaining critical biasing levels.

Comparison with other non-switching and low distortion approaches
Many non-switching linear amplifier topologies have made it into publication, patent or production. Beginning with Blomley in 1969, the 70s and 80s was a productive period of such development; certainly the golden age of the linear audio amplifier. Duncan [4] has a useful survey of these approaches.

The goal of topology modifications to produce non-switching amplifiers is to force current in the idle half of the amplifier to stay finite rather than fall to zero. This is done by smoothly converting the half-output stage to a constant current source (or sink). It allows the inactive half of a push-pull output stage to make a "soft landing" into a non-zero current state, and subsequently a "soft takeoff" into the active state. Margan [1] shows a simple, elegant and empirical way of doing this, at some expense to headroom and power dissipation.

The topology presented here achieves this in an analytically sound way, and provides design equations that allow both the quiescent and the limiting currents to be set precisely and sustained accurately over batch and temperature, without the need for any adjustment on the production line. We'll see soon that this structured approach to device biasing and the avoidance of switch-off can also fully correct for the open-loop linearity issues known to be caused by the varying combined transconductance of the paralleled output stage halves as they dance through the crossover region.

These linearity problems have also been addressed by other approaches that seek to improve linearity without a corresponding increase in the loop gain 'stick' often deployed to beat the linearity error into the ground. There come under the broad heading of 'error correction'. Cordell [5] gives a good overview of his own approach; see also Duncan [4] and Didden [9]. Such circuits generally fall into two categories. In one, a signal corresponding to the error being generated by the output stage is developed, and then structurally subtracted from the signal feeding the loudspeaker. In the other, a subtle rearrangement of feedback connections creates additional internal loop gain (sometimes non-obvious) that can suppress non-linearities, while leaving the external transfer function unchanged.

What's presented in this paper isn't error correction; it's an error avoidance scheme that uses structural cancellation between the main errors created by the two halves of the push-pull stage, leaving only the desired signal.

An evaluation methodology: treat current and voltage separately

The output stage can exhibit departures from linear behaviour that are related both to the voltage it's trying to assert onto the load, and to the current that the load demands in response. Minimizing the total output error, to create a really high quality stage, requires attending to both of these error sources independently. It's hard to separate the effects when the output is just loaded with a resistor. In the real world, significant phase shifts exist between the voltage across the load and the current flowing in it (the current is often significant when the output voltage is zero, and vice versa). This significantly affects the nature of the errors that the output stage contributes. Crossover artefacts happen at low load currents, *not* low load voltages!

The now-standard technique of plotting the incremental gain over a swept output voltage (Self [2], Cordell [5]) can be adapted to give some additional insight. To check the effect of output current, independent of voltage, the input voltage is fixed at some value and a DC sweep is done on a current source injected at the output. It's instructive to plot the partial derivative of output voltage with load current; that's the dynamic output resistance. In the ideal world, this should be independent both of the load current and of the output voltage chosen. When an audio signal is applied to the loaded output stage, the output impedance variation causes distortion, because the voltage divider between the output impedance and the load-impedance has a current-dependent value.

To check the effect only of output voltage, the source roles are reversed, and a fixed load current is taken from the output stage while the input voltage is swept over a range. This reveals how the large signal voltage gain is being affected by the static load current – and indeed, many output stages show some quite alarming deviations when tested this way. To round out the analysis, a conventional voltage sweep into a resistive load is also done.
Another useful adaptation of this method is to change the type of sweep used. The normal approach uses a sequence of DC analyses, plotting 'timeless' operating points as a function of the setup volt-

ages and currents. If instead a ramp over *time* is used, a SPICE transient analysis can show how the stage actually responds to this 'real' signal. The slew rate of the ramp can be chosen to challenge the dynamic behaviour of the output stage. Now the behaviour of the linearity in the crossover region can be tested dynamically, for any load current slew rates. Cordell [5] demonstrates that significant dynamic crossover distortion can be created by such current slew rates.

Starting point: the differential pair-based buffer

Standard power output stages aren't very precise circuits. The inherent offset voltage of base-emitter junctions (or gate-source interfaces) makes it tough to establish stable and optimum operating points. We can do a lot better than this, using local feedback techniques borrowed from precision circuit design discipline. Consider the basic forms in figures 1 (a) and (b). Familiar from the op-amp world, these are unity gain buffers (UGB) using a very tight local feedback loop. They have a small offset voltage that's only dependent on the Vbe difference between the two transistors. Form (a) has a long history in the electronics industry; at least as far back as the LM102 buffer introduced in 1967 (Addis [7], and see also Self [3]). Type (b) can also be thought of as a CFB pair whose input transistor has been replaced by a long-tailed pair (LTP).

There are two main high-quality ways of supplying the collector currents to the LTP. One is to have a current source equal to half the tail current feeding the active collector, and just short the other one to the rail. The other is to use a current mirror that forces the two currents to have some specific relationship (note: they may not be equal – see later on). Figure 1 employs ideal current mirrors made

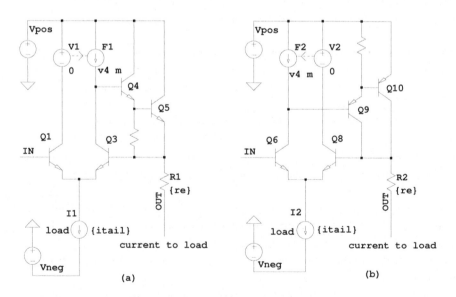

Figure 1: Two forms of the UGB output stage.

with the SPICE F primitive, where the current source senses the current in an associated voltage source.

It's tempting to try a push-pull version of this UGB circuit. The very small input offset voltage means that we now only have to create a very small extra voltage between the input transistor bases in order to define the voltage across the sensing resistors {re} and hence the quiescent current. This voltage doesn't need to track the properties or environment of the power devices, resulting in improved quiescent stability.

Such a configuration (in the complementary form of figure 1b, with simple resistive collector loads) was used in the 200W "PowerSlave" amplifier described in the April 1978 issue of ETI [6]. Figure 2 shows an adapted test circuit for simulation, derived from the PowerSlave design. Ideal transistors have been used for the input devices, which are run at a tail current of 30mA as published (they get

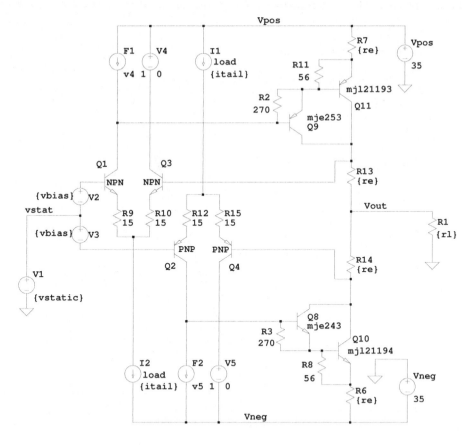

Figure 2: testing a push-pull UGB stage in simulation.

quite warm!). Emitter current sensing resistors are 0.22 ohms and the load resistance is 4 ohms. Input voltage is swept from -2V to +2V, which causes output current to vary over ~ -0.5A to +0.5A, which is where all the action is.

As the bias voltage between input bases is stepped, the circuit transitions from a gm-doubling mode (with finite quiescent current) to a zero-gm 'dead-zone' mode (with zero quiescent current). Extra emitter degeneration 'softens' the edges of the gm-doubling region but doesn't change the width or magnitude. The narrow almost-linear region is very sensitive to the value of the bias voltage forced across the emitter resistors; see figure 3, where the increments in the bias total bias voltage are 20mV per step.

Just as in the conventional case, the inactive half of the output stage will eventually turn off when enough current is drawn from the active half. It's easy to see (homework for you, if it's not!) that this

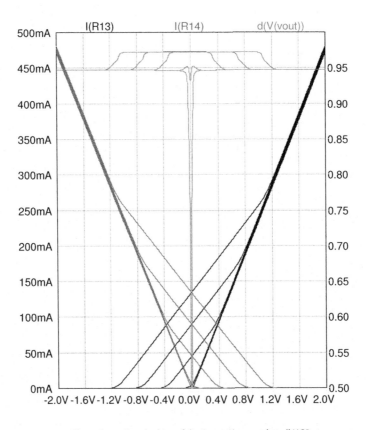

Figure 3: varying the bias of the PowerSlave push-pull UGB stage.

happens at a load current of around twice the quiescent current. This circuit definitely doesn't prevent output stage switch-off, and clearly suffers from gm-doubling.

Now, if the input LTP is built using identical, ideal transistors passing the same current, the input offset voltage is zero. But if the current is set to be *different* in the two devices, the LTP develops an offset voltage (proportional to absolute temperature). This offset voltage can be used to define the voltage across the output stage emitter resistors, so that a separately generated bias voltage between the two halves of the output stage is then not necessary. An offset voltage can also be developed by inserting a small resistor at the emitter of the feedback transistor (or unbalancing the pair of degeneration resistors). This doesn't do anything to mitigate the sensitivity to the resultant bias voltage, but it gives us a way of accurately setting it.

Introducing the Class i driver

If we don't want the current in the inactive half of the output stage to fall to zero, we need that half to transform topologically into a constant current source/sink with a predictable value. And the offset-equipped differential input amplifier just discussed immediately suggests a route to doing this. Consider the circuit of figure 4 compared to figure 1. The base of the input transistor has been connected instead to the output terminal, driving a current out to a load.

The feedback transistor runs at m times the current in the input transistor. Because of the resulting built-in offset voltage of the imbalanced long-tail pair, the effect is to produce a circuit that is un-

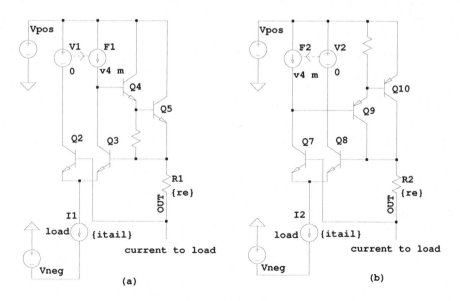

Figure 4: UGB driver reconnected as a constant current source.

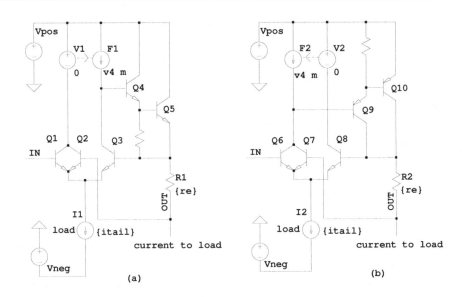

Figure 5: put the input transistor back – get the 'Class i doublet'.

willing to deliver less than a certain value of current, set by this offset voltage across Re. And that sounds like what we want out of half of our output stage; lots of current when we want current, and non-zero current (soaked up by the other half, of course) when we don't. There's just one problem, though – we lost our input terminal, in order to make this happen.

So, here's the clever part: just put another transistor back in, to act as an input path. We get the circuit shown in figure 5. The resultant input transistor 'doublet' is the characteristic sign of the Class i driver. Depending on the relationship between the voltages at the two bases, the current-splitting in the LTP is controlled either by the input signal or by the connection back to the output node.

We'll presently see that the resulting circuit neatly hands off control from one half to the other as the load current direction changes. But what makes it special is that it actually does work *exactly*, and can deliver solid design equations that can be used for quantitative work. It is possible to dimension a circuit that not only essentially eliminates both the switching and transconductance modulation components of crossover distortion, but also works out of the box in production, over temperature, with absolutely no need for any trimming components or complicated control loops.
An analytical proof of the linearity of the push-pull Class i stage is given in the Appendix. The output impedance is indeed purely resistive; under these admittedly rather ideal conditions, the output stage *cannot* introduce any current-dependent distortion. Only two parameters need to be chosen; the emitter resistor and the parameter K (equal to the ratio of the mirrors in the collector feeds). In a practical discrete circuit, this ratio is set by using unequal degeneration resistors in the collector mir-

rors. Early effect in the mirror transistor can be neglected as long as several hundred mV is dropped across those resistors.

Patent searches in the late 1990s indicated that of the many investigators of what amounts to an 'analogue OR gate' operation required for this kind of current control [11], Nakayama [12] got closest to the Class i configuration. However, his patent (filed 1983, granted 1985) shows elaborate circuits of unnecessary complexity, and he missed the atomic elegance and ideal operation of the Class i doublet.

The effects of real components on a complete circuit

A push-pull output stage using the Class i driver circuit is shown in figure 6. The small signal devices used here are the npn FMMT625 and the pnp FZT796A from Diodes, Inc. (formerly Zetex). These are high voltage SOT-23 devices whose SPICE models declare a high Early voltage (VAF). 'Ordinary' transistors could be used for the current sources and current mirrors; in simulation, changing the models for these devices has scarcely any effect.

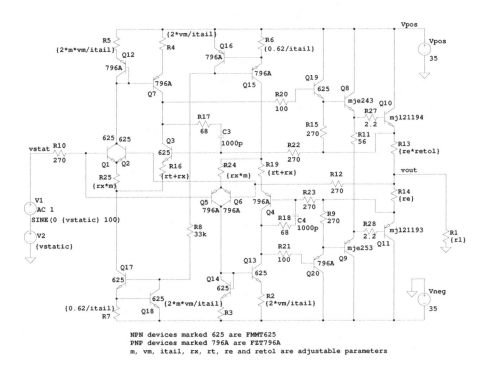

Figure 6: complete Class i push-pull output stage.

The output stage is a triplet Darlington, as recommended by Cordell, whose suggested output and driver devices are also used here [5]. By the way, when using such compound devices, always return the bleed resistors to the top of the emitter resistors, or cross-connect them to the other stage. Don't connect them directly to the output node (homework: why?).

Emitter resistors are set to 0.33 ohms, as in Cordell's circuits. In an amplifier designed to deliver higher current, I suggest reducing these resistors and accepting the higher quiescent current, to reduce the loaded voltage drop. The mirror degeneration resistors are set to drop 0.5V, and mirror imbalance parameter is set to m=1.2. Tail current of each LTP is nominally 5mA (set approximately through resistor parameters).

The circuit shows a couple of additions: unequal degeneration resistors and resistors in the doublet base connections. In the circuit analyzed, parameters rx=0 and rt=8 ohms. The reasons behind these two modifications are explained later.

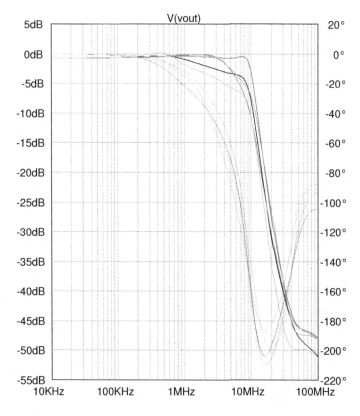

Figure 7: AC response of figure 6 as static output voltage varies from -30V to +30V.

As with all power amplifiers using slow bjt output devices, the response varies both with the current demanded and the output voltage; figure 7 shows the AC response with the static output voltage stepped from -30V to 30V onto a 4 ohm load (a highly recommendable test for all amplifiers!). The change in output device characteristics with current causes the amplitude and phase response to vary, but not in any way that's more difficult to contend with than with conventional output stages.

The poor high frequency response of large BJTs can cause even the very tight local feedback loop to exhibit some stability issues without the use of compensation. In figure 6, a simple pole-zero network has been wrapped around each feedback transistor as an example of a compensation scheme. The halves can be analyzed independently by simply breaking the connection between the emitters and loading each half separately. You should of course do detailed bench and simulation studies with your particular transistor choices. Output Zobel networks should also be used to ensure that load impedance is predictable at these high frequencies.

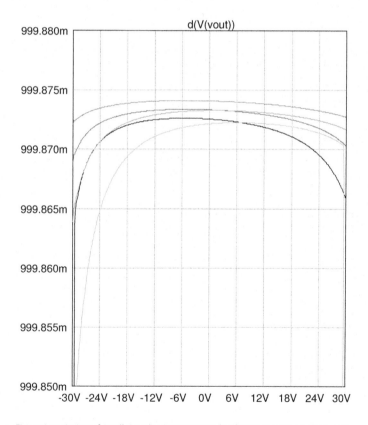

Figure 8: variation of small signal gain over ±30V, load current stepped -8A to +8A.

Figure 8 shows that the act of pulling large currents out from the output devices does not significantly change the inherent voltage gain of the stage. The peak to peak gain variation is less than 0.002%. In this plot, the output stage is not yet being presented with a resistive load, which is why the small signal gain is so close to unity.

Figure 9 shows a plot of the output impedance with injected output current of -8A to +8A and the static voltage stepped from -30V to +30V. The wobble in the output impedance curve looks alarming until you check the scale; it is ±0.16mohm, equivalent to a peak linearity error of less than ±0.004% into 4 ohms. The rapid deviation in output impedance happens only when the conducting half has almost the full supply voltage across it. This only happens when driving the amplifier into a negative resistance load (one of the pathological tests that amplifier designers love). A significant takeaway from figure 9 is that gm-doubling is completely absent over the entire current and voltage range.

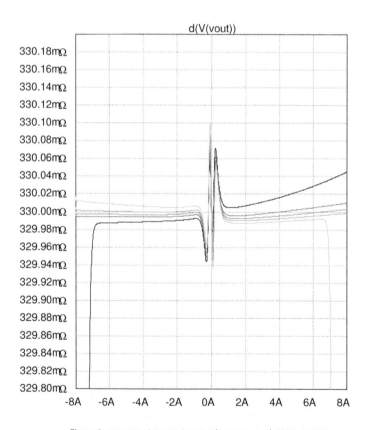

Figure 9: output resistance, input voltage stepped -30V to +30V.

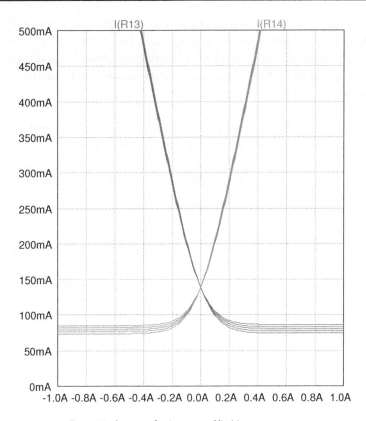

Figure 10: close-up of quiescent and limiting currents.

The detailed shape of this plot is very dependent on the simulation models used for the transistors in the LTP. The observant may notice that the 'wobble' is antisymmetric about zero, which is unusual for a symmetrical circuit. This is due to mismatch between npn and pnp small-signal devices. It's instructive (but unrealistic) to construct perfect pnp simulation complements for the npn devices used (just copy/paste a new device into your library, change its name suitably, and change the type from NPN to PNP). In such cases, the error curves become symmetric around zero.

Figure 10, which zooms in on the interesting part of the plot of the currents in the emitter resistors for the same sweep as used in figure 9, shows the very stable quiescent current point at 138mA, and the more variable limiting current value. This variation is primarily due to finite Early voltage in the Class i input doublet. The current in the outputs is held to a level that's well predicted by the design equations (allowing some leeway for the Early effect, which always tends to make the currents a little higher than expected).

If a clamping network is introduced between the doublet bases, the effect is to shut off the idling half when the clamp starts to conduct. Operating current delivery isn't affected. This will eventually happen when the base-emitter junctions break down; this should probably be avoided. The output stage can be shut down by forcing the LTP's current mirror load off, and this could form part of a protection scheme.

We can exercise the circuit with a sinewave of progressively increasing level and take an FFT to get an estimate of distortion levels. Figure 11 shows the FFT result for a 1kHz sine tone applied at the input with peak levels between 200mV and 20V. Worst-case is at 2V (this is 0.5A peak into 4 ohms; compare figure 9) where the 2nd harmonic is 95dB down on the fundamental. When overdriven, the circuit clips cleanly at around two diode drops from each rail.

The main residual sources of non-linearity in this simulation are non-ideality in the transistor models (particularly in the Class i doublet), model mismatches between pnp and npn small signal devices, and offset voltage changes caused by the difference in Is matching between the input transistors. Naturally, when building a practical amplifier to deliver this level of linearity, careful measurement and device selection will be required. Simulation can only take us so far.

As drawn, the input doublet experiences the difference between the input voltage and its local supply voltage. As this varies with applied signal, the Vbe for a given current level changes. The approach used here is to select devices whose model declares a high value of the Early voltage parameter VAF.

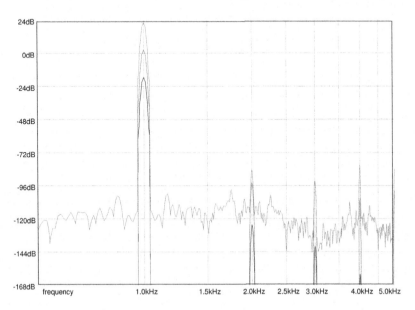

Figure 11: 1kHz tone and the first 4 harmonics. A long way down (note scale)

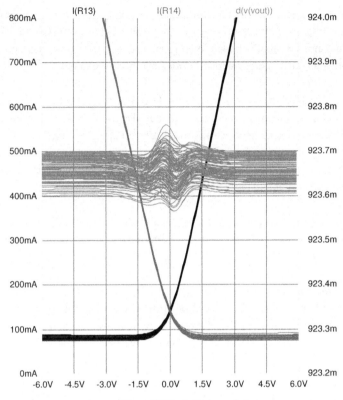

Figure 12: Monte Carlo analysis.

Suitable devices with VAF~450 were chosen from the large range of devices by Diodes, Inc. These appear to give good enough performance that the extra complexity of cascoding is unnecessary. Another contribution to non-linearity is the small imbalance in the Class i stage due to the base current into the first stage of the output triplet. This varies with load current and signal level. It can be reduced by increasing the current level in the Class i stage. But certain unsimulated effects such as self-heating will start to affect the balance. It's a tradeoff that should be assessed on the bench.

A significant advantage of the Class i configuration is that the condition for avoiding transconductance doubling or device switch-off can be met over a wide range of component tolerances and operating currents. This is demonstrated in the Monte Carlo analysis of figure 12. All the beta, VAF and Is parameters of the power devices are randomly adjusted over a +/-50% (uniform) range, and all the resistors (except for the emitter resistors, see the next paragraph) are set to 2% tolerance. None of the configurations show the development of either doubling or switch-off. No significant or egregious change in linearity or quiescent current was noticed over 100 sweeps, zoomed in to get a closer look at the critical few volts around zero.

While tolerance to active devices and setup currents is very good, one key component is critical to achieving good linearity: the current sense resistor. Mismatch between the two resistors directly causes transconductance variation between the positive and negative half-cycles, and this signifi-cantly degrades linearity much more directly than for any other component.

Because the error depends on the absolute resistance difference, the use of lower sense resistor val-ues relaxes the tolerance requirement. If not using global NFB, use precision high-power-handling metal film resistors with as close a tolerance as you can afford. Figure 13 shows an FFT of the 20Vpk 1kHz tone with equal emitter sense resistors and when one of the resistors is increased by a factor of between 0.1% and 10%. The 1% case causes a second harmonic component at about 77dB down on the fundamental. Still nothing to lose sleep about if you're using NFB.

For open-loop users prepared to contemplate a production-line distortion adjustment, the effect of this imbalance can be trimmed out (just null the 2nd harmonic) by the addition of two resistors and a potentiometer [10].

A downside: input impedance

This output stage needs to be driven by a low impedance as its input impedance is highly non-lin-ear. When one half is fully conducting, the effective AC input impedance of the LTP rises to a high value. In the handover region, the current in each input transistor is changing, resulting in a lower

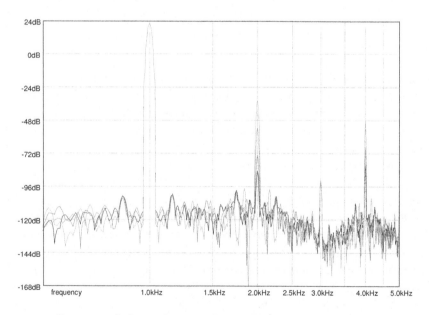

Figure 13: an elephant in the circuit: tolerance of the emitter resistors

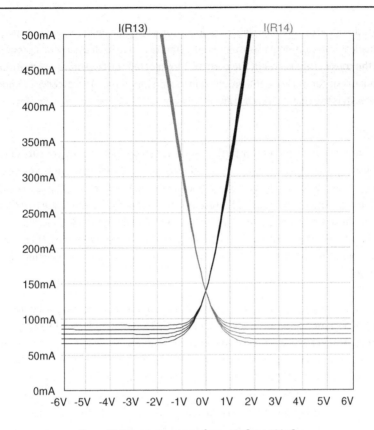

Figure 14: Temperature sweep from -40oC to +120oC.

input impedance (at least for finite beta – MOS devices operating in weak inversion wouldn't suffer from this problem).

Connecting the Class i stage to the high impedance output node of a conventional VAS will create significant distortion at its input that will need to be reduced by NFB, and the linearity advantages (not the switching advantages) are lost. The Class i doublets do tolerate equal resistances of a few hundred ohms in each base circuit. This provides some flexibility in the design of the buffer that's isolating the main gain stage; reduce the value of resistor R10 in figure 6 by the buffer output impedance.

Thermal stability
In figure 14's plot, for a 4 ohm load, the ambient temperature of the whole system in figure 6 is swept from -40°C to +120°C. Exercise caution when trying this kind of temperature sweeping with a conventionally-biased amplifier on the bench!

Without the additional unbalanced degeneration resistors {rt}, the quiescent and limiting currents in the basic circuit are proportional to absolute temperature (not in itself a particular problem). Adding resistors of the correct values, to suit the particular form of tail current source used, ensures that the simulated quiescent current is essentially constant over temperature. This excellent temperature stability indicates that the circuit will not suffer at all from load-induced operating point variation.

Conclusions

I've shown a designable high-current push-pull power stage that can deliver substantially better open-loop linearity than conventional circuits, through an analytically verifiable error cancellation scheme. Good linearity can be delivered in production over a wide active device tolerance with no trimming. The limit value of non-zero idle current in the half of the output stage that's not handling the load current can be easily set, and both this current and the no-load quiescent current are essentially independent of the output device's characteristics and environment. No thermal tracking provisions or specialized output devices are required to ensure stability over extreme operating temperature range.

The availability of a predictable high-linearity unity gain output stage gives greater flexibility to the audio amplifier designer, since lower levels of global NFB are required to meet any given distortion specification. Designers who wish to avoid global NFB entirely can, with care, gain a significant performance advantage from this configuration. With 'normal' levels of overall NFB, the dramatic reduction of distortion contributions from the output stage, achieved without any significant increase in quiescent power dissipation, enables better technical performance, and further challenges the state-of-the-art in measurement methods. Preventing device switch-off eliminates a slew (that's almost a pun) of dynamic problems that resist simple measurement but seem associated with characteristic sonic impairments.

The circuit extends readily to use of the otherwise-challenging quasi-complementary output configuration, since the output device characteristics (and their models!) have very little influence on the overall system performance. This also makes feasible an output stage entirely out of n-channel VMOS devices, taking advantage of their high current rating, robustness and low cost.

Right from the first time I built one of these amplifiers in the early 80s, replete with touchy monolithic Darlingtons and neophyte voltage amplifier design, I was bowled over by the step up both in measured performance and in sound quality that could be achieved by just adding a few transistors. Why don't you experiment with this output configuration in your own favourite amplifier design?

Acknowledgements

In the early 80s, I was able to spend a lot of time researching, building and listening to these amplifiers thanks to my very tolerant boss, Terry Grinstead. My colleagues at Burr-Brown in the late 90s were most interested in the configuration, and I had several illuminating discussions with them about

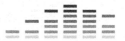

how it might be integrated onto silicon. Most recently, Bob Cordell has been very supportive on the simulation front, and where would we all be without the magnificent LTspice simulator – so thanks to Mike Englehardt. Jan Didden's persistence seeded the idea of writing the circuit up in Linear Audio, lest it be lost for ever. And, of course, huge thanks to Barrie Gilbert, whose friendship, intellectual *camaraderie* and infectious enthusiasm for all things circuitous have reaffirmed my belief that it is OK to love transistors as much as I love filters!

References

[1] "Crossover distortion in class B amplifiers", Erik Margan, Electronics & Wireless World, July 1987

[2] "Audio Power Amplifier Design Handbook", Douglas Self, Focal Press, 2009

[3] "Small Signal Audio Design", Douglas Self, Focal Press, 2010

[4] "High Performance Audio Power Amplifiers", Ben Duncan, Newnes, 1997

[5] "Designing Audio Power Amplifiers", Bob Cordell, McGraw-Hill, 2010

[6] "The PowerSlave Amplifier", Electronics Today International, April 1978 (publication rights now held by EPE, www.epemag3.com)

[7] "Good Engineering and Fast Vertical Amplifiers", John Addis, in "Analog Circuit Design: Art, Science and Personalities", ed. Williams, Newnes, 1998

[8] "Inclusive Compensation", Douglas Self, Linear Audio volume 0

[9] "the paX audio amplifier", Jan Didden, Elektor, April/May 2008

[10] Owen Jones, private communication

[11] Jon Pippard, private communication

[12] "Emitter Follower Type SEPP Circuit", US Patent 4,520,323

Appendix: Formal analysis of the Class i stage

The circuit for analysis is shown in figure 15. To simplify the analysis for this article, we'll assume that the transistors in the long-tailed pair all have identical saturation currents. We'll assume no degeneration (the effect can be added later) and we'll also ignore any base current flowing in the attached power devices. Voltage Vo is the drop across the stage when current is taken out of it.

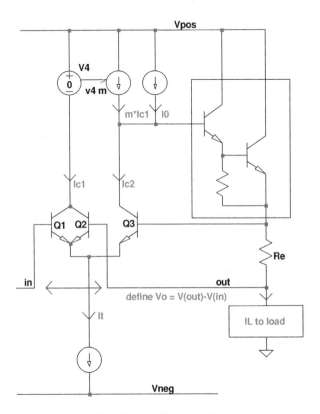

Figure 15: basic Class i stage for analysis

We first write down expressions for *Ic1* (flowing in the Class i input doublet) and *Ic2* (flowing in the feedback transistor), which sum together to give the tail current *It*:

$$I_{C2} = I_S \exp\left(\frac{V_O + I_L R_E - V_E}{V_{th}}\right) \qquad 1$$

and

$$I_{C1} = I_S \exp\left(\frac{V_O - V_E}{V_{th}}\right) + I_S \exp\left(\frac{-V_E}{V_{th}}\right) \qquad 2$$

with

$$I_T = I_{C1} + I_{C2} \qquad 3$$

Vth is the thermal voltage, kT/q for an ideal transistor with unit emission coefficient. Now from eq.2 we have

$$I_{C1} = I_S \exp\left(\frac{V_O - V_E}{V_{th}}\right) + I_S \exp\left(\frac{-V_E}{V_{th}}\right)$$

$$\therefore I_{C1} = I_S \exp\left(\frac{-V_E}{V_{th}}\right) \cdot \left(1 + \exp\left(\frac{V_O}{V_{th}}\right)\right)$$

$$\therefore I_S \exp\left(\frac{-V_E}{V_{th}}\right) = \frac{I_{C1}}{1 + \exp\left(\frac{V_O}{V_{th}}\right)} \qquad 4$$

and we can substitute this back into eq.1:

$$I_{C2} = I_S \exp\left(\frac{V_O + I_L R_E - V_E}{V_{th}}\right)$$

$$\therefore I_{C2} = I_S \exp\left(\frac{V_O}{V_{th}}\right) \cdot \exp\left(\frac{I_L R_E}{V_{th}}\right) \cdot \exp\left(\frac{-V_E}{V_{th}}\right)$$

$$\therefore \frac{I_{C2}}{I_{C1}} = \exp\left(\frac{I_L R_E}{V_{th}}\right) \cdot \frac{1}{1 + \exp\left(\frac{-V_O}{V_{th}}\right)} \qquad 5$$

The discussion on the UGB driver indicated that we could bias the collectors with either a current source or a mirror. Let's assume the general case where we use both, i.e. the value of the current in the working collector (feeding the output device) is the sum of a constant current portion and the output of a current mirror driven by the other collector. We can solve this equation using eq.3 to get expressions for the device currents involving only the constant current source values

$$I_{C2} = I_0 + m I_{C1} \qquad 6$$

(with $I_0 = 0$ if just a mirror, and $m = 0$ if just a current source)
and since

$$I_T = I_{C1} + I_{C2}$$

we can write

$$I_{C2} = \frac{m I_T + I_0}{m+1} \text{ and } I_{C1} = \frac{I_T - I_0}{m+1} \qquad 7$$

So plugging eq.7's expressions into eq.5 and rearranging:

$$\frac{mI_T + I_0}{I_T - I_0}\cdot\left(1+\exp\left(\frac{-V_O}{V_{th}}\right)\right) = \exp\left(\frac{I_L R_E}{V_{th}}\right)$$

and defining

$$K = \frac{mI_T + I_0}{I_T - I_0}$$

we get

$$I_L = \frac{V_{th}}{R_E}\ln K + \frac{V_{th}}{R_E}\ln\left(1+\exp\left(\frac{-V_O}{V_{th}}\right)\right) \qquad 8$$

which is our precious relationship between the current this half-stage is delivering and the voltage that appears at the output. We can see immediately that the quiescent current when the output voltage drop is zero is

$$I_Q = \frac{V_{th}}{R_E}\ln K + \frac{V_{th}}{R_E}\ln(1+1) = \frac{V_{th}}{R_E}\ln(2K) \qquad 9$$

and the limiting current when the output voltage is many times the thermal voltage is

$$I_{min} = \frac{V_{th}}{R_E}\ln K + \frac{V_{th}}{R_E}\ln(1+\sim 0) \Rightarrow \frac{V_{th}}{R_E}\ln K \qquad 10$$

This shows that solely by choosing the currents in the Class i driver's *input* pair we can set both the quiescent and the minimum current levels (they differ by a constant that's only dependent on the emitter resistor value). Note that the current as defined here is *always positive* for all values of output drop.

The minimum current can be chosen to be quite low even with low value emitter resistors. If all current sources in the amplifier have the same tempco, K is independent of temperature. Current mirror tolerance can be made pretty independent of transistor parameters. So the minimum and quiescent current settings are really quite stable over large production volumes.

The thermal voltage is proportional to absolute temperature, and therefore so are the quiescent and limiting currents in the output devices. Don't be tempted to make the emitter resistors out of normal metal wire with PTAT resistivity to compensate. It will lead to signal-dependent distortion, because the resistors will vary with load current.

We can correct for the temperature variation of the quiescent current in the suggested embodiment of figure 7. The tail current sources have a roughly ITAT behaviour, and so a low-value resistor (or resistance difference) in series with the emitter of the feedback transistor can provide an extra voltage that falls with temperature just as the LTP's offset is rising. We can therefore stabilize the offset voltage in just the same way as a bandgap reference is stabilized.

This additional resistor does not affect the ideal linearity in any way; it just increases the effective value of the constant K. In practice, the reduction in loop gain around the driver does eventually increase the sensitivity of the circuit to non-idealities in the output devices, but not until the local loop gain has been significantly reduced. The increase in the limiting and quiescent currents can be easily calculated because the change in offset voltage is just the device current flowing in the effective resistance delta of the degeneration resistors. Surely you must have been expecting *some* homework!

Meanwhile, going back to eq.8 and developing the matching expression for the other half of the stage, we can write

$$I_{L+} = \frac{V_{th}}{R_{E+}} \ln K_+ + \frac{V_{th}}{R_{E+}} \ln \left(1 + \exp\left(\frac{-V_O}{V_{th}} \right) \right)$$

and

$$I_{L-} = \frac{V_{th}}{R_{E-}} \ln K_- + \frac{V_{th}}{R_{E-}} \ln \left(1 + \exp\left(\frac{+V_O}{V_{th}} \right) \right)$$

Now the actual current into the load is just the difference between these two. Assuming that the K and emitter resistor values are the same for the two half-stages, we have

$$I_L = \frac{V_{th}}{R_E} \ln \left(1 + \exp\left(\frac{-V_O}{V_{th}} \right) \right) - \frac{V_{th}}{R_E} \ln \left(1 + \exp\left(\frac{+V_O}{V_{th}} \right) \right)$$

$$\therefore I_L = \frac{V_{th}}{R_E} \ln \frac{\left(1 + \exp\left(\frac{-V_O}{V_{th}} \right) \right)}{\left(1 + \exp\left(\frac{+V_O}{V_{th}} \right) \right)}$$

$$\therefore I_L = \frac{V_{th}}{R_E} \ln \left(\exp\left(\frac{-V_O}{V_{th}} \right) \frac{\left(\exp\left(\frac{+V_O}{V_{th}} \right) + 1 \right)}{\left(1 + \exp\left(\frac{+V_O}{V_{th}} \right) \right)} \right)$$

$$\therefore I_L = \frac{V_{th}}{R_E} \ln \left(\exp\left(\frac{-V_O}{V_{th}} \right) \right)$$

$$\boxed{\therefore I_L = \frac{V_{th}}{R_E} \cdot \frac{-V_O}{V_{th}} = \frac{-V_O}{R_E}}$$

11

This rather simple result delivers the Class i punch: the output impedance of the full stage, assuming matching between the devices, has a *theoretically perfect linear output impedance equal to the value of one emitter resistor*. And if this is the case, the stage cannot cause any non-linearity, whatever the load current. Note, by the way, that the sign in eq.11 results from our choice of variables – it *is* a positive output resistance!

The alternate configuration using a complementary power device driven from the collectors of the

input transistors analyzes out to exactly the same result; the characteristics of the output devices don't enter into these expressions at all, and create only second order effects. And interestingly, when the effect of device base current is taken into account, we see that both configurations also behave the same way. The emitter follower based circuit steals current from the feedback transistor, whereas the complementary form injects extra current into the input transistors. In either case, base current is only an issue when one half of the circuit is strongly conducting, and it causes a small additional curvature to the output as the offset of the driver stage changes (the effective value of K changes a little at high output currents). It has little effect in the region where both halves are conducting and doesn't disrupt the good linearity in the crossover region.

A New Amplifier Topology with Push-Pull Transimpedance Stage

Samuel Groner

Abstract

In this article I introduce an amplifier topology which uses a novel push-pull transimpedance stage. Compared to known standard amplifier configurations, the new circuit offers a substantial improvement in power supply rejection. Furthermore secondary slew rate limits are addressed, and sensitivity to loading from the output buffer is reduced. This makes this amplifier architecture particularly suitable for high quality audio power amplifier designs. Experimental results using model amplifiers are presented.

1. Introduction

Power amplifier design is a topic which finds wide interest in the audio community—not only in the sense of commercial concerns, but also as a fascinating and often demanding challenge for electrical engineers and do-it-yourself enthusiasts. The trade-offs involved are numerous; from the basic requirements for accurate audio signal reproduction (such as good frequency response, low noise and distortion, etc.) over contemplations regarding efficiency, safety and complexity to constraints as a result of current fashion, which might favour certain design techniques for no particular objective reason. As there will never be a solution which simultaneously fulfills all demands, we can expect an ongoing development in this field and I hope to add to the state of the art with the humble contribution of this article.

Most audio power amplifiers have been built around topologies with two gain stages; the first gain stage forms a transconductance stage (i.e. a voltage-to-current converter, typically implemented by a simple differential pair), and the second a transimpedance stage (i.e. a current-to-voltage converter, usually a common-emitter transistor configuration) which also provides Miller compensation. A full audio power amplifier capable of driving a speaker load is completed by the addition of a unity gain power output stage, e.g. a complementary Darlington emitter follower.[1] As explained by Self [1] in

---

[1] I should add that some authors count the output buffer as explicit gain stage, so the standard amplifier topology is then referred to as three-stage amplifier. Personally I prefer the other nomenclature which is in line with the large IC operational amplifier literature, and which appreciates that for the basic conceptional functionality of amplifiers the output stage is not strictly necessary.

great detail this configuration is very suitable to build discrete power amplifiers, as it offers potentially excellent performance at low complexity.

There are amplifier topologies which use three gain stages; however proper compensation is usually
difficult to achieve, and the possible performance improvement is often benign compared to the increase in complexity. On the other hand, it is also possible to build amplifiers with just one gain stage.
Unfortunately they require a power output stage with very high and constant input impedance for
reasonable distortion performance; furthermore typical topologies show rather high sensitivity to
transistor and resistor mismatch. This makes them less suitable for discrete implementation and the
required complexity for a given performance goal will often be higher than with the use of a two-
stage topology.

In this article I will consider—once more—the two-stage topology. Before I present the new amplifier architecture in section 3, I'll first discuss typical prior-art topologies and some of their shortcomings in section 2. Later in this text (sections 4–7) detailed advise for the optimum practical
realisation of the novel amplifier topology is given. Section 8 considers several possible adaptations
and alterations of the presented circuit, while in section 9 I show experimental verifications of the new
amplifier concept. This article is finished with a brief conclusion, and an appendix covering noise
sources in folded cascode stages.

2. Review of Typical Two-Stage Topologies

Figure 1 depicts a conceptual schematic of what is generally accepted to be the standard two-stage
amplifier topology. Q1 and Q2, together with the current source I1, form a differential pair which is
loaded by a Widlar current mirror (Q3 and Q4). These parts make up the first stage; as noted above
it is a transconductance gain stage. The second gain stage with transimpedance behaviour is formed
by Q5, Q6 and I2. C1 is the Miller compensation capacitor; it defines, together with the transcon-

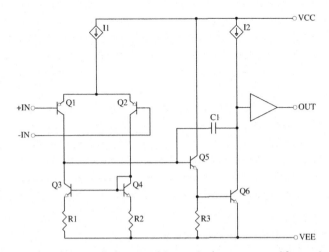

Figure 1: Conceptual schematic of the standard two-stage amplifier topology.

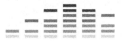

ductance of the first stage, amplifier open-loop gain at high frequencies and hence stability margins [1, 2, 3]. Towards high frequencies the compensation capacitor transfers global loop gain to local second stage feedback.

This feedback reference voltage connection of the Miller compensation loop creates several problems. One of these is a reduction in power supply rejection; as the base of Q5 is referenced to the negative supply by the base-emitter junctions of Q5 and Q6, the ripple of the negative power supply rail voltage is superposed to the intended output signal. This effect is reduced by the global feedback loop. The rail injection hence increases towards high frequencies, where less global feedback is available to suppress the effect. In other words, available amplifier loop gain sets an upper limit to power supply rejection; with standard Miller compensation power supply rejection decreases at 20 dB per decade, and becomes 0 dB at the unity loop gain frequency. With a unity loop gain frequency of 700 kHz, which can be considered a typical figure for audio power amplifiers, power supply rejection is hence limited to about 30 dB at 20 kHz.[2] This estimate ignores second-order effects which depend on the exact implementation, but the result is still useful and valid for a rough analysis. Note that for the positive power supply there is no such primary injection path; the power supply rejection will be largely independent of frequency, and thus is usually much less critical.

Power supplies of power amplifiers are typically unregulated for efficiency reasons [1, 2]. This means that they carry substantial ripple related both to the mains frequency and harmonics of the output signal; it is highly undesirable that this ripple content be superposed to the audio signal. Yet it is difficult to give exact figures for the needed power supply rejection, as this depends on the expected performance level, output power and power supply design details. However it is unlikely that the above quoted figure of 30 dB at 20 kHz is sufficient for any quality power amplifier. Also note that ripple related to the harmonics of the output signal extends well above the audio frequency range; hence the region of high power supply rejection should reach at least up to 100 kHz.

To improve the power supply rejection of the basic two-stage topology from figure 1, several solutions have been presented in the literature. The simplest one uses a RC low pass filter, inserted between power output stage and transimpedance stage, to reduce the ripple content on the power supply before it feeds the transimpedance stage. To be appreciably effective, the low pass filter requires a rather large time constant. If the capacitor shall not become unreasonably large, the resistor must have a sufficiently high value. The inevitable DC voltage drop across this resistor will reduce maximum output voltage swing in many cases. This is further exacerbated by the fact that Q6 will need, in a practical implementation, an emitter resistor for current limiting. This further reduces available output voltage swing.

To avoid this issue, a separate additional negative power supply for the small-signal stages has been used [1, 2]. This supply is, for example, derived from an additional mains transformer secondary winding and has rather low current requirements; hence it can easily be arranged to have both sufficient voltage and very low ripple. While the cost of such a solution is modest (at least in the context of a

---

[2] Note that this figure is related to the output, not the input, of the amplifier. This is unlike the figures quoted in operational amplifier data sheets. Figures related to the output show a value which is lower by the noise gain of the used amplifier configuration—typically 20–30 dB for audio power amplifiers.

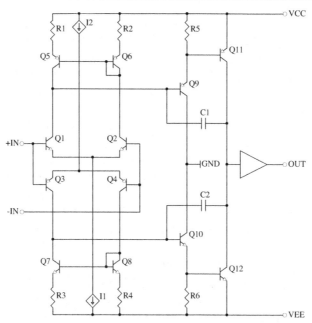

Figure 2: Basic two-stage amplifier with push-pull transimpedance stage. Necessary bias control circuit for the second stage is omitted.

commercial design where a custom power transformer is usually specified anyway), it remains a rather inelegant brute force solution.

Conceptually more pleasing is the use of Ahuja compensation [1, 4]. By means of a cascode the input node of the transimpedance stage is referenced to ground rather than a power supply rail. This removes the basic power supply injection route, however in many cases second-order effects make this arrangement less effective than the previously discussed means. Furthermore certain implementations can suffer from local instability of the Miller compensation loop (which now includes at least one additional transistor), or may contribute significantly to the voltage noise of the amplifier. The last difficulty of the two-stage topology shown in figure 1 which I'll discuss here is related to slew rate. While the output of the second stage can sink very high currents by turning on Q6, current sourcing is limited by I2. This can lead to a slew rate limitation, particularly as under transient conditions the output current of I2 may be reduced by junction capacitances [1], and if the output stage demands high drive currents. I have presented a solution to this in [5], but there are some limits to its effectiveness. Of course it is very arguable whether there are any audible artefacts from such slew rate limitations within a well designed amplifier [6]. Nonetheless, at least from a marketing point of view, it is desirable to tackle this issue.

To make the sourcing and sinking output current capabilities of the second stage equal, and as a first-order approximation unlimited, many prior art amplifiers have implemented a push-pull arrangement similar to that shown in figure 2. To derive the complementary drive signals required for the

transimpedance stage formed by Q9–Q12, two complementary differential pairs (Q1–Q4) are employed. Not shown in the schematic diagram is the bias current control necessary for the second stage; some solutions for this are presented in [2, 5, 7, 8].

While this amplifier topology, with some minor modifications of the input stage, easily supports very high slew rates (see e.g. [8]), it does not fully solve the power supply rejection issue discussed above. Due to the complementary nature of the topology both power supply rails now act as main injection route. However, as is easily shown by simulation or other forms of sufficiently detailed theoretical analysis, the injection from the negative power supply rail is reduced by 6 dB compared to the amplifier from figure 1 for a given amount of loop gain. Furthermore ripple signals which are present in a complementary form on both power supply rails are theoretically rejected. But this rejection mechanism is not particularly reliable, as it depends e.g. on the matching of the smoothing capacitors employed in the positive and negative power supply rail. So this amplifier architecture has again to rely on either RC filtering, additional power supplies for the small-signal stages or Ahuja compensation for excellent power supply rejection.

Further minor problems with this topology arise from gain mismatch in the two complementary halves.[3] This can lead—according to simulation results—to both additional distortion and instability, although at least the latter is easily fixed by connecting a small capacitor across the inputs of the second stage (i.e. the bases of Q9 and Q10).

Excellent power supply rejection can be achieved by the use of a differential transimpedance stage as shown in figure 3. The second stage is formed by Q5–Q8, and its output is converted to single ended by the current mirror realised by Q9 and Q10; biasing is provided by I2. Besides the Miller compensation capacitor C2 there is now an additional capacitor (C1) which has an (although only second-order) influence on compensation. It is required to make the drive from the input stage single-ended at high frequencies, as otherwise the output current of Q2 would bypass the Miller compensation loop at high frequencies. The conversion of the differential output current of the input stage to a single-ended output voltage is, thanks to the ground connection of C1, carried out with respect to ground. Ripple of the negative power supply is present at the base of both Q5 and Q6; however this appears as a common-mode signal to the transimpedance stage and hence is rejected because of the differential nature of this stage. The rejection is mainly limited by mismatch of C1 and C2; for best results these should hence be 1% parts.

It cannot be stressed enough that C1 needs to be grounded for good power supply rejection. Most amplifiers that use a similar topology (and that I've evaluated), connect this capacitor to the collector of Q7; presumably in an attempt to make it a Miller compensation capacitor as well, but this cannot happen as there is no significant voltage swing at this node. However this arrangement will effectively connect C1 to the positive power supply rail through the current mirror input, putting power supply rejection back to the point of the simple two-stage amplifier of figure 1. Also detri-

---

[3] The gain of one complementary half is defined as the transconductance of that differential pair times the corresponding Miller compensation capacitor. Gain mismatch can hence arise both from the input stage transconductances or the compensation capacitors.

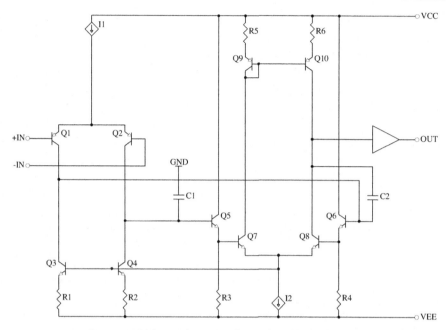

Figure 3: Amplifier topology with differential transimpedance stage.

mental to the performance of this topology is the use of a standard current mirror instead of the active load formed by Q3 and Q4. The main disadvantage of this topology relates to the voltage headroom required by I2; it directly reduces available output voltage swing which is highly undesirable. Also both sourcing and sinking output current capability of the second stage is limited by I2; hence the support of very high slew rates will again be difficult at some point, particularly if the output stage demands substantial drive current.

As we have seen from this discussion of two-stage topologies there is no known architecture which simultaneously achieves inherently excellent power supply rejection and freedom from second-stage slew rate limits. In the following section I will present a novel amplifier topology which does just this.

3. New Push-Pull Transimpedance Stage

As shown above the main power supply rejection limitation in typical two-stage amplifier topologies arises from the reference of the input of the transimpedance stage to at least one supply rail. More specific, the emitter of the common-emitter transistor in the transimpedance stage is connected directly to the power supply, which then forwards power supply ripple to the input of the transimpedance stage. From this node Miller compensation transfers the ripple to the second stage output. Can't we simply connect the emitter of the common-emitter transistor in the transimpedance stage to ground, in order to also reference the Miller compensation loop to ground? This is not straightforward, because the collector of this transistor needs to be able to swing nearly all the way from the negative to the positive power supply; furthermore, the input voltage of the second stage is then

at a potential which is inconvenient to drive from the input stage without greatly limiting the common-mode input range of the differential pair.

Fortunately *not straightforward* does not mean *impossible* in this case. We can use folded cascodes both to level shift the output current of the first stage to the input of the transimpedance stage, and to free the collector of the common-emitter transistor from any significant voltage swing. Folded cascodes are non inverting stages and, being common-base transistor configurations, typically reduce stability margins of the global feedback loop by a small amount only. Hence there are only minor fundamental implementation problems to be expected.

Figure 4 depicts a first attempt to design such an amplifier. Q5 forms the folded cascode which acts as level shifter for the output current of the input stage, and Q8 provides the folded cascode for the output of the basic transimpedance stage realised by Q6 and Q7. The input node of the transimpedance stage (the base of Q6) is now indeed, through the base-emitter junctions of Q6 and Q7, referenced to ground. It results that the basic power supply rejection will be high and independent of frequency. At first it might look as if the collector current of Q7 were undefined; however, V2 forces a fixed voltage across, and hence a fixed current through, R5. Ignoring the base current loss of Q8, the difference between this current and that set by I3 is then, by the action of global feedback, enforced as collector current for Q7. Also noteworthy is the fact that there is just one compensation capacitor needed—there is no chance that capacitor mismatch can introduce distortion, instability or a power supply rejection limitation as observed for some prior art topologies.

While practical implementation of such a circuit is perfectly feasible, the output of the transimpedance stage is not yet a push-pull configuration and will have similar slew rate limits as the one from figure 1. The amplifier revealed by figure 5 fixes this. The transimpedance stage (Q7–Q12) is now

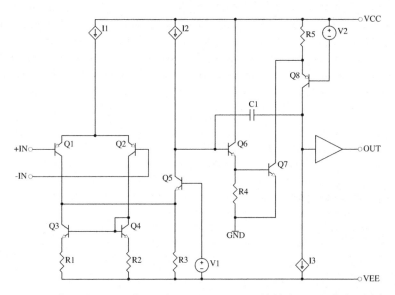

Figure 4: Amplifier with ground referenced second gain stage and folded cascodes for level shifting.

95

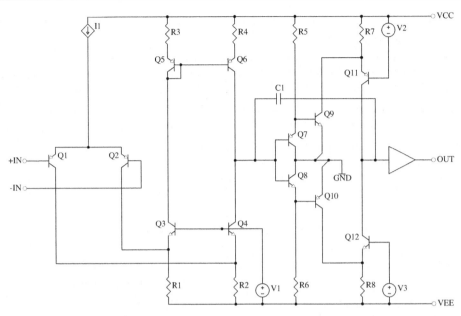

Figure 5: Basic amplifier with novel push-pull transimpedance stage.

arranged as complementary push-pull configuration. Unlike the amplifier from figure 2, there is no need for an explicit bias current control circuit; the voltage from Q7 emitter to Q8 emitter provides bias for Q9 and Q10. The input node of the transimpedance stage (the bases of Q7 and Q8) is still referenced to ground by the emitters of Q9 and Q10. Hence the basic power supply rejection is good. As an additional change, both collectors of the input pair are now level shifted with folded cascodes (Q3 and Q4), and the current mirror (formed by Q5 and Q6) is placed after the cascodes. This minimises the impact of the folded cascode to collector current balance of the differential pair of the input stage, and with the dual folded cascode the differential pair is operated at very nearly equal collector voltage; this reduces secondary limitations to offset, drift, common-mode rejection and power supply rejection.

In the next sections we will look into the optimum practical realisation of amplifiers with this novel transimpedance stage, and explore several extensions and adaptations of it.

4. Biasing Considerations

The first thing to get right in a circuit design is the biasing conditions. So I will, first of all, discuss the necessary considerations in this respect. Please consider figure 6 for this, which shows several additional circuit elements that are essential, or at least very helpful, for a practical realisation.

There are three fundamental bias currents to be chosen for this novel transimpedance stage: the collector current of the emitter followers Q8 and Q9, that of the common-emitter transistors Q10 and Q11, and finally the current in the folded cascodes formed by Q14 and Q15. Needless to say, the col-

lector current of complementary pairs (e.g. Q8 and Q9) should be set to approximately equal values. There are various trade-offs associated with the selection of these bias conditions. Detailed discussion of these is beyond the scope of this article, so I'm just quoting suggested values which will be found to work well in most typical power amplifier designs:

- 0.5–1 mA for Q8 and Q9
- 5–20 mA for Q10 and Q11
- Use the same, or a slightly higher, collector current for Q14 and Q15 as for Q10 and Q11.

The collector current for Q8 and Q9 is easily set by selecting appropriate values for R7 and R8. Biasing Q10 and Q11 requires a bit more thought, however. As mentioned in the previous section, an explicit bias current control circuit will not be required for the new push-pull transimpedance stage. However, to mitigate the sensitivity to transistor tolerances and thermal effects, the addition of emitter resistors is necessary. In figure 6, R11 and R12 realise this. In most cases choosing their values such that they each carry about a 100 mV voltage drop at the nominal collector current of Q10 and Q11 will be sufficient for good bias current stability. Minimising the value of the emitter resistors is advantageous as this lowers the sensitivity to loading of the second stage output node (details on this can be found in [5]), so going above the suggested 100 mV voltage drop is not advised. Once the

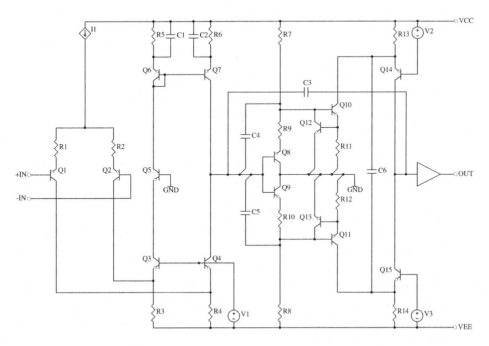

Figure 6: More detailed amplifier schematic using the new second stage topology.

emitter resistor value is determined, an appropriate bias voltage is set up by selecting R9 and R10. Simulation can be helpful to derive an initial estimate for the value of these parts, however experimental verification will usually be needed.

The collector current of the folded cascodes (Q14 and Q15) is set both by the emitter resistors (R13 and R14) and the base reference voltage sources V2 and V3. To maximise available output voltage swing the DC voltage drop across the emitter resistors should be minimised; a lower limit of about 200 mV is set by the need that the emitter impedance of the folded cascode transistor (given by the reciprocal of its transconductance) is small compared to the emitter resistor, such that most of the AC collector current of Q10 and Q11 actually flows into the emitter of the corresponding folded cascode (and thus to the output node), rather than into the emitter resistor (and thereafter into the power supply, where it does not produce any usable output).

After discussion of the biasing considerations of the transimpedance stage, we will turn our attention to the folded cascodes of the input stage (Q3 and Q4 in figure 6). As these folded cascodes are part of the input stage, they must be carefully designed to not impair the voltage noise of the amplifier (such considerations are essentially negligible in the second stage, where there is a substantial amount of loop gain available to reduce the impact of the corresponding folded cascodes). That's particularly important if, as routinely done in audio power amplifiers, the input stage transconductance is reduced by the addition of emitter resistors in the differential pair (note R1 and R2). While the emitter degeneration is very useful for improving input stage distortion and slew rate [1, 2], it also pronounces noise contributions from following stages.

As detailed in the appendix, there are several design strategies available to minimise the impact of the folded cascodes:

- Maximise the value of the emitter resistors by minimising the quiescent current of the folded cascode transistor and the use of a voltage reference with large DC voltage.
- Use a voltage reference with low noise and low impedance.
- Choose transistors with high h_{FE} and low excess noise.

If these strategies are combined they will ensure that amplifier performance is not significantly degraded by the presence of the folded cascodes. There's one caveat regarding the quiescent current of the folded cascode transistors: if it is chosen lower than the collector current of the input differential pair, additional distortion at high frequencies might result (because at peak output currents of the differential pair one or the other folded cascode transistor will switch fully off). Usually the most suitable bias condition for the folded cascode transistors is hence a collector current equivalent to, or slightly above, that of the transistors of the input differential pair.

The current mirror (Q6 and Q7 in figure 6) has a very similar impact on the voltage noise of the amplifier as the folded cascodes Q3 and Q4. As indicated in the appendix, the procedures to minimise its contribution are very similar to those of the folded cascode. Most important, the emitter resistors R5 and R6 should have a large value [5, 9]. Unlike the prior art topologies from figure 1–3, there is plenty of voltage headroom at the current mirror output available, which allows the use of rather

large emitter resistors without pushing the current mirror close to saturation.

Figure 6 reveals a last enhancement for the input stage. The common-base transistor Q5 is introduced to keep the folded cascode transistors Q3 and Q4 at approximately the same collector-emitter voltage. This minimises offset due to Early effect and different thermal operating points. Moreover, the base current of this additional transistor partially cancels the base current errors of the current mirror. This further reduces amplifier offset voltage.

5. Stability and AC Performance

Having clarified the basic biasing conditions, let us focus on stability and AC performance. The stability of the global feedback loop does not need any special attention (in this article, not as general design practice!), as AC open-loop gain is defined the same way as for prior art two-stage topologies—namely by the input stage transconductance and the Miller compensation capacitor C3 [1, 2, 3]. However the stability of the local Miller compensation loop should be considered, as additional transistors (the folded cascodes in the second stage, Q14 and Q15 in figure 6) are now included within this loop. These necessarily contribute some delay and phase shift, which could impact stability margins. I have stated above that folded cascodes reduce stability margins by a small amount only; this applies solely to the global feedback loop (and hence to the folded cascodes of the input stage), which, for audio power amplifiers, typically has a unity loop gain frequency in the order of 1 MHz or less. However the bandwidth of the local Miller loop of the second stage can extend into the 100 MHz region, and here the effects of an additional common-base stage are not negligible.

The additional delay and phase shift typically manifests itself as gain peaking in the 10–100 MHz region. Generally associated with this is a peak in second stage output impedance, which interacts as LC resonant network with the input capacitance of the output power buffer. As the latter can be substantially dependent on output voltage and output current, a potential instability mechanism may only be triggered under certain load and signal conditions. To largely eliminate these effects I've found the use of feed-forward capacitors in the emitter followers of the second stage to be the most dependable and powerful technique [10, 11]. C4 and C5 implement these capacitors. They bypass Q8 and Q9 such that, at high frequencies, the local Miller loop consists of a cascaded common-emitter (Q10 or Q11) and common-base transistor (Q14 or Q15) only. Such a transistor arrangement has excellent stability margins within the local Miller compensation loop, and no significant gain peaking is observed. At low frequencies, where the impedance of the feed-forward capacitors is large, the emitter followers are fully in the signal path, and improve amplifier performance (in particular low-frequency open-loop gain and distortion).

As suitable measurement equipment to quantify gain peaking above the 10 MHz region (i.e. a network analyzer) is not routinely found in audio engineering laboratories, the value of these feed-forward capacitors will in most cases be determined by simulation. The smallest value which still minimises gain peaking is usually the most suitable—typically around 100 pF. It should however be appreciated that, with the standard SPICE transistor models, characterisation of transistor behaviour near the cut-off frequency f_T may be rather inaccurate. If experimental verification reveals a remaining instability mechanism in the Miller compensation loop, the choice of a larger feed-forward ca-

pacitor should be considered.

I have promised that the novel amplifier topology will bring absence of slew rate limitations in the transimpedance stage; this was, admittedly, a bit cheating at first. To support very high slew rates the output current of the second stage must be able to dynamically exceed the quiescent current by a substantial amount (at least as long as we apply a reasonable upper limit for quiescent current, for practical reasons). This however is not the case for the new push-pull transimpedance stage, because the output current of the folded cascodes is limited by their bias voltage sources and emitter resistors.

Fortunately there is an easy fix for this; with the use of capacitor C6 (in figure 6) greatly increased transient output currents are made possible. This capacitor acts as high-frequency level shifter, such that the common-emitter transistor of one half of the transimpedance stage (e.g. Q11) can dynamically increase the collector current of the folded cascode in the other half (Q14). Thereby the operation mode of the transimpedance stage is changed to class AB. There is no primary limit for the value of this capacitor; however its presence means that high-frequency power supply ripple modulates the quiescent current of the folded cascodes. Hence its value should not be chosen larger than necessary. Usually 1 nF is perfectly adequate, and 10 nF should suffice to support even very high slew rates.

It must be appreciated that this slew rate enhancement capacitor cannot increase the second stage output current at low frequencies. It is still necessary to choose a sufficiently high quiescent current to drive the output power buffer. However, as typically the required drive currents increase towards high frequencies (due to the capacitive portion of the input impedance of the output power buffer), the slew rate enhancement capacitor will nonetheless reduce the need for high quiescent currents. Above I suggested that the emitter resistors of the current mirror (R5 and R6 in figure 6) should have a large value to minimise the noise contribution of the current mirror. However at some point large emitter resistor values will introduce a detectable pole to the open-loop gain of the amplifier, and under some conditions also present a large-signal limitation.[4] The capacitors connected in parallel with the emitter resistors (C1 and C2) avoid this, while preserving the improvement from the emitter resistors at audio frequencies. Typical values for these capacitors range from 100 pF to 10 nF.

6. Current Limiting

Another view on figure 6 reveals two last components whose function I've not yet disclosed—Q12 and Q13. These transistors limit the collector current of Q10 and Q11 to a value of about six times the quiescent current. This is necessary because otherwise overload conditions can increase the collector current and power dissipation beyond the maximum rating of typical low power parts. Usually this current limiting scheme will not interfere with the slew rate capability of the amplifier; if necessary, the emitter resistors R11 and R12 may be bypassed with a capacitor to restrict the current limiting to

---

[4] The large-signal limitation follows from increased transient output currents in the current mirror, which occur during signals with fast rate of change. With such transient currents the current mirror output may be pushed into saturation, as the voltage across the emitter resistors of the current mirror momentarily increases.

lower frequencies.

The emitter followers (Q8 and Q9) in the transimpedance stage need no explicit protection, as R7 and R8 inherently limit their collector current. Similarly, the average collector current of the folded cascode transistors is limited by their emitter resistors and bias voltage sources, as noted above. The slew rate enhancement capacitor C6 enables increased transient output currents; however, as these are of short duration only, they will not usually trigger a failure condition for the folded cascode transistors.

7. Further Improvement of Power Supply Rejection

As analysed in some detail in the previous sections, the basic power supply rejection limitation of prior art amplifier architectures is absent in the novel topology presented in this article. However, we also need to consider second-order effects at some point. If the power supply rejection of a typical implementation, based on figure 6, is simulated it is found that the power supply rejection is indeed independent of frequency (that is, at least up to about 10 kHz), but limited to roughly 60 dB (figure related to the output). At high frequencies this is a definite improvement over the performance of standard amplifier topologies, but the restless urge for perfection asks for more.

It is possible to remove many of the second-order effects by circuit modifications (e.g. by replacing R7 and R8 in figure 6 with current sources, or by substituting the simple Widlar current mirror formed by Q6 and Q7 with a more elaborate implementation) and thereby improve power supply rejection, but a far more powerful and yet simpler approach exists. Due to the voltage gain of typical power amplifier implementations the output voltage swing is far greater than the voltage swing at the amplifier input. Thanks to the structure of the novel topology, only the folded cascodes in the transimpedance stage will see the full output voltage swing. This means that only these circuit elements, which represent a very minor ripple injection route, need to be connected to the main high voltage power supply. All preceding stages are easily powered from a supply with lower voltage, which must just accommodate the input voltage swing. Such a low voltage power supply is straightforward to derive from the main power supply by the use of simple voltage regulators; note that this comes without the cost of additional mains transformer secondary windings, rectifiers, large smoothing capacitors and so forth. It is hence a very economical solution, adopted without hesitation even for cost sensitive applications.

In figure 7 a possible basic implementation of such an amplifier with regulated supplies for the amplifier front-end is shown. Even if the used shunt regulators (D1, D2, R7 and R8) are just implemented with resistors and discrete zener diodes as shown, the ripple rejection will approach 40 dB, pushing the overall amplifier power supply rejection to 100 dB. At low frequencies, it is possible to advance things another order of magnitude by the use of more elaborate regulators (e.g. by replacing R7 and R8 with current sources). At high frequencies, the output buffer also contributes some power supply rejection limitations which are not easily removed, and layout effects will be more difficult to control. Currently these figures are based merely on simulation results; however, I have no indication that these should be misleadingly optimistic.

Besides the power supply rejection improvement, there is another benefit from the use of such low

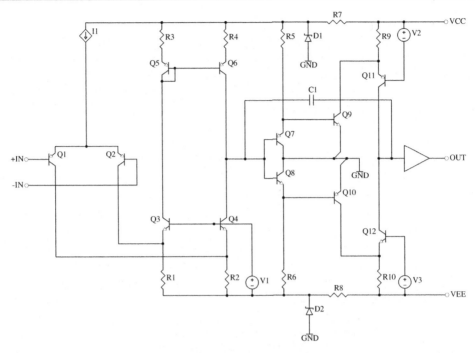

Figure 7: Conceptual amplifier with shunt regulators for the front-end added.

voltage, regulated power supplies for the amplifier front-end: the need for transistors with large break-down voltage ratings is eliminated, and we can choose from a far greater range of transistors with improved performance, e.g. with lower noise and higher h_{FE}. Also as power dissipation is reduced, smaller (and standard surface mounted) packages might be used which is beneficial to reduce cost.

I shall not fail to point out that the use of very low power supply voltages for the input stage may pronounce common-mode distortion at some point. If supply rails substantially below ±15 V are used, this should be carefully evaluated. Usually the use of a bootstrapped cascode [1, 2] for the input differential pair will be a complete cure.

8. Adaptation to Other Input Stage Topologies

So far we have considered the application of the new transimpedance stage to standard voltage feedback input stages with one differential pair only. However, it is perfectly feasible to adapt the new second stage to other input stage structures. Below I will give some examples of this.

In figure 8, an amplifier with complementary differential input pairs is sketched. The output current of each differential pair is made single-ended by an according current mirror (Q5 and Q6, or Q7 and Q8) and subsequently level-shifted to the common input node of the transimpedance stage by folded cascodes Q9 and Q10. With suitable, minor input stage modifications [8] such an amplifier can be designed to support very high slew rates. Note that, compared to the topology from figure 2, there is only one compensation capacitor and no need for a second stage bias control circuit. As

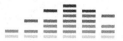

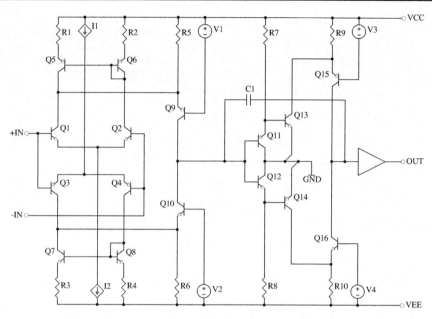

Figure 8: Novel transimpedance stage adapted to an input stage with complementary differential pairs.

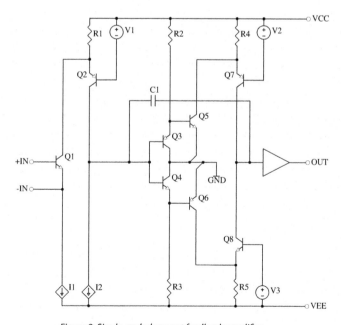

Figure 9: Single-ended current feedback amplifier.

Samuel Groner

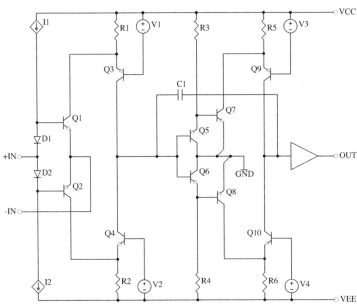

Figure 10: Complementary current feedback input stage combined with new push-pull second stage.

for any of the following examples, the use of low-voltage regulated power supplies for the amplifier front-end (as detailed in section 7) is fully supported.

The simplest form of current feedback is implemented as shown in figure 9. This topology is particularly applicable to low level preamplifiers, as only one transistor, Q1, acts as primary noise source. I1 is optional to reduce the rather large bias current flowing from the inverting input terminal. Two amplifiers of this structure may be used to form the front-end of an instrumentation amplifier, such as is in frequent use in transformerless microphone preamplifiers [12].

Further improvements regarding large-signal performance may be made with a complementary current feedback input stage (see figure 10). Most complementary current feedback amplifiers are based on one-stage topologies; figure 10 however represents a full two-stage architecture, with the resulting advantages regarding open-loop gain (in the context of current feedback amplifiers usually referred to as *transimpedance*), insensitivity to loading from the power output stage and distortion. Although not discussed further, the use of two transimpedance stages and a suitable amplifier subcircuit for common-mode feedback will permit the design of fully differential amplifiers [13].

9. Experimental Verification

To compare the audio performance of the new transimpedance stage to the standard amplifier topology from figure 1, a model amplifier (that is, an amplifier with a small-signal output buffer only, which is powered from low voltage regulated supplies [1]) for each topology was built. Figure 11 depicts the implementation which was chosen for the standard topology, and in figure 12 the model amplifier for the novel transimpedance is shown. To make the results as fair as possible, the input differential

104

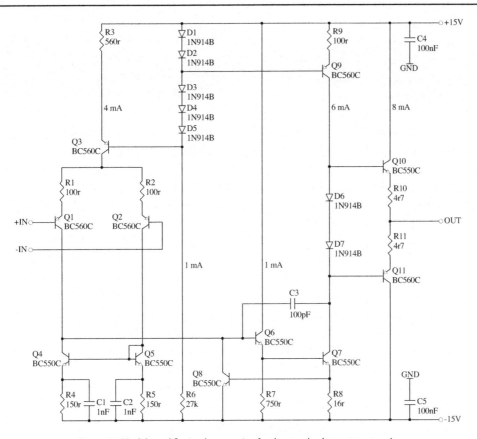

Figure 11: Model amplifier implementation for the standard two-stage topology.

pairs have the same quiescent current and emitter degeneration, and the compensation capacitors have alike values. Furthermore, the quiescent current of the emitter followers and the common-emitter transistors in the transimpedance stage, as well as the emitter resistor values of the common-emitter transistors, are made equal. Obviously, also the small-signal class A output stage details are equivalent. For simplicity, the use of voltage regulators for the front-end of the new amplifier was omitted.

If measured at a noise gain of 22 (which gives a unity loop gain frequency of about 700 kHz), +20 dBu output level and within a 80 kHz bandwidth, THD+N of both amplifiers is below –112 dB across the full audio frequency range, and dominated by amplifier noise and residual contributions of the oscillator and analyzer. This indicates that both topologies have no inherent distortion mechanisms in the small-signal stages which were significant in the context of a full power amplifier design. Substantial differences however are observed if the two amplifiers are evaluated for their sensitivity to loading at the second stage output node. In [5] I have introduced the use of a voltage-dependent net-

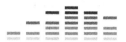

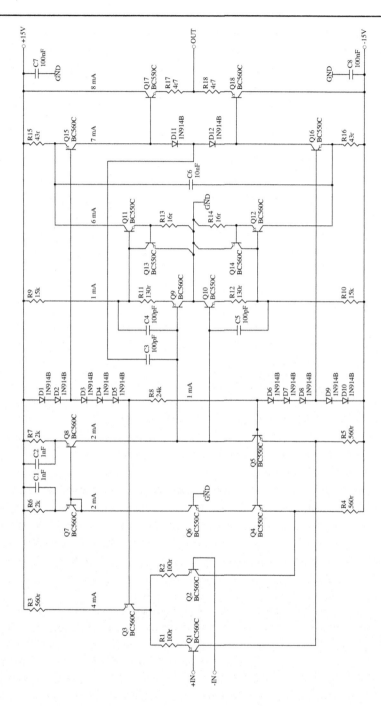

Figure 12: Implementation of the model amplifier for verification of the new transimpedance stage.

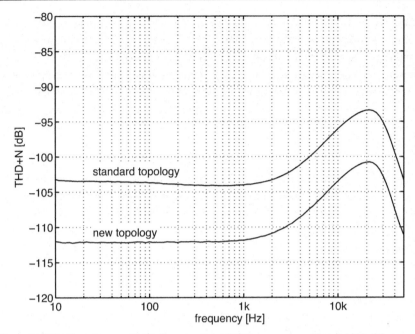

Figure 13: THD+N measurement (+20 dBu output level, 80 kHz measurement bandwidth) of the two model amplifiers with voltage-dependent loading of the second stage output node.

work, consisting of two back-to-back connected 3.3 V zener diodes in series with a 10 kΩ resistor, to roughly model the loading behaviour of power output stages. There is no reason to suspect that this modeling is particularly accurate, however it enables the easy comparison of amplifier topologies regarding the sensitivity to this distortion mechanism, which is just what we need here. Figure 13 discloses the measurement results; without doubt they provide little evidence for arguing against the novel transimpedance stage. At low frequencies, the standard amplifier topology shows a mixed distortion residual, while the new amplifier architecture is still limited by noise and oscillator/analyzer contributions. Above 1 kHz, both model amplifiers show increasing distortion levels, however the magnitude observed for the novel transimpedance stage remains about 8 dB below that of the conventional arrangement. Note that the decrease in distortion above 20 kHz is due to the bandwidth limiting filter and not actual circuit behaviour.

Unfortunately detailed discussion of the reasons which lead to the superiority of the new second stage with regard to output loading are beyond the scope of this article. I can just refer to the analysis I presented in [5], and give some food for thought in the following listing:

• The lumped resistance at the input node of the second stage is considerably higher for the new topology; this is because of the use of folded cascodes (which have higher output resistance than a differential pair), the current mirror with high emitter resistor values (which increases its output resistance), and the high-value resistors which are used to bias the emitter followers (R9

and R10 in figure 12). The high lumped resistance leads to low second stage output impedance.

- The complementary push-pull arrangement further reduces second stage output impedance, and mitigates the dependence of output impedance on output current.
- The novel transimpedance stage shows reduced nonlinear modulation of the compensation capacitor reference voltage (i.e. the second stage input node voltage). This is because the complementary topology cancels even-order harmonics present at the transimpedance stage input node.

Next I have evaluated the equivalent input noise of both amplifiers. Measured in a 22 Hz–22 kHz bandwidth, the amplifier from figure 11 achieves –122.6 dBu (this includes the noise from the feedback network, with an effective total resistance of 98 Ω). While this is already an excellent figure, the new amplifier topology does even better with –124.5 dBu. This surprisingly large difference cannot be attributed to the input differential pair, as its implementation is equal for both amplifiers, and spread in transistor performance is probably lower than the measured deviation. To the extent that I have investigated this, I can explain the observed behaviour with the current mirror noise contribution. As noted in section 4, the new amplifier topology allows the choice of much larger emitter resistors for the current mirror (for the presented implementations the values are 2 kΩ for the new push-pull stage, and 150 Ω for the standard amplifier), which reduces current mirror noise. Despite the additional noise contribution of the folded cascodes, this leads to overall better noise performance for the novel amplifier architecture. The emitter resistors of the standard topology cannot be made significantly larger without further circuit changes, as the current mirror output might become saturated under certain conditions.

Well-mannered overload behaviour is, particularly with more complex amplifier topologies, not always easily achieved. Typical artefacts include [2]:

- Polarity reversal during clipping
- Oscillation during, or during recovery from, clipping
- Prolonged recovery from clipping

Fortunately the basic overload behaviour of the novel amplifier topology is quite good; figure 14 depicts the output voltage of the model amplifier from figure 12 attempting to provide a 10 kHz, 40 V_{PP} triangle waveform output with ±15 V power supplies. There is some prolonged recovery from clipping discernible, but no polarity reversal or instability. In contrast, the standard amplifier topology shows distinctly asymmetric overload behaviour, and for negative clipping, considerable artefacts (see figure 15). While I do not believe that there are drastic audible differences between the overload behaviour of the two amplifier topologies—last but not least, serious clipping sounds pretty bad anyway, and the observed artefacts occur in the µs range—an oscilloscope display similar to figure 14 will surely please a reviewer's eyes much more than one close to figure 15.

These measurements neglect the contribution of the power transistors in the output buffer. Often these suffer themselves from considerable recovery time [2], and it may be desirable to prevent sat-

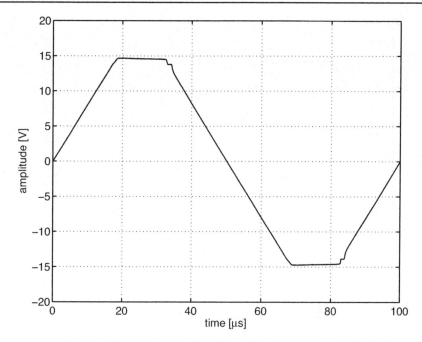

Figure 14: Overload behavior of the model amplifier from figure 12.

uration of these transistors by clamping the output voltage of the transimpedance stage to a well defined threshold below the power supply voltage. Implementation of such a clamping arrangement
is often difficult, particularly because it must not impair the distortion performance of the amplifier
below clipping. Some possible implementations may be found in [2].

As the model amplifier from figure 12 does not implement voltage regulators for the amplifier front-
end, and hence the potential power supply rejection advantage of the new topology is not fully realised, I have not carried out detailed power supply rejection measurements yet. Initial measurements
however indicate that the main injection mechanism is indeed absent, and that the model amplifier
from figure 12 has—even without the voltage regulators—overall better power supply rejection
than the standard amplifier implementation shown in figure 11.

Last but not least the slew rate of these two model amplifiers was evaluated. The measurement results were +46.8 V/µs and −45.6 V/µs for the standard topology and +42.3 V/µs and −43.4 V/µs for
the novel amplifier. These results are mainly determined by the primary slew rate limitation (finite output current of the input stage), which masked the expected advantage of the novel topology. The
overall lower slew rate of the novel amplifier is probably just a result of parts tolerances, which lead
to lower input stage quiescent current; possibly there is also a minor systematic effect from the input
stage folded cascodes.

To also model the, at high frequencies potentially considerable, drive current demand of a power
output stage, I've added a 3.3 kΩ resistor from the second stage output node to ground. This was suf-

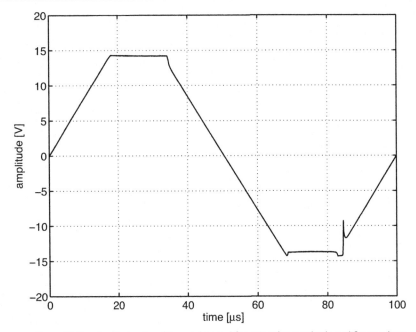

Figure 15: Overload behavior of the model amplifier using the standard amplifier topology.

ficient to make the slew rate behaviour of the standard topology more asymmetric (the measured values are +42.4 V/µs and –44.6 V/µs). The new push-pull configuration however easily supported the increased output current. The resulting slew rates are +41.4 V/µs and –42.6 V/µs, which is nearly the same as what is observed without the loading resistor.

To more thoroughly verify the absence of slew rate limitations in the second stage, I have also constructed a model amplifier based on the topology sketched in figure 8, using the input stage modifications derived in [8] and the very same second stage implementation as shown in figure 12. With a total input stage quiescent current of about 20 mA, and a compensation capacitor of 100 pF, the achieved slew rate was +226.6 V/µs and –228.3 V/µs. Additional loading at the transimpedance stage output altered this to just +223.5 V/µs and –222.4 V/µs. This is enough evidence to conclude that the novel transimpedance stage indeed supports very high slew rates; simulation results indicate that, with appropriate changes to the input stage, much higher values are theoretically possible. However the effects from finite small-signal bandwidth soon makes further efforts in this direction meaningless.

10. Conclusion

In this article I have presented a new transimpedance topology, suitable for combination with a wide range of input stages to form amplifiers with two gain stages. Compared to prior art amplifier designs, the novel architecture shows distinct advantages. First of all, it features inherently good power supply rejection, which is easily improved further by the use of voltage regulators for the amplifier front-

end. These voltage regulators are easily implemented at low cost and complexity. The transient current output capability of the new transimpedance stage is considerably enhanced as well, and will easily support the design of amplifiers with very high slew rate. This comes along with reduced sensitivity to loading at the second stage output node—this is a very welcome property, as it simplifies the design of the power output stage. Also the clipping behaviour was shown to be superior to the standard amplifier topology.

The novel second stage topology requires level shifting at the input stage via folded cascodes. I have outlined how their impact on offset and voltage noise can be minimised, and shown that the noise performance of an amplifier using the new transimpedance stage may even be superior to prior art implementations; that is because of reduced current mirror noise contribution. There is a complexity penalty associated with the new circuits, compared to the standard amplifier implementation. However, there is no significant cost increase to be expected, as just small-signal transistors and standard passive components are needed. Also the increased quiescent current is usually of no relevance within the context of a full power amplifier design.

I must leave the design of a fully worked out power amplifier design, using the new concepts presented here, to future research. However, the interested reader will find it easy to derive his own implementation from the presented model amplifier. If, as suggested in section 7, voltage regulators for the amplifier front-end are used, the design from figure 12 will only need minor modifications in the folded cascodes of the transimpedance stage to accept high voltage power supply rails. With the addition of a suitable power output buffer, and the necessary control and protection circuitry, a complete power amplifier is realised.

To the best of my knowledge this new amplifier topology is first officially published in this article. However it is not possible to investigate all prior art, particularly all the information buried within the extensive patent repository. I shall be happy to hear about any findings with this respect from my valued readers.

11. Acknowledgements

I'm very grateful to Bob Cordell for reviewing this text and for providing valuable thoughts on it. I'd like to express my thanks to Jan Didden for his efforts in publishing this article and for providing us with an excellent resource on audio electronics.

Bibliography

[1] Douglas Self: *Audio Power Amplifier Design Handbook,* 5th edition, Focal Press, 2009

[2] Bob Cordell: *Designing Audio Power Amplifiers,* 1st edition, McGraw-Hill, 2010

[3] J. E. Solomon: *The Monolithic Op Amp: A Tutorial Study,* IEEE J. Solid-State Circuits, vol. 9, no. 6, pp. 314–332, December 1974

[4] Bhupendra K. Ahuja: *An Improved Frequency Compensation Technique for CMOS Operational Amplifiers,* IEEE J. Solid-State Circuits, vol. SC-18, no. 6, pp. 629–633, December 1983

[5] Samuel Groner: *Comments on Audio Power Amplifier Design Handbook by Douglas Self,* February 2011, available for download from

www.sg-acoustics.ch/analogue_audio/power_amplifiers/pdf/audio_power_amp_design_comments.pdf

[6] Bruno Putzeys: *The F-word—or, why there is no such thing as too much feedback,* Linear Audio, vol. 1, pp. 112–132, April 2011

[7] Royal A. Gosser, Jeffrey A. Townsend: *Integrated-Circuit (IC) Amplifier With Plural Complementary Stages,* US Patent 5,537,079, filed December 1994, issued July 1996

[8] Giovanni Stochino: *Ultra-fast amplifier,* Electronics & Wireless World, pp. 835–841, October 1995

[9] Alberto Bilotti: *Noise Characteristics of Current Mirror Sinks/Sources,* IEEE J. Solid-State Circuits, vol. SC-10, no. 6, pp. 516–524, December 1975

[10] William H. Gross: *New High Speed Amplifier Designs, Design Techniques and Layout Problems,* Analog Circuit Design: Operational Amplifiers, Analog to Digital Convertors, Analog Computer Aided Design, Springer, 1993

[11] William F. Davis, Robert L. Vyne: *Design Techniques for Improving the HF Response of a Monolithic JFET Operational Amplifier,* IEEE J. Solid-State Circuits, vol. SC-19, no. 6, pp. 978–985, December 1984

[12] Graeme John Cohen: *Double Balanced Microphone Amplifier,* AES preprint, no. 2106, August 1984

[13] Bruno Putzeys: *High-Performance Discrete Building Blocks for Balanced Audio Signal Processing,* AES preprint, no. 6294, October 2004

Appendix: Noise in Folded Cascode Stages

The noise contribution of folded cascodes is a major consideration for the newly introduced amplifier topology. In this appendix I will thus present a brief analysis of the major noise sources in folded cascodes. For an exact analysis the mathematical expressions quickly become rather involved. I will hence apply several simplifications; however it is ensured that the result is still valid at least to the extent that it leads to the correct conclusions and design guide lines in typical implementations.

The basic folded cascode consists of three fundamental circuit elements: a common-base transistor, an associated emitter resistor and a voltage reference which is connected to the base of the cascode transistor. The input of such a stage is in the form of a current, which is applied to the emitter of the common-base transistor. The output is also in the form of a current, available at the collector of the common-base transistor. In the following we will consider the three fundamental circuit elements to be noise-free (which is denoted by the addition of an asterisk to the according denominator), and model their actual noise contribution by the addition of explicit voltage and current noise sources. In figure A1, Q* embodies the cascode transistor; its voltage and current noise generators are combined and referred to the input by E_{nQ} and I_{nQ}. R* forms the emitter resistor, and its noise contribution is represented by the series voltage source E_{nR}. Finally, the voltage reference is shown as V*, with associated noise generator E_{nV}. The incremental impedance of the voltage reference is of some importance

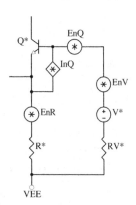

Figure A1: Folded cascode noise generators.

as well, and represented as RV*.

We will now independently analyse every of the four noise generators, and derive their contribution at the output of the folded cascode, i.e. the contributions to the collector current of Q*. The total of these contributions may then be derived by the usual root-mean-square summation, which needs to be applied for uncorrelated sources. For the analysis we will make the following assumptions: the h_{FE} of Q* is much larger than unity such that base current losses are negligible, the reciprocal of Q* transconductance is much smaller than R*, and $h_{FE} \cdot R^*$ is much larger than RV*. All assumptions are valid for typical implementations.

The voltage noise sources of Q* and V* (E_{nQ} and E_{nV}) effectively appear as input signal to an emitter degenerated common-emitter stage. Their contribution at the cascode output is then given by:

$$I_{n|E_{nQ}} \approx \frac{E_{nQ}}{R*} \qquad (1)$$

$$I_{n|E_{nV}} \approx \frac{E_{nV}}{R*} \qquad (2)$$

Similarly the noise generator E_{nR} appears in the folded cascode output current as:

$$I_{n|E_{nR}} \approx \frac{E_{nR}}{R*} \qquad (3)$$

The current noise generator of Q* (I_{nQ}) has two different contribution paths. First of all, it appears directly in the collector current. That is seen by considering that the sum of the Q* emitter current and I_{nQ} is constant (as set by V*, R* and Q* base-emitter voltage); hence I_{nQ} must modulate the emitter current of Q*. As the collector current is equal to the emitter current, the emitter current modulation also appears at the collector of Q*. However, I_{nQ} also flows trough the voltage reference. There RV* converts the noise current to a corresponding voltage, which again drives an emitter degenerated common-emitter stage. Note that this mechanism is fully correlated to the first contribution path, and hence the two terms must be linearly added:

$$I_{n|I_{nQ}} \approx I_{nQ} + \frac{I_{nQ} \cdot RV*}{R*} \qquad (4)$$

Contemplation of (1) trough (4) reveals that, everything else equal, the contribution of any of the four noise generators is reduced by increasing R*. Increasing R* however also increases E_{nQ} (as this transistor is then operated at lower collector current, which increases its voltage noise) and E_{nR} (higher resistance values imply higher voltage noise); yet this increase is typically proportional to the square-root of R* only. Thus overall a net improvement of about $\sqrt{2}$ (or 3 dB) for doubling R* is gained. I_{nQ} reduces itself as well at lower quiescent currents (lower base current implies lower base current noise). From this discussion it follows that, as a first means to reduce the noise contribution of a folded cascode, the emitter resistor value should be chosen as large as possible. This corresponds to the choice

of a low quiescent collector current, and a voltage reference with large DC value. There is usually a lower limit on quiescent current, dictated by distortion concerns. Further noise improvements beyond this point must hence be achieved solely by the increase in reference voltage.

There are various types of voltage reference elements available, which offer different tradeoffs for a low noise cascode implementation. Forward-biased diodes (standard small-signal parts or light emitting diodes) usually offer low voltage noise; however, their forward voltage is low, and several parts might need to be put in series to realise a sufficiently high emitter resistor value. Besides increasing the voltage noise generator E_{nV}, this also augments incremental impedance RV^* and its detrimental effect on noise as shown in (4). Zener (and avalanche) diodes are available with a wide range of voltages. Yet their voltage noise is at least an order of magnitude, for parts with high reverse breakdown voltage even more, higher than that of forward-biased diodes. In most cases this will necessitate the use of an RC filter to make this noise contribution negligible at audio frequencies. Similar concerns apply for the various bandgap voltage references available as integrated circuits.

If a differential folded cascode (as e.g. formed by Q3 and Q4 in figure 5 of the main text) is used, the noise contribution of the common voltage reference is theoretically rejected by the common-mode rejection of the following stage (e.g. a current mirror). However, as the common-mode rejection is subject to resistor and transistor tolerances, it is not very dependable without further precautions. Hence sufficient attention to the performance of the voltage reference must be given nonetheless.

From (1) to (4) it is seen that for increasing R^* values the total noise contribution of a folded cascode with given quiescent current converges towards I_{nQ}. Hence the last step in minimising folded cascode noise is the choice of a transistor with low current noise. This corresponds to a device with high h_{FE} and low excess noise. Note that the choice of a transistor with low voltage noise is not necessary; once the emitter resistor R^* is chosen large enough, the contribution from E_{nQ} is easily reduced well below that from E_{nR}.

By now it might have occurred to you that figure A1 also represents a typical current source implementation; a folded cascode is essentially a current source, where the emitter of the pass transistor is used as input node. Hence all the noise reduction strategies outlined above are applicable to the design of current sources as well. This however is often of less practical relevance for power amplifier design. The noise of the current source which biases the input differential pair is mitigated by the common-mode rejection of the amplifier; current sources in later stages are fed to nodes with comparably low impedance, and also a substantial amount of loop gain is available to reduce any remaining contribution.

Even current mirrors are closely related to figure A1—just consider that the voltage reference is implemented with a series-connection of a resistor and a forward-biased diode. The base of Q^* then forms the input node, and the collector of Q^* the output node of a standard Widlar current mirror. Noise reduction in current mirrors is hence again done by the means outlined above. As the voltage reference is now replaced with a diode and a resistor with fixed relation to R^*, the available design freedom reduces to the choice of large resistor values and a pass transistor with low current noise.

Simple Loudspeaker Correction Filters

Marcel van de Gevel

1. Introduction

Active filter stages having two (usually complex) poles and two (usually complex) zeroes can be very useful in applications such as active loudspeakers. For example, they can be used for correcting or extending the bass response of a woofer or for correcting for the roll-off of the tweeter in an active crossover circuit.

A well-known circuit in this category is the Linkwitz transform circuit. This circuit is versatile and the equations to calculate the component values are relatively simple, but a disadvantage is that it needs four capacitors to realise two poles and two zeroes. Theoretically, only two capacitors are needed to make a two-pole, two-zero circuit. Moreover, the capacitors typically have non-standard values, which means that in practice they may have to be constructed from series or parallel connections of capacitors. This increases the cost, especially when accurate and audiophile capacitors are used.

Another option is a state variable filter. This can be made with only two capacitors with standard values, but the number of operational amplifiers in the circuit is relatively high. This again increases the costs, especially when the op-amps are actually discrete circuits constructed of special-quality audiophile valves.

In this article, a modified Sallen and Key filter is proposed as a bass extending correction filter with two poles and two zeroes. It can be constructed with two capacitors with standard values. The active part is only a voltage follower. Tweeter response correction can be done with a filter based on an inverting second-order low-pass.

The proposed circuits also have disadvantages: the calculations are relatively complex, the output impedance is not zero but a constant resistance and not all possible combinations of poles and zeroes can be made. With the Linkwitz correction circuit it is possible to use the main amp that drives the loudspeaker as the amplifier for the correction circuit (just scale the impedances in the feedback network until you have the desired gain). With my circuits you really need an extra op-amp or other type of low-level amplifier.

2. Typical applications in active loudspeakers

2.1. Bass correction/extension

The most well-known application is bass correction and extension in closed-box loudspeaker systems, but bass correction can also be applied to bass reflex speakers. In both cases you have to be careful not to boost the bass too much because of the risk of low-frequency overload.

For low frequencies, where the loudspeaker and its enclosure are small compared to the wavelength, closed-box loudspeakers and bass reflex loudspeakers behave as lumped systems. Like any lumped system, their small-signal response can be described with a finite number of poles and zeroes.

The voltage to sound pressure response of a closed-box loudspeaker is a second-order high-pass, having two zeroes at zero and two poles. A bass reflex loudspeaker has a fourth-order high-pass response with four zeroes at or near zero and four poles. The current to sound pressure response is similar, but with more complex pole pairs because the electromagnetic damping of the loudspeaker resonance disappears with current drive.

In terms of poles and zeroes, an inadequate bass response is due to improper pole positions. The ratio of the imaginary to the real part of the poles is related to the quality factor of the loudspeaker and therefore to whether the bass sounds boomy. The distance of the poles from the origin is related to the cut-off radian frequency. For a second-order high-pass filter, the poles and zeroes are:

two zeroes at 0

$$\text{poles} \quad -\frac{\omega_0}{2Q} \pm j\sqrt{\omega_0^2 - \frac{\omega_0^2}{4Q^2}}$$

For a closed box, $\omega_0 = 2\pi f_c$ and $Q = Q_{TC}$, where

$$Q_{TC} = Q_{TS}\sqrt{1 + \frac{V_{AS}}{V_{AB}}}$$

$$f_c = f_s\sqrt{1 + \frac{V_{AS}}{V_{AB}}}$$

V_{AB} is the effective acoustic volume of the closed box. For a box filled with damping material, this is some 25 % greater than the actual inner volume. All other variables on the right hand sides of the equations are Thiele and Small parameters of the driver. The equation for the quality factor does not include acoustic losses in the box.

It is more complicated for a bass reflex loudspeaker system. When you know that the box is designed for a Butterworth or Chebyshev transfer and you also know the cut-off frequency and the ripple (for a Chebyshev), you can simply look up the normalised low-pass pole positions in standard filter tables

and apply a high-pass transformation.

If this is not the case, the articles of Thiele and Small ([1] and [2]) explain how to calculate the coefficients of the fourth-order denominator polynomial of the transfer function of the bass reflex loudspeaker system. The roots of this fourth-order polynomial can then be found numerically or analytically, as explained on Wikipedia [3]. See the sidebar for an alternative method based on impedance measurements of the whole system.

Traditionally loudspeaker boxes are designed for flat(-ish) response under voltage drive. Using a correction filter to obtain a flat response, the designer can optimise the box for other parameters, such as large-signal behaviour or spouse acceptance factor. An example is tuning a bass reflex box to minimise cone excursions over the frequency range of interest.

Correcting the low-frequency response comes down to putting the zeroes of the filter on top of the poles of the loudspeaker and putting the poles of the filter in the locations where you would like the poles of the entire system to be. For a closed-box system a single correction filter section with two zeroes and two poles will do the job. Two sections are required for a bass reflex system.

2.2. Tweeter response correction

A tweeter in a sealed enclosure also has a second-order high-pass response from voltage (or current) to sound pressure (at least as long as baffle step issues do not occur in the tweeter's frequency range). Usually tweeters are not designed to be used down to their natural cut-off frequency. As a typical example, take a tweeter that has a high-pass response at 860 Hz with $Q=0.77$ (Peerless WA10/8, also known as 811815) that you want to use in a system with a fourth-order Linkwitz-Riley crossover at 2 kHz.

The response of the tweeter has the following poles and zeroes:

2 zeroes at 0
poles at -3508.8 rad/s $\pm$ 4109.3 j rad/s

A fourth-order Linkwitz-Riley high-pass at 2 kHz has these poles and zeroes [4]:

4 zeroes at 0
2 poles at $(-2000 \cdot \sqrt{2} \cdot \pi + 2000 \cdot \sqrt{2} \cdot \pi \ j)$ rad/s
2 poles at $(-2000 \cdot \sqrt{2} \cdot \pi - 2000 \cdot \sqrt{2} \cdot \pi \ j)$ rad/s

You obtain the desired Linkwitz-Riley response when you combine the tweeter with the following two filter sections:

zeroes at -3508.8 rad/s $\pm$ 4109.3 j rad/s

poles at (-2000·√2·π ± 2000·√2·π j) rad/s

2 zeroes at 0
poles at (-2000·√2·π ± 2000·√2·π j) rad/s

The first section is a correction filter, the second is a simple second-order 2 kHz Butterworth high-pass.

3. The proposed filters

3.1. Bass extension filter

The filter for bass extension is shown in figure 1. It is clear from the picture that it has an output impedance of $R_4R_5/(R_4+R_5)$, that the DC gain is 1 and the gain at high frequencies is $R_4/(R_4+R_5)$.

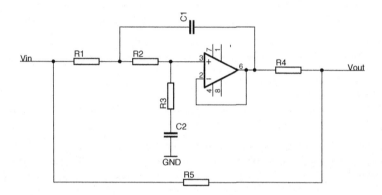

Figure 1. Bass extending correction filter based on a modified Sallen and Key low-pass filter

The transfer function can be written as:

$$H(s) = \frac{a_2 s^2 + a_1 s + 1}{b_2 s^2 + b_1 s + 1}$$

A straightforward but tedious calculation (see the appendix) shows that:

$$a_2 = R_1 R_2 C_1 C_2 \frac{R_4}{R_4 + R_5}$$

$$a_1 = R_3 C_2 + (R_1 + R_2)C_2 \frac{R_4}{R_4 + R_5}$$

$$b_2 = R_1 R_2 C_1 C_2$$

$$b_1 = (R_1 + R_2 + R_3)C_2$$

After solving the component values for given a_2, a_1, b_2 and b_1, this results in the following design procedure:

-Calculate the desired values of a_2, a_1, b_2 and b_1 from the desired pole and zero positions, or from the desired quality factors and natural frequencies.

The relation between the zeroes z_1 and z_2 and the coefficients a_2 and a_1 is:

$$a_2 = \frac{1}{z_1 z_2}$$

$$a_1 = -\frac{1}{z_1} - \frac{1}{z_2}$$

The relation between the poles p_1 and p_2 and the coefficients b_2 and b_1 is:

$$b_2 = \frac{1}{p_1 p_2}$$

$$b_1 = -\frac{1}{p_1} - \frac{1}{p_2}$$

In the case of a closed-box loudspeaker with quality factor Q_{TC}, resonant frequency f_c, desired quality factor after correction Q_{TC}' and desired resonant frequency after correction f_c', this becomes:

$$a_2 = \frac{1}{(2\pi f_c)^2}$$

$$a_1 = \frac{1}{2\pi f_c Q_{TC}}$$

$$b_2 = \frac{1}{(2\pi f_c')^2}$$

$$b_1 = \frac{1}{2\pi f_c' Q_{TC}'}$$

-Choose values for R_5, C_1 and C_2
-Calculate R_4:

$$R_4 = R_5 \frac{a_2}{b_2 - a_2}$$

-Calculate R_3:

$$R_3 = \frac{a_1 b_2 - a_2 b_1}{(b_2 - a_2)C_2}$$

-Calculate R_1:

$$R_1 = \frac{\dfrac{b_1}{C_2} - R_3 \pm \sqrt{\left(R_3 - \dfrac{b_1}{C_2}\right)^2 - 4\dfrac{b_2}{C_1 C_2}}}{2}$$

-Calculate R_2:

$$R_2 = \frac{b_2}{C_1 C_2 R_1}$$

The following are necessary requirements to get real and positive solutions (assuming a_1, a_2, b_1 and b_2 to be positive, as they normally are):

$$\frac{C_2}{C_1} \le \frac{b_2 (a_1 - b_1)^2}{4(b_2 - a_2)^2}$$

To avoid extreme resistor ratios, it is advisable to choose the ratio C_2/C_1 as large as possible without violating this constraint (and without spending fortunes on parallel connections). That is, given a chosen value for C_1, take the largest standard value for C_2 that meets the constraint.

$$b_2 > a_2$$
$$b_1 > a_1$$
$$\frac{a_1}{a_2} \ge \frac{b_1}{b_2}$$

3.2. Bass-cut filter (for tweeter correction, for example)

The proposed filter is shown in figure 2. The output impedance is clearly $R_5 R_6/(R_5+R_6)$, while the gain at high frequencies is $R_5/(R_5+R_6)$.

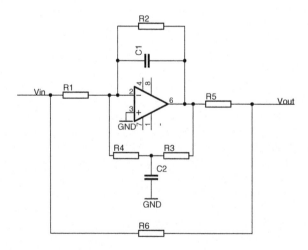

Figure 2. Bass-cut correction filter (for example for tweeter response correction) based on an inverting low-pass filter

The response can be written as:

$$H(s) = K\frac{a_2 s^2 + a_1 s + 1}{b_2 s^2 + b_1 s + 1}$$

where K is the DC gain factor (which will be ignored from now on).

To simplify the equations somewhat, the resistor values will be replaced with their reciprocals, the conductances:

$G_1 = 1/R_1$

$G_2 = 1/R_2$

$G_3 = 1/R_3$

$G_4 = 1/R_4$

$G_5 = 1/R_5$

$G_6 = 1/R_6$

A long calculation with lots of terms to rearrange shows that:

$$b_2 = \frac{C_1 C_2}{G_3 G_4 + G_2 G_4 + G_2 G_3}$$

$$b_1 = \frac{G_4 C_1 + G_3 C_1 + G_2 C_2}{G_3 G_4 + G_2 G_4 + G_2 G_3}$$

$$a_2 = \frac{C_1 C_2}{G_2 G_4 + G_2 G_3 + G_3 G_4 - \dfrac{G_1 G_4 G_5}{G_6} - \dfrac{G_1 G_3 G_5}{G_6}}$$

$$a_1 = \frac{G_4 C_1 + G_3 C_1 + G_2 C_2 - C_2 \dfrac{G_1 G_5}{G_6}}{G_2 G_4 + G_2 G_3 + G_3 G_4 - \dfrac{G_1 G_4 G_5}{G_6} - \dfrac{G_1 G_3 G_5}{G_6}}$$

C_1 and C_2 can be chosen, although there is a constraint on their ratio. If the DC gain is considered to be unimportant, two out of the three resistors R_1, R_5 and R_6 can be freely chosen. The third then follows from the relation:

$$\frac{R_6}{R_1 R_5} = C_1\left(\frac{b_1}{b_2} - \frac{a_1}{a_2}\right)$$

Further,

$$G_2 = C_1\left(\frac{b_1}{b_2} - \frac{a_2 - b_2}{a_2 b_1 - a_1 b_2}\right)$$

$$G_3 + G_4 = C_2\frac{a_2 - b_2}{a_2 b_1 - a_1 b_2}$$

$$G_3 G_4 = \frac{C_1 C_2}{b_2} - G_2(G_3 + G_4)$$

There are two solutions for G_3 and G_4:

Solution 1:

$$G_3 = \frac{G_3 + G_4 + \sqrt{(G_3 + G_4)^2 - 4G_3 G_4}}{2}$$

and

$$G_4 = \frac{G_3 + G_4 - \sqrt{(G_3 + G_4)^2 - 4G_3 G_4}}{2}$$

Solution 2:

$$G_3 = \frac{G_3 + G_4 - \sqrt{(G_3 + G_4)^2 - 4G_3 G_4}}{2}$$

and

$$G_4 = \frac{G_3 + G_4 + \sqrt{(G_3 + G_4)^2 - 4G_3 G_4}}{2}$$

That is, when the solution with the plus sign is chosen for G_4, the solution with the minus sign must be used for G_3 and vice versa.

The following are necessary conditions to get positive real component values:

$$\frac{C_2}{C_1} \geq 4\frac{(a_2 b_1 - a_1 b_2)^2}{b_2(a_2 - b_2)^2} - 4\frac{b_1(a_2 b_1 - a_1 b_2)}{b_2(a_2 - b_2)} + 4$$

$$\frac{b_1(a_2 - b_2)}{a_2 b_1 - a_1 b_2} - \left(\frac{a_2 - b_2}{a_2 b_1 - a_1 b_2}\right)^2 b_2 < 1$$

$$b_1 a_2 > a_1 b_2$$

$$a_2 > b_2$$
$$\frac{b_1}{b_2} > \frac{a_2 - b_2}{a_2 b_1 - a_1 b_2}$$

4. Checking filter calculations

It is very easy to make mistakes in filter calculations. One way to check whether the calculations are correct is to simply do them again to see if you get the same answer. Besides, there are computer programmes that can extract the pole and zero locations from an electronic network, so you can input the filter design and let the computer calculate whether the poles and zeroes are where you wanted them to be. My favourite in this category is the old DOS programme LINear Dynamic circuit Analyzer, LINDA for short, from Catena Microelectronics. Unfortunately, it isn't supported anymore. A reasonable alternative is the Windows-version of LINDA that was written by the Delft University of Technology a couple of years ago. ANP3 is another programme in this category; I can't comment on it because I've never used it.

5. Examples

5.1. Bass extension from 80 Hz Butterworth to 40 Hz Butterworth for a closed box

As an example, suppose you have a closed box with f_C=80 Hz and Q_{TC}=√2/2≈0.7071068 (second order Butterworth high-pass). Say you want to extend the bass response by an octave using the circuit of figure 1.

The required values for a_2, a_1, b_2 and b_1 are:

a_2=1/(2Π f_C)²≈3.957858736·10⁻⁶ seconds²
a_1=1/(2Π f_C Q_{TC})≈2.813488488·10⁻³ seconds

b_2=1/(2Π f_C')²≈15.83143494·10⁻⁶ seconds²
b_1=1/(2Π f_C' Q_{TC}')≈5.626976976·10⁻³ seconds

C_2 and C_1 must be chosen according to the following inequality:

$$\frac{C_2}{C_1} \le \frac{b_2\left(a_1 - b_1\right)^2}{4\left(b_2 - a_2\right)^2}$$

That is, C_2/C_1≤0.2222...

Take C_1=1 μF and C_2=220 nF and choose R_5=10 kΩ.

$$R_4 = R_5 \frac{a_2}{b_2 - a_2} = 3.33333... \text{ k}\Omega$$

$$R_3 = \frac{a_1 b_2 - a_2 b_1}{\left(b_2 - a_2\right)C_2} \approx 8.52572269 \text{ k}\Omega$$

$$R_1 = \frac{\dfrac{b_1}{C_2} - R_3 \pm \sqrt{\left(R_3 - \dfrac{b_1}{C_2}\right)^2 - 4\dfrac{b_2}{C_1 C_2}}}{2}$$

Arbitrarily choosing the solution with the plus sign:

$$R_2 = \frac{b_2}{C_1 C_2 R_1} \approx 7.673150407 \text{ k}\Omega$$

Rounding the resistances to the nearest E96 values gives:

R_1=9.31 kΩ
R_2=7.68 kΩ
R_3=8.45 kΩ
R_4=3.32 kΩ
R_5=10 kΩ

The final circuit is shown in figure 3. LINDA simulations indicate that the pole and zero positions are:

poles (-177.9 ± 178.672 j) rad/s
zeroes (-355.883 ± 358.332 j) rad/s

Ideally, the poles should be at (-177.715317... ± 177.715317... j) rad/s and the zeroes at (-355.430635... ± 355.430635... j) rad/s. The small differences are due to rounding all resistances to E96 values; when the resistances are not rounded, all six digits of the LINDA output are according to expectation.

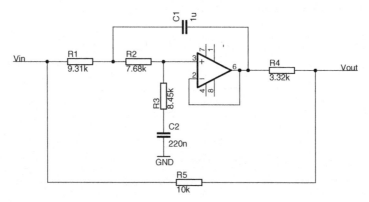

Figure 3. Example bass extension circuit, that extends the bass from 80 Hz to 40 Hz

5.2. Tweeter correction example of section 2.2

As explained in section 2.2, a filter with the following poles and zeroes

zeroes at -3508.8 rad/s $\pm$ 4109.3 j rad/s
poles at $(-2000 \cdot \sqrt{2} \cdot \Pi \pm 2000 \cdot \sqrt{2} \cdot \Pi j)$ rad/s

is useful as part of a cross-over filter for a Peerless WA10/8 tweeter. As this is a filter that reduces the low frequencies, we can try to realise it with the circuit of figure 2.

The values for a_2, a_1, b_2 and b_1 follow from:

$a_2=1/(z_1 z_2) \approx 34.24889309 \cdot 10^{-9}$ seconds²
$a_1=-1/z_1-1/z_2 \approx 240.3450321 \cdot 10^{-6}$ seconds
$b_2=1/(p_1 p_2) \approx 6.332573978 \cdot 10^{-9}$ seconds²
$b_1=-1/p_1-1/p_2 \approx 112.5395395 \cdot 10^{-6}$ seconds

The ratio of C_2 to C_1 must comply with

$$\frac{C_2}{C_1} \geq 4\frac{(a_2b_1-a_1b_2)^2}{b_2(a_2-b_2)^2} - 4\frac{b_1(a_2b_1-a_1b_2)}{b_2(a_2-b_2)} + 4$$

so $C_2/C_1 \geq 2.47001459$

Try $C_1=1$ nF and $C_2=3.3$ nF. Arbitrarily choosing $R_1=R_5=10$ kΩ:

$$\frac{R_6}{R_1 R_5} = C_1\left(\frac{b_1}{b_2} - \frac{a_1}{a_2}\right)$$

so $R_6 \approx 1.075393175$ kΩ

As this value is a bit small for most op-amps, it may be more convenient to use higher values for C_1 and C_2. Taking $C_1=10$ nF and $C_2=33$ nF:

$R_6 \approx 10.75393175$ kΩ

$$G_2 = C_1\left(\frac{b_1}{b_2} - \frac{a_2-b_2}{a_2b_1-a_1b_2}\right) \approx 58.02360893 \text{ µS}, \text{ hence } R_2=1/G_2 \approx 17.23436405 \text{ k}\Omega$$

$$G_3 + G_4 = C_2\frac{a_2-b_2}{a_2b_1-a_1b_2} \approx 3.949826382 \bullet 10^{-4} \text{ siemens}$$

$$G_3 G_4 = \frac{C_1 C_2}{b_2} - G_2(G_3+G_4) \approx 29.1931931 \bullet 10^{-9} \text{ siemens}^2$$

Taking the first solution for G3 and G4:

$$G_3 = \frac{G_3 + G_4 + \sqrt{(G_3 + G_4)^2 - 4G_3G_4}}{2} \approx 2.965348854 \cdot 10^{-4} \text{ siemens}$$

$$G_4 = \frac{G_3 + G_4 - \sqrt{(G_3 + G_4)^2 - 4G_3G_4}}{2} \approx 9.844775281 \cdot 10^{-5} \text{ siemens}$$

Hence, $R_3 = 1/G_3 \approx 3.372284508$ kΩ and $R_4 = 1/G_4 \approx 10.15767218$ kΩ.

Rounding all resistances to the nearest E96 values:
$R_1 = 10$ kΩ
$R_2 = 17.4$ kΩ
$R_3 = 3.4$ kΩ
$R_4 = 10.2$ kΩ
$R_5 = 10$ kΩ
$R_6 = 10.7$ kΩ

The complete circuit is shown in figure 4.

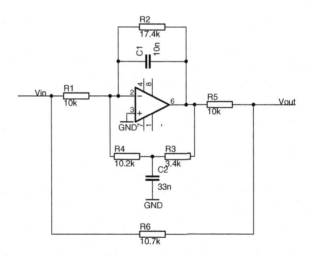

Figure 4. Example correction filter for a Peerless WA10/8 tweeter.

With these rounded values, LINDA finds the following pole and zero locations, which are all close to what we ordered:

poles at $(-8815 \pm 8830j)$ rad/s
zeroes at $(-3465 \pm 4064j)$ rad/s

6. References

[1] A. N. Thiele, "Loudspeakers in vented boxes", *Proceedings of the IRE Australia*, vol. 22, pages 487 to 508, August 1961, reprinted in the *Journal of the Audio Engineering Society*, vol. 19, number 5, pages 382 to 391 and number 6, pages 471 to 483, May and June 1971

[2] Richard H. Small, "Vented-box loudspeaker systems", *Journal of the Audio Engineering Society*, vol. 21, number 5, pages 363 to 372, number 6, pages 438 to 444, number 7, pages 549 to 554 and number 8, pages 635 to 639, June to October 1973

[3] Wikipedia, Quartic function, http://en.wikipedia.org/wiki/Quartic_function

[4] Siegfried H. Linkwitz, "Active crossover networks for noncoincident drivers", *Journal of the Audio Engineering Society*, vol. 24, number 1, pages 2 to 8, January/February 1976

[5] Chris Verhoeven and Arie van Staveren, private communication, 1993

Finding the poles of an unknown loudspeaker system by impedance measurement

A lumped linear time-invariant system has only one characteristic polynomial [5]. That means that as long as the driving and loading conditions remain the same, all transfers have the same poles. A snag is that some of these poles may be poorly observable because they are covered or nearly covered by zeroes. I'll get back to this later, assume for the time being that there is no problem with observability.

This means that at low frequencies, where a closed box or bass reflex box can be regarded as a lumped linear time-invariant system, the transfer from voltage to sound pressure has the exact same poles as the transfer from voltage to current (that is, the admittance of the loud-speaker). The transfer from current to sound pressure has the exact same poles as the trans-fer from current to voltage (that is, the impedance of the loudspeaker). The zeroes of the transfer from voltage or current to sound pressure are already known: two at 0 for a closed-box system and four at or close to 0 for a bass reflex box ([1], [2]).

As the admittance is the reciprocal of the impedance, the poles of the admittance are the ze-roes of the impedance. So when you measure the impedance graph and manage to extract the poles and zeroes from the measured impedance graph, the pole-zero patterns of the transfers to sound pressure are:

Closed box case:
Voltage to sound pressure:
Two zeroes at 0
Poles are identical to the two low-frequency zeroes of the impedance

Current to sound pressure:
Two zeroes at 0
Poles are identical to the two low-frequency poles of the impedance

Bass reflex case:
Voltage to sound pressure:
Four zeroes at or near 0
Poles are identical to the four low-frequency zeroes of the impedance

Current to sound pressure:
Four zeroes at or near 0
Poles are identical to the four low-frequency poles of the impedance

"Low-frequency poles" and "low-frequency zeroes" means the poles and zeroes that are related to the one or two bumps in the impedance graph related to the loudspeaker and box resonances. In fact Thiele [1] already made extensive use of this.

Extracting the poles and zeroes from the impedance plots is fairly simple when you have a circuit simulator available that can extract poles and zeroes and magnitude and phase plots from a circuit model (such as the Windows version of LINDA, or the original DOS LINDA combined with PLEX). Just enter an impedance model for the loudspeaker and keep tweaking its

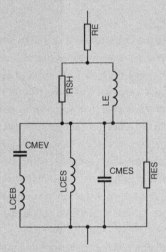

Impedance model for a loudspeaker in a bass reflex box according to Thiele [1]. C_{MES}, R_{ES} and L_{CES} are related to the loudspeaker resonance, L_{CEB} and C_{MEV} model the box and the vent, R_E is the voice coil DC resistance, L_E the voice coil self inductance and R_{SH} roughly models the voice coil eddy current losses. Replace C_{MEV} with a short in case of a sealed box. The pole and zero introduced by L_E and R_{SH} are usually outside the frequency range where the loudspeaker can be regarded as a lumped system and should be ignored.

parameters until the impedance plots match the measurements as much as possible. The programme will then tell you what the pole and zero locations are.

There are computer programmes that can directly extract poles and zeroes from magnitude and phase versus frequency plots, although these do not always work reliably in the presence of measurement errors. It should also be doable with a plain old spreadsheet; if you neglect the voice coil self inductance, you can write the impedance as the ratio of two products of second-order polynomials, tweak the coefficients until it matches the measurements and then calculate the poles and zeroes from the second-order polynomial coefficients. If you write the impedance with neglected voice coil inductance as:

$$Z = R_E \frac{\left(a_2 s^2 + a_1 s + 1\right)\left(c_2 s^2 + c_1 s + 1\right)}{\left(b_2 s^2 + b_1 s + 1\right)\left(d_2 s^2 + d_1 s + 1\right)}$$

then the following equations help to narrow down the search space:

$a_2 c_2 = b_2 d_2$ (which means that the impedance for low and high frequencies is the same when you neglect the voice coil inductance)

$$a_2 + a_1 c_1 + c_2 = b_2 + b_1 d_1 + d_2$$

Of course there are cases where the loudspeaker is driven by something in between voltage and current, like from an open-loop triode amplifier. In this case again the poles of all transfers are the same, so you can measure the transfer from amplifier input to the voltage across the loudspeaker terminals, extract the poles, and correct for the response of the combination of amplifier and loudspeaker. Any amplifier that has a low-frequency roll-off will also add zeroes. If nothing exotic is done in the amplifier, these zeroes will all be at or very close to 0.

If you try the same with a negative-feedback amplifier with 0.01 ohm output impedance, the output voltage will be almost independent of the variations in loudspeaker impedance. This is a case of poor observability. A workaround is to measure the transfer from the amplifier input voltage to the current through the loudspeaker instead.

Another example of poor observability would be to measure the impedance graph of a loudspeaker system having an impedance correction network that suppresses the bump related to the fundamental resonance. In this case, the only workaround is to disconnect the impedance correction network for the measurement.

Automatic response equalisation
With DSP techniques, it should be possible to automate the whole procedure. That is, one could make an amplifier with built-in self-adjusting correction filter. It would have a "calibrate" button. When you press the button, the system would ask whether the connected loudspeakers are closed boxes or bass reflex systems, how much bass extension you want and whether you want a flat or a bumpy response (a loudspeaker designer once told me that he always designs for a low-frequency response peak, because loudspeakers with a flat response don't sell). It then measures the impedance, extracts the pole and zero locations, calculates the required correction, transfers this into the z-domain and programs the result into digital IIR filters and into non-volatile memory.

Appendix A.
Calculating the transfer functions of the filters - a crash course in network theory

The editor of Linear Audio insisted (suggested! – *ed* ;-) that I should include the derivation of the transfer functions in this article. The problem with this is that the derivation is not particularly interesting for people who have followed electric network theory classes, as they know how to do such a calculation, and it is impossible to understand for people who have no knowledge of network theory. In my opinion, the only way out was to turn this appendix into a crash course in network theory. I assume that the reader has a good working knowledge of elementary algebra, differential calculus and complex numbers.

A.1. Modelling the circuit
Calculating the transfer of an electric or electronic filter usually goes in two steps:

1. Draw a network model that is a mathematical abstraction of the real-life filter
2. Calculate the transfer of this model

Regarding the first step: the simplest model for a capacitor is an ideal linear capacitor (which my former network theory professor Fred Neerhoff always called a 'lineaire capaciteit', a linear capacity), the simplest model for a resistor is an ideal linear resistor, the simplest model for an inductor is an ideal linear inductor (linear inductivity), the simplest model for an amplifier with well-defined gain is a linear controlled source, the simplest model for a high-gain amplifier used in a feedback configuration is a nullor (combination of a nullator and a norator, see below) and the simplest model for an interconnecting wire is a node.

If you are worried about second-order effects, you need to use more elaborate models. To give two examples that are relevant to audio: an inductor in a passive crossover could be represented by the series connection of a linear inductivity and an ideal linear resistor if you are worried about the effect of its DC resistance. An amplifier could be represented by an ideal controlled source plus a resistor representing its output resistance, if there is reason to believe that the output resistance might not be negligible. In this appendix, we will only use ideal models with no second-order effects.

A.2. Transfer functions
The transfer of a filter can be described by a transfer function consisting of the ratio between two polynomials in *s*, which in older literature is denoted as *p*. (This actually only applies when the filter is linear, time invariant, continuous time and lumped, but analogue filters used for audio are usually close enough to being all of that to model them with a linear, time-invariant, continuous-time lumped network model). Personally I think the old notation *p* is much clearer than *s*, because *s* is too similar to s, the SI symbol for second. Still, since *s* is the more usual notation, I will stick to it.

Depending on the type of calculation one wants to do, *s* can be regarded as the Laplace variable

(outside the scope of this article), as a differentiation to time operator, or as $j\omega$, where ω is the radian frequency ($\omega=2\Pi f$) and j is the imaginary unit number ($j^2=-1$).

The transfer functions of the filter network models that this article deals with are all of the form:

$$H(s) = \frac{V_{out}}{V_{in}} = K\frac{a_2 s^2 + a_1 s + 1}{b_2 s^2 + b_1 s + 1}$$

Interpreting s as a differentiation-to-time operator, this means that the relation between the input and output voltage is given by this differential equation:

$$b_2\frac{d^2 v_{out}}{dt^2} + b_1\frac{dv_{out}}{dt} + v_{out} = K\left(a_2\frac{d^2 v_{in}}{dt^2} + a_1\frac{dv_{in}}{dt} + v_{in}\right)$$

Using complex numbers, calculating the output signal becomes relatively simple when the filter does not oscillate and when the input signal is a stationary sine or cosine wave (that is, a sine or cosine that has been there long enough for initial transients to damp out). A cosine equals the sum of two complex exponential functions:

$$\cos(\omega t) = \frac{1}{2}e^{j\omega t} + \frac{1}{2}e^{-j\omega t}$$

As the network model is linear, we may use the superposition principle. That is, we may calculate the response to each complex exponential signal independently and simply add the results.

The time derivative of a complex exponential signal is:

$$\frac{de^{j\omega t}}{dt} = j\omega e^{j\omega t}$$

Hence, when

$$v_{in} = \frac{1}{2}e^{j\omega t}$$

we get

$$b_2\frac{d^2 v_{out}}{dt^2} + b_1\frac{dv_{out}}{dt} + v_{out} = K\left(a_2(j\omega)^2 + a_1 j\omega + 1\right)\frac{1}{2}e^{j\omega t}$$

This equation is satisfied when the output signal is also a complex exponential signal of the same frequency, but multiplied with some complex multiplication factor. That is, assume that

$$v_{out} = Xe^{j\omega t}$$

This results in

$$\left(b_2(j\omega)^2 + b_1 j\omega + 1\right)Xe^{j\omega t} = K\left(a_2(j\omega)^2 + a_1 j\omega + 1\right)\frac{1}{2}e^{j\omega t}$$

$$X = \frac{1}{2}\cdot\frac{K\left(a_2(j\omega)^2 + a_1 j\omega + 1\right)}{b_2(j\omega)^2 + b_1 j\omega + 1} = \frac{1}{2}H(j\omega)$$

and

$$\frac{v_{out}}{v_{in}} = \frac{X}{\frac{1}{2}} = H(j\omega)$$

So when you substitute $s=j\omega$, the transfer function turns into a complex-valued gain factor for complex exponential input signals. Note that $H(j\omega)$ can also be written in a polar form:

$$H(j\omega) = |H(j\omega)|e^{j\varphi}$$

with

$$\varphi = \arctan\bigl(\mathrm{Im}(H(j\omega))/\mathrm{Re}(H(j\omega))\bigr) + k\pi$$

when the real part of $H(j\omega)$ is not zero and where k is an integer. The factor $|H(j\omega)|$ represents the actual gain, while the factor $e^{j\varphi}$ just gives a phase shift of φ.

In the end, we are interested in the response to the real-valued cosine wave rather than to the complex exponential waveform. Hence, when

$$v_{in} = \cos(\omega t) = \frac{1}{2}e^{j\omega t} + \frac{1}{2}e^{-j\omega t}$$

then

$$v_{out} = \frac{1}{2}e^{j\omega t}H(j\omega) + \frac{1}{2}e^{-j\omega t}H(-j\omega)$$

It can be shown that $H(j\omega)$ and $H(-j\omega)$ must have equal real parts and opposite imaginary parts for any filter that produces a real-valued output signal for each real-valued input signal. This results in equal magnitudes, but opposite phases for $H(j\omega)$ and $H(-j\omega)$. Hence,

$$v_{out} = \frac{1}{2}e^{j\omega t}|H(j\omega)|e^{j\varphi} + \frac{1}{2}e^{-j\omega t}|H(j\omega)|e^{-j\varphi} = |H(j\omega)|\frac{1}{2}\left(e^{j(\omega t+\varphi)} + e^{-j(\omega t+\varphi)}\right) = |H(j\omega)|\cos(\omega t + \varphi)$$

That is, also for a normal cosine wave $|H(j\omega)|$ represents the gain, while the phase shift is φ.

A.3. Poles and zeroes

The values of s for which the denominator of the transfer function is zero are called the poles of the transfer function. The values of s for which the numerator of the transfer function is zero are called the zeroes. The number of poles of a lumped system can never exceed the number of energy-stor-

ing parts (such as capacities and inductivities in an electric network, or masses and springs in a me-chanic system).

An interesting property is that all transfers of a system with multiple in- or outputs have the same poles, although in some of these transfers some poles may be covered by zeroes. This is a very use-ful property for loudspeaker design, as it allows one to partly determine the electro-acoustic trans-fer by simple impedance measurements. See also the sidebar.

A.4. Calculating the transfer function for a given filter network

The transfer of any network consisting of impedances, independent sources, linear controlled sources, nullators and norators can be calculated with a method called modified nodal analysis. The procedure is as follows:

A. For a network with n nodes, number the nodes from 0 up to and including n-1. Node 0 will be the reference node (also known as the datum), all voltages are with respect to node 0. The ground node is usually taken as node 0, although this is not necessary (in fact the term ground has no meaning in network theory).

B. For each of the n-1 nodes that have a number different from 0, write down the nodal equation. This is an equation expressing how much current flows into and out of the node as a function of the node voltages. Of course all current that flows into a node also has to flow out of the node again (Kirchhoff's current law).

C. For each voltage source and each nullator or norator, you have to introduce additional equations.

D. The last step is to solve the unknown node voltages from the resulting set of equations. With lin-ear equations there is a simple trick for this, which is known as Gaussian elimination. The trick is best illustrated by an example. Suppose you have the following set of equations:

$$3a + 2b + 3c = 0$$
$$2a + 5b + 8c = 0$$
$$a + 6b + 4c = 12$$

By subtracting two thirds of the first equation from the second equation and one third of the first equation from the third equation, you can eliminate a from the second and third equations:

$$3a + 2b + 3c = 0$$
$$\frac{11}{3}b + 6c = 0$$
$$\frac{16}{3}b + 3c = 12$$

By subtracting 16/11 times the second equation from the third equation, b is eliminated from the third equation and we get:

$$3a + 2b + 3c = 0$$
$$\frac{11}{3}b + 6c = 0$$
$$-\frac{63}{11}c = 12$$

The third equation now has only one unknown left (c) and is quite easily solved. Once the third equation is solved, you can substitute the result in the second equation, which then also becomes a simple equation with only one unknown (b). Substituting b and c in the first equation then results in a simple equation with only the unknown a.

$$-\frac{63}{11}c = 12 \Leftrightarrow c = -\frac{11 \cdot 12}{63} = -\frac{132}{63} = -\frac{44}{21}$$

$$\frac{11}{3}b + 6 \cdot \left(-\frac{44}{21}\right) = 0 \Leftrightarrow b = \frac{3}{11} \cdot 6 \cdot \frac{44}{21} = \frac{3 \cdot 6 \cdot 4}{21} = \frac{24}{7}$$

$$3a + 2 \cdot \frac{24}{7} + 3 \cdot \left(-\frac{44}{21}\right) = 0 \Leftrightarrow a = \frac{1}{3}\left(-2 \cdot \frac{24}{7} + 3 \cdot \frac{44}{21}\right) = \frac{1}{3}\left(-\frac{4}{7}\right) = -\frac{4}{21}$$

It is clear that the amount of work increases rapidly with increasing number of equations (though not as rapidly as with other algorithms for solving systems of linear equations). As the number of equations in modified nodal analysis depends on the number of nodes, it is advisable to eliminate any node that can easily be eliminated before doing the analysis.

A.5. The transfer of the bass extending filter

Figure 5 shows a network model for the bass extending filter. The op-amp has been replaced with an ideal controlled voltage source with unity gain and all resistors and capacitors have been replaced with ideal ones.

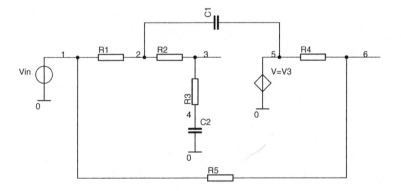

Figure 5. Network model for the bass extending filter.

Two nodes can easily be eliminated:

1. It is clear from inspection of the network that the output impedance is constant and equal to R_4 in parallel with R_5. Hence, we might as well short-circuit the output and calculate the output current, the unloaded voltage is then simply R_4 in parallel with R_5 times the short-circuit current.

2. Node 4 can be eliminated by replacing the series connection of R_3 and C_2 with an impedance $R_3+1/(sC_2)=(sR_3C_2+1)/(sC_2)$.

These simplifications result in the network of figure 6.

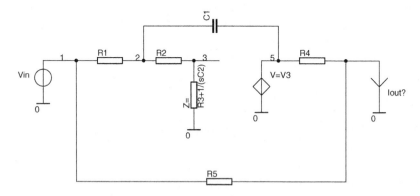

Figure 6. Simplified network model.

The nodal equations are:

$$(G_1 + G_5)V_1 - G_1V_2 = I(V_{in}) \text{ for node } 1,$$
$$-G_1V_1 + (G_1 + G_2 + sC_1)V_2 - G_2V_3 - sC_1V_5 = 0 \text{ for node } 2,$$

$$-G_2V_2 + \left(G_2 + \frac{sC_2}{sR_3C_2 + 1}\right)V_3 = 0 \text{ for node } 3,$$
$$-sC_1V_2 + (sC_1 + G_4)V_5 = I(\text{controlled source}) \text{ for node } 5$$

In these equations, $G_x=1/R_x$ for $x=1, 2, 3, 4$ or 5. Note that the admittance (reciprocal of the impedance) of a capacity with capacitance C is sC.

The extra equations are:

$$V_1 = V_{in}$$
$$V_5 = V_3$$

Note that the equations for nodes 1 and 5 contain unknowns that do not occur in any other equation, namely the current through the input signal source $I(V_{in})$ and the current through the controlled source I(controlled source). We can eliminate these unknowns by simply disregarding these equations. The remaining system of equations becomes:

$-G_1 V_{in} + (G_1 + G_2 + sC_1)V_2 - (G_2 + sC_1)V_3 = 0$ for node 2,

$-G_2 V_2 + \left(G_2 + \dfrac{sC_2}{sR_3 C_2 + 1}\right)V_3 = 0$ for node 3.

Adding $G_2/(G_1 + G_2 + sC_1)$ times the first equation to the second equation to eliminate node voltage 2:

$$-G_1 V_{in}\dfrac{G_2}{G_1 + G_2 + sC_1} + \left(-\dfrac{G_2(G_2 + sC_1)}{G_1 + G_2 + sC_1} + G_2 + \dfrac{sC_2}{sR_3 C_2 + 1}\right)V_3 = 0$$

Hence,

$$V_3 = G_1 V_{in}\dfrac{G_2}{(G_1 + G_2 + sC_1)\left(-\dfrac{G_2(G_2 + sC_1)}{G_1 + G_2 + sC_1} + G_2 + \dfrac{sC_2}{sR_3 C_2 + 1}\right)} =$$

$$= \dfrac{G_1 G_2 V_{in}}{-G_2(G_2 + sC_1) + G_2(G_1 + G_2 + sC_1) + \dfrac{sC_2}{sR_3 C_2 + 1}(G_1 + G_2 + sC_1)} =$$

$$= \dfrac{(sR_3 C_2 + 1)G_1 G_2 V_{in}}{-G_2(sR_3 C_2 + 1)(G_2 + sC_1) + (sR_3 C_2 + 1)G_2(G_1 + G_2 + sC_1) + sC_2(G_1 + G_2 + sC_1)}$$

After multiplying both the numerator and the denominator with $R_1 R_2$, using $R_1 = 1/G_1$ and $R_2 = 1/G_2$:

$$V_3 = \dfrac{(sR_3 C_2 + 1)V_{in}}{-R_1(sR_3 C_2 + 1)(1/R_2 + sC_1) + (sR_3 C_2 + 1)(1 + R_1/R_2 + sR_1 C_1) + sC_2(R_2 + R_1 + sR_1 R_2 C_1)}$$

When you write out the denominator, you find that lots of terms cancel, and you are left with:

$$V_3 = \dfrac{(sR_3 C_2 + 1)V_{in}}{s^2 R_1 R_2 C_1 C_2 + s(R_1 + R_2 + R_3)C_2 + 1}$$

The output short-circuit current equals:

$$I_{out} = \dfrac{V_5}{R_4} + \dfrac{V_{in}}{R_5} = \dfrac{V_3}{R_4} + \dfrac{V_{in}}{R_5} =$$

$$V_{in}\dfrac{\dfrac{R_5}{R_4 + R_5}\dfrac{R_5}{R_4 + R_5}(sR_3 C_2 + 1) + \dfrac{R_4}{R_4 + R_5}(s^2 R_1 R_2 C_1 C_2 + s(R_1 + R_2 + R_3)C_2 + 1)}{R_4 R_5 \quad s^2 R_1 R_2 C_1 C_2 + s(R_1 + R_2 + R_3)C_2 + 1}$$

The unloaded output voltage equals the short-circuit current times the value of R_4 and R_5 in parallel, which is:

$$V_{out,\,unloaded} = V_{in}\dfrac{\dfrac{R_5}{R_4 + R_5}(sR_3 C_2 + 1) + \dfrac{R_4}{R_4 + R_5}(s^2 R_1 R_2 C_1 C_2 + s(R_1 + R_2 + R_3)C_2 + 1)}{s^2 R_1 R_2 C_1 C_2 + s(R_1 + R_2 + R_3)C_2 + 1}$$

After defining the transfer function as the ratio between the unloaded output voltage and the input voltage and simplifying the numerator:

$$H(s) = \frac{V_{out,\,unloaded}}{V_{in}} = \frac{s^2 \dfrac{R_4}{R_4+R_5} R_1 R_2 C_1 C_2 + s\left(\dfrac{R_4}{R_4+R_5}\left(R_1+R_2\right)+R_3\right)C_2 + 1}{s^2 R_1 R_2 C_1 C_2 + s\left(R_1+R_2+R_3\right)C_2 + 1}$$

A.6. The transfer of the bass-cut filter

Figure 7 shows a network model for the bass-cut filter. The op-amp has been replaced with a nullator (drawn as a single circle) and a norator (drawn as two circles). The output is again shorted to reduce the number of nodes.

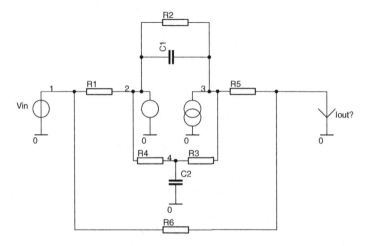

Figure 7. Network model for the bass-cut filter.

A nullator is a two-terminal network element with the properties that there is no voltage across it and no current flowing through it. A norator is a two-terminal network element with the properties that there can be any voltage across it and any current flowing through it. The combination of a nullator and a norator is also known as a nullor. Tellegen came up with the concept of nullors in 1954 as a way to model high-gain negative-feedback circuits. The name nullor was only introduced a decade later.

In order to get a network that has a finite and non-zero number of solutions, the number of nullators in the network must be the same as the number of norators, and there must be some sort of path from each norator to a nullator. What happens is that the norators supply whatever voltage and current is needed to make the voltage across and current through the nullators equal to zero.

Suppose you have an amplifier and you use it in a negative-feedback configuration. When you let the open-loop voltage, current, transimpedance and transadmittance gains of the amplifier approach infinity, the input voltage and current will approach zero and the output will supply whatever voltage and current it needs to supply. So a nullator basically models the input of the amplifier and the norator the output.

A nullor is basically the same as an ideal op-amp, except that an ideal op-amp has one of the terminals of its norator implicitly tied to the power supply pins, which is very inconvenient when you want to use series feedback at the output.

The nodal equations for figure 7 are:

$$(G_1 + G_6)V_1 - G_1V_2 = I(V_{in}) \text{ for node } 1,$$
$$-G_1V_1 + (G_1 + G_2 + G_4 + sC_1)V_2 - (G_2 + sC_1)V_3 - G_4V_4 = 0 \text{ for node } 2,$$
$$-(G_2 + sC_1)V_2 + (G_2 + G_3 + G_5 + sC_1)V_3 - G_3V_4 = I_{norator} \text{ for node } 3,$$
$$-G_4V_2 - G_3V_3 + (G_3 + G_4 + sC_2)V_4 = 0 \text{ for node } 4.$$

Additional equations:

$$V_1 = V_{in}$$
$$V_2 = 0$$

The nodal equations for nodes 1 and 3 contain unknowns that do not occur anywhere else, we will remove these from the system of equations. After substituting the additional equations, it all simplifies to:

$$-(G_2 + sC_1)V_3 - G_4V_4 = G_1V_{in}$$
$$-G_3V_3 + (G_3 + G_4 + sC_2)V_4 = 0$$

Adding $G_4/(G_3+G_4+sC_2)$ times the second equation to the first equation to eliminate the voltage at node 4, we get:

$$\left(-G_3 \frac{G_4}{G_3 + G_4 + sC_2} - (G_2 + sC_1)\right)V_3 = G_1V_{in}$$

$$V_3 = -V_{in} \frac{G_1}{\dfrac{G_3G_4}{G_3 + G_4 + sC_2} + G_2 + sC_1}$$

The exact same result can be obtained in a different way by first analysing the voltage to current transfer of the sub-circuit R_3-C_2-R_4. One can show that the transfer from the voltage at node 3 to the current that flows out of R_4 is the same as when the sub-circuit R_3-C_2-R_4 had been replaced with the series connection of an inductivity with inductance $R_3 R_4C_2$ and a resistor with resistance R_3+R_4. The

gain from the input voltage to node 3 then follows from the well-known equations for a negative gain op-amp amplifier. After a bit of rewriting, this gives the same equation for the transfer to node 3.

The transfer from the input voltage to the short-circuit output current now follows from adding G_5 times the voltage at node 3 to G_6 times the input voltage. After a lot of rearranging terms, this leads to the equations given earlier in this article.

SIT Nemesis!

Nelson Pass

Introduction

In Linear Audio Volume 0 I presented a redux of the 1985 Hiraga design, the Nemesis. The article explored some of the issues and variations that accompany the use of a simple single-ended Class A design coupled to the loudspeaker through an output transformer. This is an addendum to that piece.

The Arch Nemesis

The "Arch Nemesis" had a central theme – the performance of a Common-Source mode power FET operating without feedback into an output coupling transformer. The transformer was originally commissioned by Jan Didden (our publisher) from Electra-Print in Las Vegas. Everything else was up for grabs, and so I played with a number of different Mosfet and Jfet devices, varying the supply voltage, bias current and resistive loading in an effort to locate the "sweet spot" for each device, and then compared the measured result.

You can see it all there, but to summarize, the best general result came from a new depletion mode Jfet, the SemiSouth SJDP120R085. Here is figure 10 from that article showing the specific circuit (**Figure 1**):

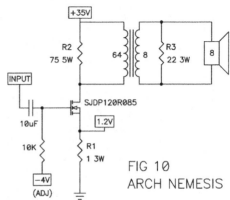

Figure 1: Original Arch Nemesis diagram from the article in Vol 0

R1 was used to degenerate the gain of the Fet for lower distortion and increased bias stability with vertical Fets. The values of R2 and R3 here were used to give a damping factor of 1 for the load. Without R3 and R2 the output impedance of the amplifier was about 28 ohms, which is considered quite high. There is another reason for R2 – a transformer works best when the source impedance is a small fraction of the primary impedance. This primary is 64 ohms, and the Drain resistance driving it is about 80 ohms.

Driven by 80 ohms, the distortion and bandwidth figures for this transformer are not very good. Setting R2 at 75 ohms lowers the source impedance seen by the transformer and improves the lower frequency performance. Still lower values cause increased distortion in the power transistor.

If this were a SET amplifier with a 300B operated without feedback we could be looking at a damping factor of 2 or 3 at the speaker terminals, the result of a relatively low 700 ohm plate resistance working with maybe a 2500 ohm transformer primary. Non-feedback amplifiers of this type with very high quality transformers do better on the bottom end but suffer more tube distortion.

If only there were a good linear Fet with a low Drain resistance...

The Pentode Character of a Mosfet

The characteristics of an amplifying device's curves are quite important to the performance. Your ordinary Jfet or Mosfet has a set of curves which resemble those of a Pentode tube (**Figure 2**).

The current passing from Drain to Source (Ids) in a Mosfet is reflected in the vertical scale in Amps, and the voltage from Drain to Source (Vds) is the horizontal scale. Ten different curves are shown,

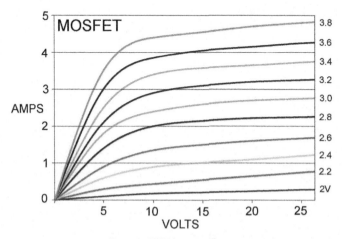

Figure 2: FET Vds versus Ids curves

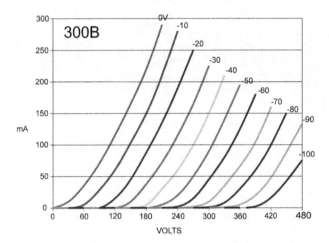

Figure 3: 300B tube Vak versus Ia curves

each for a different value of the Gate to Source control voltage (Vgs). We see that for a given value of Vgs the current rises proportionally with Vds from 0 to roughly 5 volts and then levels off. This region from 0 to 5 volts is known as the "linear" or "ohmic" region, where the Fet acts like a variable resistor. The region above about 5 volts is known as the "saturation" region where the current through the device is much less dependent on Vds and acts like a variable current source.

We could also say that in the linear region the device acts mostly like a voltage controlled resistor, and in the saturation region it acts mostly like a voltage controlled current source. Because the current Ids is very dependent on Vds at low voltage values, in the linear/ohmic region the output resistance at the Drain is quite low - in this case as low as 1 ohm or so. In the saturation region the Drain resistance increases dramatically to 100 ohms or more.

By contrast, here are the curves of a 300B power Triode tube (**Figure 3**).

The voltages are much higher and the current much lower than that of the Mosfet example. In a Triode the Plate current is dependent on the Grid to Cathode voltage but also on the Plate to Cathode voltage, much as with the linear region of the Mosfet. However the curves do not flatten out at higher voltages, and the Plate resistance of the Triode remains relatively low (in this case about 700 ohms – low for a tube!)

Enter the SIT

SIT stands for *Static Induction Transistor*. It is a form of power Jfet invented in Japan by Professor Junichi Nishizawa which found its way into audio in the form of the Vfet power amplifiers produced by Yamaha and Sony in the mid-1970's.

They were called Vfets at the time because they have a vertical structure, but the subsequent inven-

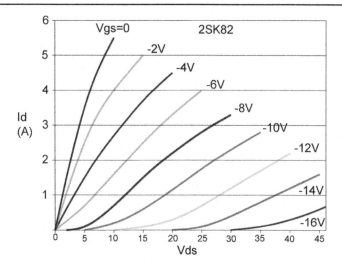

Figure 4: Sony 2SK82 VFET (SIT) Vds versus Id curves.

tion and dominance of vertical Mosfets has made use of the term confusing. SITs are very fast devices and have found use in radar and power conversion, but since Sony and Yamaha ceased production, versions suitable for audio amplification have been rare and expensive.

SITs look very much like solid state versions of Triodes, except that the voltage and current values are scaled differently. Tubes work at high voltages and low currents, and transistors are good at lower voltages and higher currents. The advantage for transistors is that these voltages and currents are convenient for driving loudspeakers directly and do not generally require an output transformer.

Why are we bothering with a transformer at all? A Fet driving a coupling transformer is the *raison d'e-tre* of this design based on Hiraga's Nemesis.

Here is a curve (**Figure 4**) of a Sony 2SK82 VFET (SIT) with a transconductance of about 0.5 S and a Drain impedance of about 10 ohms at about 40V and 1.5 amps

And here (**Figure 5**) is an example of the Yamaha 2SK77 with a transconductance of about 1.25 S and output impedance of about 5 ohms It has more gain, but is virtually unobtainable.

As you can see from the slopes of the curves, these devices have a linear/ohmic character throughout their operating region much like a power triode.

Those comfortable with tubes should feel reasonably at home. Like a Triode, the SIT is a depletion mode device – the Gate voltage operates at a negative voltage with respect to the Source. The notion of "Mu", the amplification factor, is also familiar – it is the product of the transconductance times

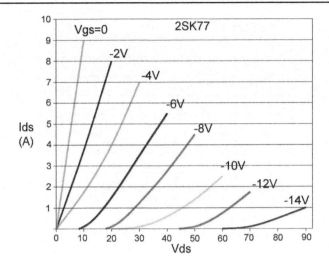

Figure 5: Yahama 2SK77 Vds versus Id curves.

the output (Drain) resistance. As with a Triode, the Mu of the SIT is relatively constant because there is a reciprocal relationship between the transconductance and the output resistance. This makes for convenient adjustment for different loads by simply altering the voltage and current ratios in equal proportions while remaining near the optimal operating point.

In addition to delivering a low output Drain impedance, the SIT allows you to "work the load line" like a Triode. The gain increases with current, but also increases with voltage across the device. Variation in gain creates distortion, but the operating point of the device can be chosen to have these variations cancel. You can read more about that in "The Sweet Spot" to be found at www.passdiy.com.

SIT Nemesis
Already having a pair of Arch Nemesis laying around, I have tried the Sony 2SK82's, but I was a little disappointed as the transconductance was low and they did not develop much voltage gain. So instead I had some custom SITs made (**Figure 6**).

Figure 6: Custom Pass Labs SIT: the PASS-SIT-1.

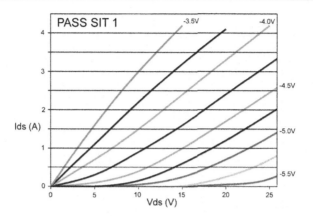

Figure 7: Vds versus Id curves for the PASS-SIT-1.

I had a small batch of these made last year with an eye toward putting them into a First Watt product. I've spent a year getting acquainted with them and exploring the potential for power amplifiers, including of course, the Nemesis.
It has a transconductance of about 2 and a Drain resistance of about 7 ohms (**Figure 7**).

It's a nice looking part, so in it goes. After a little playing around, the circuit looks like **Figure 8**.

It's a somewhat simpler circuit than the original Arch Nemesis. Gone are the 1 ohm resistor degenerating the Source connection to ground, as well as the primary and secondary load resistors. The amplifier biases up at about 0.9 Amps with a Gate voltage of about -7 volts. The gain is about 17 dB into 8 ohms and the damping factor is about 2.

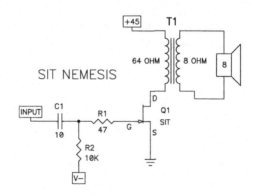

Figure 8: SIT-1 based Arch Nemesis.

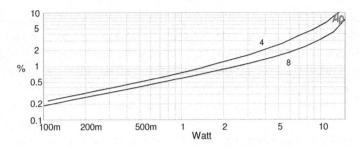

Figure 9: SIT 1 Arch Nemesis distortion versus output power into 4 and 8 ohms.

The gain is 3 dB higher, the output impedance has been halved from 8 ohms to 4 ohms and the low frequency distortion of the transformer has been about halved. As seen in the curves, we also have much better performance into 4 ohms. The frequency response of the transformer has not improved, nor has the midband distortion, where the transistor appears to be responsible for about one third of the harmonic content. **Figure 9** shows the distortion versus output power into 4 and 8 ohms, while **Figure 10** gives you the distortion versus frequency at 1W. The frequency response is shown in **Figure 11**.

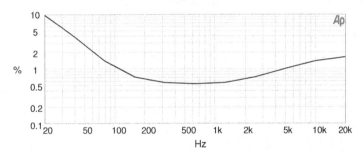

Figure 10: SIT-1 Arch Nemesis distortion versus frequency at 1W.

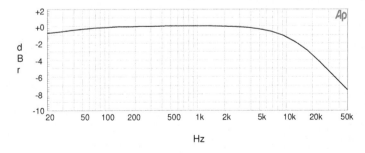

Figure 11: SIT-1 Arch Nemesis frequency response.

The real question of course is how is it different sonically? Having only two transformers, there was not an opportunity to compare versions side-by-side, but I didn't have any problem preferring the SIT version. The R085, the best of the previous batch, was somewhat dry by comparison and the SIT was more lively and had better depth. It shared something interesting with some other SIT prototypes, which when properly adjusted have the ability to present instruments in ensemble with a very individual character. You can easily focus on one instrument individually from the others.

This quality seems to be dependent on the specifics of the load-line. The amplitude distribution of the 2nd and 3rd harmonic and phase of the 2nd harmonic distortion vary as you adjust the supply voltage and the bias current. You can simply adjust for lowest distortion, or you can tweak these parameters to vary the sonic signature. It seems that Hiraga favored a ratio of 2nd to 3rd harmonic with the 2nd harmonic being dominant, but I am not aware that he specified the phase.

Clearly one potential improvement is to seek out *and pay a lot more for* a better transformer, one with more and perhaps better magnetic material and a wider high frequency bandwidth. As I understand it, Jan's copies of the Nemesis had an enormous transformer with much better high frequency bandwidth. From the measurements he has shared, though, it did not look to have lower distortion in the bass, likely because of the high Drain impedance of the Mosfet used.
Possibly Jan will follow up on this in the future with his better transformers.

Another possibility is to eliminate the transformer altogether and bias SITs to directly drive the load impedance. I am working on this, and I expect to present some interesting results in the near future.

Also I have reason to believe that we will see some new SIT parts from a couple of sources in the coming year – parts that you should be able to actually buy.

You should probably start saving for them now...

© 2011 Nelson Pass

Zen → Cen → Sen - Evolution of a Minimalistic IV Conversion Circuit

EUVL

How it started

I have to admit that the AD844 based RIAA preamp circuit from LC Audio [1] fascinates me. I was look-ing, once again, at their "optical supply" MC head amp [2] the other night, only to find out that it was adopted from Leach's common-base MC head amp [3] published a while ago.

There are already detailed descriptions of how the circuit works at both the LC Audio and the Leach websites, so I am not repeating that here. What interests me about the Leach head amp is that it is not a voltage amplifier. Rather it is a current conveyor, at the output of which the current is con-verted to voltage by means of the output resistor (Riv). There are a quite few threads on DIY Audio about the Leach Head Amp, and various people have commented about its noise level and distor-tion level, not always positively.

It still appealed to me somehow, because of its simplicity, and I thought something similar could be very useful for IV conversion for current-output DACs. I spent some time figuring out how to do it with JFETs instead. And the solution in the end was obvious.

Using JFETs in this circuit has some key advantages, at least for DAC IV conversion. It eliminates all the biasing resistors and capacitor around the base of the bipolar transistors, and you only need to tie both JFET gates to the DAC ground, thus simplifying the circuit even further. All is left now are a pair of complementary JFETs with matched Idss, a (battery) floating power supply, 2 decoupling caps, and one IV-conversion resistor. It all seems obvious, but the elimination, or at least drastic reduction, of the base current through the BJT's back to the DAC Gnd is a key performance advantage of this JFET based circuit compared to the original, as will be explained later.

I then noted the similarity of this circuit to Nelson Pass's Zen IV [4] (**Figure 1**) in terms of components, though there are also some key differences in circuitry. In the Zen IV, the IV conversion is done by the two 1k resistors at the positive and negative rails, connected to the output via two high-pass filters in parallel. Thus, the 10uF coupling caps are working in voltage mode, and their non-linearities will

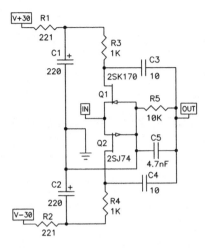

ZEN I–V CONVERTER
(C) 2010 PASS LABS

Fig 1: Nelson Pass' Zen IV.

appear as output distortion. On top of that, any noise on either power supply rail will be fed directly through to the output, i.e. there is no PSRR. This adds to the requirement for the power supply.

As I pointed out at the beginning of the Zen IV thread [5], there are a few more limitations of the Zen circuit. Let's take a DAC like PCM1704 with 1.2mA output. To get 2Vrms out, one needs to use 4.7k resistors at both rails for IV conversion. And in order to keep the current swing small compared to bias (for low distortion), the bias current, in this case also Idss, of the JFETs wants to be, say, 6mA minimum. This means, however, 28V across the 4.7k resistors, requiring +/- 37V rails or higher. The resistors see continuous dissipation of 170mW, increasing thermal noise in the resistors.

The equivalent input resistance of the Zen IV equals to the reciprocal of the sum of transconductances of the JFET pair, and is about 17 ohm. If one wishes to keep this lower, to say <10R, one needs to use 2 pairs of complementary JFETs in parallel, each with 6mA+ Idss. This, however, means +/- 65V rails, and 0.7W continuous dissipation per resistor.

Most of these drawbacks are not applicable to the JFET "Leach" circuit, which I nicknamed Cen IV (to reflect its complementary nature; **Figure 2**). An 18V supply across the two JFETs is quite sufficient, though you can go further to 27V or 36V if you wish. The benefit of higher voltage is lower JFET capacitances, which in turn means higher bandwidth and lower distortion. The Riv only carries the signal current from the DAC, and no quiescent current. Changing the IV conversion gain (from say 500R to 2.7k), or increasing the number of JFETs in parallel, does not affect the rest of the circuit – no changes in rail voltages, or resistor wattage, etc. And the battery only sees a constant current load, as the DAC current runs in a separate loop and does not go through the batteries at all. The only

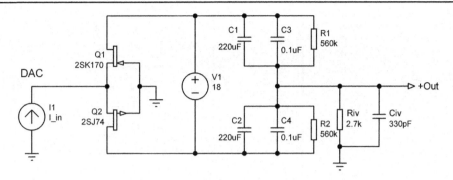

Fig 2: The Cen IV (2SK170 / 2SJ74, matched Idss)

drawback is the necessity of a floating power supply. But two 9V-block NiMH rechargables would easily provide 10 hours of operation. So this is not a real problem.

I made a direct comparison between the distortion performance of the Zen IV vs. the Cen IV in Spice, using the same JFET Spice models in both circuits. The Zen IV is the original circuit as published, and the Cen IV has a Riv of 500R for the same transimpedance gain as the Zen. The results are somewhat surprising. For a current input signal of +/- 1mA, 1kHz sine, THD is 0.000257% for Zen, and 0.000066% for Cen. The JFET models being identical, this is pure circuitry difference; a factor of four improvement. My interpretation is that the Zen IV is a push pull transimpedance amplifier, whereas the Leach circuit is a pure current conveyor, as the power supply is not connected to the DAC ground and therefore runs in a current loop totally separate from the signal current loop. Except for the JFET gate connections to DAC Gnd, the entire input signal current has to return to DAC Gnd via Riv. Thus, whatever non-linearities there are in the devices, Kirchhoff's law ensures near-zero distortion (the resistor Riv is also not 100.000000% distortion free [6]). However, because of the presence of Cgd and Cgs of the JFETs, there is a very tiny leakage current through the gates to DAC Gnd in the presence of an AC signal, and this tiny current is not flowing though Riv. If this current is not perfectly linearly proportional to the input current signal (and it is not), it is precisely this non-linearity that contributes to distortion in the CEN circuit. We shall expect that distortion decreases with JFET capacitances, and increases with frequency. What about a higher transimpedance than 500R? Using Riv of 2.7k in the Cen circuit, THD is 0.0019% at 1kHz. The floating PSU essentially swings together with the output signal relative to DAC Gnd. And the higher the output swing, the higher the leakage current through the JFET gates, and thus the higher the distortion. But still, the performance is very respectable by any standard.

I could have stopped here. But 2SJ74s are becoming increasingly difficult to get. And the 2J103 / 2SK246 pair is of little use here due to its low transconductance. So I wanted to come up with a design with only N-JFETs, and at the same time make use of their lower capacitance to reduce distortion further. The new circuit, which I named Sen IV (S for Single Ended; **Figure 3**), is much akin to the

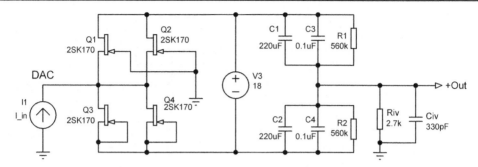

Fig. 3: The Sen IV (4x 2SK170, matched Idss).

current-source-loaded JFET follower, published by Curl, Borbely, Feucht, and Pass on various occa-sions. To get close to the same input impedance as the 2SK170 / 2SJ74 pair, a total of 4x 2SK170's are used, as the two lower ones merely acts as current source and play no part in determining the input impedance. One penalty is increased current consumption. But even at about 20mA total bias, this is still not unacceptably high. Distortion now is 0.0012% (-98.4dB) with 2.7k Riv, a touch lower than Cen. As already mentioned, only the top two 2SK170's are contributing to gate leakage related dis-tortion. Since the 2SK170 has lower capacitance as the 2SJ74, it is not too surprising that the distor-tion in the Sen IV is further reduced.

These THD figures do not necessarily represent reality, as they are only as accurate as the Spice mod-els themselves, and all passive components, current sources, power supplies are assumed ideal. It does, however, indicate that the development of the circuitry itself is going in the right direction.

Bread-boarding & First Measurements

Once I was happy with the circuit, it was time to build and test. Idss-matched devices (8.5mA) were dug out from my JFET stock and breadboard circuits were quickly assembled. Two important issues became obvious at this point – a true floating supply with no coupling to Ground (I used 2x 9V bat-teries which gave no problems at all), and the need of a potential divider to set the floating power supply symmetrically about Input Ground during start up. The latter was easily achieved by adding a pair of resistors of identical values in parallel to the output coupling caps. I tried anything from 68k to 560k, and they all worked fine, so the value is not critical. Eventually I settled on 560k.

For measurement purposes, the two decoupling capacitors are not so critical. I just used a pair of or-dinary electrolytic capacitors, such as Panasonic FC 100uF 16V. There is room for experiment in the eventual application, where I plan to start off using German-made Frolyt Bipolar (220uF 25V), fol-lowed by ELNA RBP 220uF 16V bipolar, and Nichicon Muse ES 100uF 16V bipolar, in parallel with WIMA MKP2 0.1uF 250V. One could also use large-value film caps, such as WIMA MKS2-XL 15uF. The minimum value of the capacitance should not be less than 4.7uF, assuming a Riv of 2.7k at the out-put. If you use a lower Riv value because of higher DAC current output, you should consider in-

creasing the minimum value of the capacitors accordingly. The choice of capacitor is endless but at the same time controversial, so I shall leave you to experiment with whatever unobtainium caps you have in your stock.

To simulate a current-output DAC for testing purposes, I had to build a high bandwidth, ultra low distortion VCCS (voltage controlled current source). The circuit in Fig. 9 of National Semiconductor's AN1515 was chosen, and implemented using an OPA1642 dual opamp, 4 Caddock MKV132 10k re-sistors matched to 0.01%, and a 1k 0.1% Vishay Dale CMF55 as gain resistor (R13). It is essential to use very low distortion components, and I consider a JFET input opamp to be advantageous here. Meas-urements verified that the VCCS was low enough in distortion (<-90dB) and high enough in band-width (> 1MHz) to be not limiting the first measurements. Here are a few initial measurements.

Figure 4 and 5 show the measurements for the Cen IV circuit. The -3dB bandwidth is around 220kHz

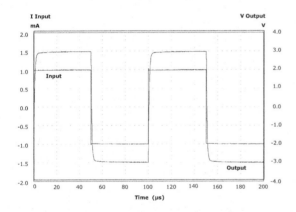

Fig 4: Cen IV 10kHz +/-1mA Square Wave (Riv = 3k; smaller curve = Vin for VCCS, larger curve = Vout Cen IV, unfiltered)

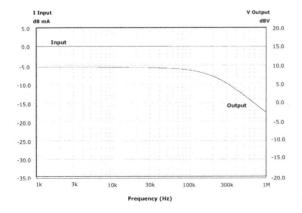

Fig 5: Cen IV Frequency Response at +/-1mA sine wave input (Riv = 3k; top = Vin for VCCS, bottom = Vout Cen IV, unfiltered)

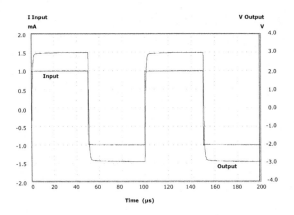

Fig 6: Sen IV   10kHz +/-1mA   Square Wave (Riv = 3k; smaller curve = Vin for VCCS, larger curve = Vout Sen IV, unfiltered)

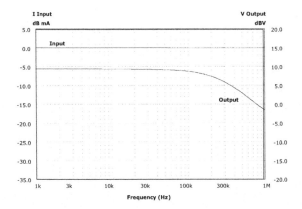

Fig 7: Sen IV   Frequency Response at +/- 1mA sine wave input (Riv = 3k; top = Vin for VCCS, bottom = Vout Sen IV, unfiltered)

This is followed in by the results for the Sen IV in **figures 6 and 7**. The -3dB bandwidth is now around 300kHz due to the lower capacitances of the N-JFETs.

Circuit Variants

Now that the basic circuits have been proven, we can look at a couple of variants, apart from playing with passive components.

As already mentioned, both Cen (with one 2SK170 / 2SJ74 matched pair) and Sen (with 4x 2SK170 matched) have an input resistance of about 15R. If this is too high for your DAC, you can half that in value by using 2 pairs of 2SK170 / 2SJ74 for Cen, and 4 matched 2SK369 for Sen. The input capacitances will double in both cases, and so would distortion. So low input impedance comes at a cost, and has to be balanced against distortion reduction in the DAC itself with various input impedance values of the IV circuit.

The use of only N-JFETs in the Sen makes it really versatile. You can basically use any TO92 N-JFET at

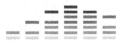

Idss. If you can live with a slightly higher input resistance, say 25R, you may use 4 matched 2SK117BL; this device has 1/3 of the capacitance of the 2SK170. The bandwidth can then be increased to near 1MHz, and the distortion reduced by another 10dB. A truly excellent performer !!

Application Limitations

As is the case for the Zen IV, these circuits work with DACs with symmetrical current outputs and at 0V DC nominal. With slight modifications and added complexity, however, it is possible to adapt the circuit for single rail DACs with DC biased voltage and/or current at their outputs. E.g. you can hang the gates of the JFETs at an elevated voltage from DAC to cater for voltage bias, or you can pick JFETs with different Idss on purpose to cope with current bias. I shall leave this as an exercise to those skilled in the art.

Also, using 4 FETs at 10mA Idss as in the Sen IV, the total quiescent current is 20mA. I would not swing more than 25% of this, so the i_out of your DAC should not be >5mA. If your DAC has a higher current output, you just have to put more JFETs in parallel, or use devices with an even higher Idss. With 9V across each JFET, 20mA bias is still not excessive in terms of dissipation, especially if you use a small heat sink on the devices.

PCB Layout

A couple of PCBs were quickly put together (**Fig 8**). The most critical passive component for the entire circuit is probably Riv. The PCBs were designed to accept Caddock MKV132 or Texas TX2575. You may use other resistor types, and I recommend you to solder the resistor directly at the output connector anyhow. If you are using non-oversampling DACs and want to limit the bandwidth further, you can solder a film cap at the position marked Civ, such as WIMA FKP2 or MKP2. A 330pF film cap in combination with a Riv of 2.7k will form a first order LP filter at 180kHz, for example. For optimal thermal tracking, I made use of our famous JFET heat sinks produced by wire cut EDM.

Fig 8: The Prototypes

Final Measurements

I took the prototypes together with the VCCS to Jan Didden's one evening. Before measuring the IV circuits, we first checked the signal source. To measure the VCCS, we connected a 20R resistor to its output, so as to simulate the input impedance of the IV circuit.

The FFT of the analogue generator of the AP at 1Vrms output shows a HD of -100dB for 2nd and 3rd, and -105dB at 4th. Adding the VCCS to that, and with a 20R load resistor at its output the distortions all rose to about -90dB (**Fig 9**). This might well be due to the fact that the signal level is low (20mVrms) and thus the relative noise level as well as the preamp distortion of the AP might add to the distortion of the VCCS itself.

After some discussions and experiments, Jan and I decided to use a 20k resistor directly in series with the AP analogue generator output set at 20Vrms output to simulate a 1mA rms current source. This might still not be totally distortion free, but it appears that we can get better results than the VCCS. It just proves once again that measuring very low distortion levels is not a simple matter.

At 20Vrms output, the HD of the signal source is -115dB for 2nd, and about -105dB for 3rd and 4th. Almost identical or a very slight improvement relative to 1Vrms

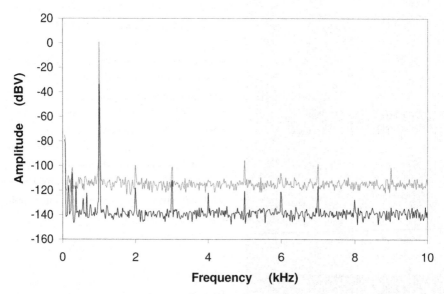

Fig 9: FFT of VCCS with 20R resistor at output (top : Signal Source 1Vrms, bottom : VCCS Voltage Output at 20mV RMS)

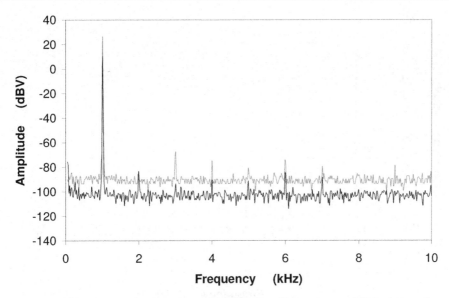

Fig 10: FFT of Sen IV using 20k series resistor at input (top : Signal Source, bottom : IV Voltage Output)

Then we proceeded to measure both the Cen & Sen IV's, each using 2.7k in parallel with 330p at the output. As the measurement was done at 1kHz, we would not see too much of a LP filter at 180kHz, but noise floor will improve at HF.

Apply 20Vrms input to the 20k series resistor, the input current is 1mA rms. The measured distortion of the Sen (**Fig 10**) circuit (after correcting for the distortion of the signal source) is -93dB 2nd, -100dB 3rd, and -110dB 4th. For any of the values to be totally reliable below -100dB, we need a much better signal source, and ideally a current signal source first.

Similarly, for the Cen circuit (**Fig 11**), the corrected distortions are -92dB for 2nd, -101dB 3rd, and -110dB 4th, essentially identical to the SEN and indicating that the distortion in the current signal source is masking the accuracy of the measurement of the IV circuit. Reducing the input amplitude by half reduces THD by some 4dB, but again the signal source is likely to be masking the performance of the IV circuit itself.

The orders of magnitude of these values are similar to those of the simulation. Rather than chasing academically perfect figures and 100% correlation between theory & measurement, I consider these decent enough. In practice, one can easily reduce all even harmonics further by running two of them in balanced mode.

We also did a quick frequency sweep to verify the hypothesis that THD increases with frequency (**Fig 12**).

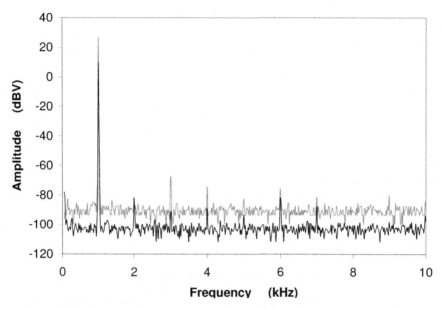

Fig 11: FFT of Cen IV using 20k series resistor at input (top : Signal Source, bottom : IV Voltage Output)

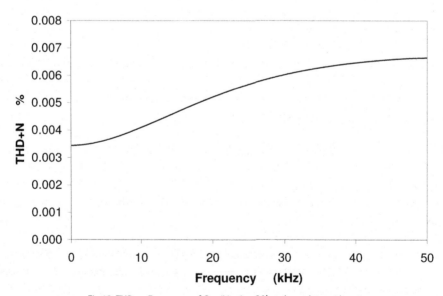

Fig 12: THD vs. Frequency of Cen IV using 20k series resistor at input

The inevitable question now is – how does it sound? We cannot possibly give you a neutral opinion, and shall therefore only urge you to try these simple yet high performance circuits for yourselves.

Support

To enable the reader to experiment with these two simple yet elegant circuits themselves, an evaluation pack will be made available as a Group Buy on DIY Audio after the publication of the article. Each pack will include :

2x   Cen IV PCBs (4 single ended or 2 balanced IV in total), single sided 35um copper, 1.6mm FR4

2x   Sen IV PCBs (4 single ended or 2 balanced IV in total) , single sided 35um copper, 1.6mm FR4

4x   Quad JFET heat sink Type 10 (for Sen IV)

4x   Dual JFET heat sink Type 0 (for Cen IV)

Optionally

2x   Idss matched 2SJ74BL

I included the 2SJ74 (limited to 40 pairs) as they are now hard to get, but 2SK170 and others are still easily available, so I shall leave you to source those separately.

Acknowledge

Most sincere thanks to Jan Didden and WK Lai, for the many interesting discussions during the circuit development, and for helping with the simulation work, the measurements, and arranging the prototype PCBs. Nelson Pass kindly allowed the inclusion of the schematic for his Zen IV circuit for which I thank him.

References

1.   http://www.lcaudio.com/index.php?page=8
2.   http://www.lcaudio.com/images/Accessories/mcstepbig.gif
3.   http://users.ece.gatech.edu/mleach/headamp/
4.   http://www.passdiy.com/pdf/Z-IV.pdf
5.   http://www.diyaudio.com/forums/pass-labs/173291-zen-i-v-converter.html#post2297965
6.   Resistor non-linearity – there's more to Ω than meets the eye", Ed Simon, Linear Audio Vol 1, p138

Paragraphing

"The division of discourse next above the Sentence is the Paragraph. It is a collection, or series, of sentences, with unity of purpose – an orderly collection, a natural sequence.

Look to the Paragraphs, and the Discourse will take care of itself: Each paragraph (or, on a larger scale, each section of a chapter) corresponds to a point to be made, described, narrated; to a head of discourse, a topic, an aspect.

If you establish the ordonnance of your theme, you will find that there is one order superior to all others; in establishing the order in which you desire to make the points of your exposition or your argument, to set forth the incidents in your narrative, the aspects in your description, you simultaneously and inevitably establish the division into paragraphs and the order of those paragraphs. That is the nearest sensible thing to a general rule"

Alexander Bain, philosopher and rhetorician, 1818-1903

Testing One, Two, Three

Stuart Yaniger

Have you ever watched a talented close-up magician? Coins seemingly appear and vanish in defiance of the laws of physics. Handkerchiefs are cut to bits, then are made whole. Bullets are caught in teeth. Amazing! And watching the show, it all looks real, even when your conscious brain KNOWS that the magician is trying to fool you- and if the magician is skilled, even when you know the trick, you're still fooled (I used to work with a fellow whose Three Card Monte would buffalo experienced street hustlers). Our brains and sense organs, as a system, are limited in what they can do and how they can efficiently process the sort of data that kept our ancestors from being eaten or trampled. Magicians know how to exploit the sensory system's "shortcuts" and use that knowledge to entertain.

Unfortunately, that knowledge can be used by charlatans and fraudsters- if the fellow bending spoons or the lady talking to the dead tell their audiences that it's not an act, it's real, they can be quite convincing to the majority of people who do not have experience with the arts of conjuring or cold reading. As with the ethical performer, the audience can be fooled into believing that they saw or heard things that they didn't actually see or hear. Does that make the audience stupid? Not at all. They're human, with all the basic hardware issues that go with having a human brain.

The difference between the audiences of a magician and a charlatan is not intelligence or perceptiveness but rather gullibility and ego. The audience at a magic show knows they're being fooled and will not walk away convinced that the magician really materialized doves out of thin air or read their thoughts. The audience for spoonbenders and channelers often think that they are too smart to be fooled. Unfortunately, being fooled by one's senses is universal, and many scientists have had careers ruined by endorsing transparent frauds (1). One magician I know told me that he LOVED having scientists and academics for an audience- "They're much easier to fool than children or bus drivers since they rely on their intellect and always assume they're the smartest person in the room. And they usually are, but they're not working in their environment, they're working in mine."

It's important, when trying to get to objective truth about subjective judgments, that one's ego is left standing outside. This isn't about who's smarter or whose ears are better, it's about determining what's important in your designs and making design decisions with ones, errr, eyes open. And that requires controls on our listening tests.

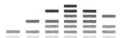
1. Our Purpose

"I changed the cathode resistor in the first stage and the difference was staggering!"

As the wise philosopher Alvarado asked, "What is reality?" (2) Philosophers have been philosophizing over this question for millennia, yet have come to no definitive answer. Thus, we can safely and swiftly leave them to their own devices. With the philosophers safely receding in the rear-view mirror, we can now ask the fundamental question of concern to the audio designer, "Is doing X instead of Y really an improvement? Can I actually even hear a difference between X and Y?" The naïve and obvious answer is, "Trust your ears. If you hear it, it's real." And like most obvious statements, it's a truism. And that's the object of this article- how to evaluate sonic differences at a designer level with accuracy and confidence, to KNOW what's coming from the sound and what's coming from other factors. The important thing in audio is what you HEAR, not what you hope you hear, believe you hear, or think you hear.

The rational audiophile will accept as axiomatic the proposition that if the 3 dimensional soundfield of an acoustic event is reproduced accurately, the listener will be unable to distinguish it from the original- his ears and brain will be fooled. In reality, this is impossible with current technology (where the 3d soundfield around the listener is collapsed to two to five points remote from the listener, each having a single valued function of time), and audio systems must rely on tricks and illusions to fool the listener. The best-known "trick" is stereo- the center image is a pure illusion, there really is no singer standing between the two speakers!

If, like the magic show, the goal of a hifi audio system is to provide entertainment by creating an illusion, there's more than just the pure soundfield to be considered. But the informed designer needs to know what counts for the actual auditory parts of that sonic illusion and separate that from the rest. That's the purpose of this little exposition- controlled subjective testing is a powerful tool which has contributed hugely to audio in general. It is a method and philosophy that can be inexpensively and (relatively) easily used by individual designers and experimenters.

2. Define the Problem

When we are trying to evaluate the subjective sonic impact of a design choice, we need to first define what it is we are trying to find out:

1. Can the consequences of this choice be heard by me?
2. Can the consequences of this choice be heard by an average listener?
3. Can the consequences of this choice be heard by *anyone*?
4. If the answer to 1, 2, or 3 is "yes," then which choice is preferred?

This seems trivial, but it's not- it's a natural tendency among audiophiles to want universal answers. As a result, the boundaries between these questions get blurred- each of these questions is quite different from the others, and naturally, the means by which they can be answered is also quite different. In particular, Question 4 is a distinctly different one when applied to the population at large

or the target market- the usual term for experimentally determined preference is "Hedonic." Getting reliable hedonic data is a massive undertaking- an excellent example in the audio realm is the work by Toole (3) in determining listener preference for loudspeaker frequency response and polar pattern. In this article, we'll look at methods appropriate to answer the question appropriate to the main issues facing high end audio designers- Question 1. We will touch on Questions 2 and 3, but only long enough to determine that this is the sort of issue best left to others- our focus will be in properly framing the questions and designing experiments appropriate to answering those questions- and avoiding the error of designing a test to determine the answer to one of the questions, but really wanting the answer to a different one (this is far more common than one would expect!). I'll also review some common ways in which typical audiophile approaches to listening tests can be misleading and how to do it better.

This is *not* a guide to testing the claims of others (except in a limited sense), to do scientifically rigorous sensory analysis, or to determine the limits of human sensory performance, but we will borrow from the methods that researchers use in these areas (4) to allow you to get useful results that will allow you to focus your design efforts on things that matter- that is, matter to you, the designer or to the people that you design for. The false dichotomy of "subjectivists" and "objectivists" is one of the most destructive notions that high quality audio has ever had inflicted on it. That notion has unnecessarily poisoned useful discussion of design issues and led to a comic book view of rational approaches to making real design improvements. Subjective auditory impressions, when controlled to be by ear alone, are hardcore objective data.

The assumption here is that, as a designer, you want to get the right answer, not the answer you're hoping for (unless it's right). If you are testing strangers or groups or there is some interest at stake by the listeners, controls have to be structured quite differently, beyond the scope of this short article.

We start with a quick review of what we're trying to accomplish, the ways we unwittingly sabotage our determinations of audibility and preferences, talk about how listening tests should be structured, then give a few case studies as examples. The assumption is that you don't want to run full University trials or the complex methods outlined in the standard BS.1116-1 ("Methods for the subjective assessment of small impairments in audio systems including multichannel sound systems"), that you have a couple of friends- at most- to help out, and that you either want to satisfy your own curiosity or drive design decisions.

Remember: Trust your ears, but don't trust your lying brain!

3. Non-Auditory Cues
As we already touched on, what we are interested in finding out is if a design choice is audible. Whether it looks cool, comports with audio fashion, satisfies philosophical urges, gives you pride of ownership, or it just makes you happy to have when playing your music are separate design issues

beyond the scope of this short article. But fundamentally, to evaluate audibility, we have to trust our ears, and not help them out by using other senses or our conscious or unconscious preconceptions. We will begin by reviewing some of the principal ways we cheat ourselves into hearing things that may not be there and how to avoid them.

3a. Placebo Effect

I don't think we need to rehash the placebo effect- just about everyone is familiar with it. You perceive a change because you *think* there's a change, whether or not there's been one. It's programmed into how our brains work, and is probably a result of the relative impact of false negatives (I thought I heard something, I figured that I was imagining things, did nothing, and got eaten by a sabertooth tiger) and false positives (I thought I heard a sabertooth tiger, there wasn't one, so I ran for no reason) on our distant ancestors. This is the major reason why any serious auditory (or haptic or organoleptic, for that matter) inquiry must be done blind, i.e., that the test subjects- whether you or your Trusty Assistant- are unaware about whether or not there's been a change of the variable under test except by their subjective reactions to the sound. For example, we love big, heavy, shiny, artfully designed boxes for our electronics. But does the cheap, flimsy amplifier actually sound different than the 100 kilo three chassis monster? Maybe, but if we see them both, the answer will almost assuredly be "yes." So to determine whether the actual sound is different, it's necessary to hide their identities during audition. You may know that the comparison is between a $100 Flanasonic DX-5000 and a gorgeously constructed $10,000 Dominator Beethoven Mark IV, but at any given time, you don't know which of the two units you're listening to. If they sound different, your ears will tell you. If they don't, your ears will tell you that as well.

One interesting corollary to this is the observation by several cynics that amplifiers with black front panels tended to have their sound described as "dark" when compared with amplifiers having light colored front panels…

Listen with your ears, not your eyes.

3b. My Wife, or The Need for Double Blind

It's become an audio cliché- "The change was so obvious that my wife, who wasn't even in the room and doesn't care about audio, immediately asked me, 'What did you change? It sounds better.'" And that does happen- as I will relate shortly, it's happened to me. The cliché provides an insight into a unique way in which you fool yourself with the unconscious help of others.

Many years ago, a German teacher named Wilhelm von Osten had a horse, Hans. Hans was particularly notable because, it was claimed, he could do arithmetic. If he was asked, "Hans, what is four plus three?" Hans would respond by pawing the ground seven times. He could do all sorts of arithmetic, not just addition. That indeed is remarkable, for it demonstrated not only mathematical ability, but also language capacity and understanding. By all accounts, von Osten was an honest (though ill-

tempered) man, so no guile was suspected. Hans's performances attracted large crowds, and the high public interest prompted a psychologist, Oskar Pfungst, to investigate.

Pfungst noticed several things. First, the trick worked even when von Osten wasn't present- this eliminated the idea that von Osten was consciously signaling the horse. Second, the horse wouldn't perform properly when it had blinders on. Third, and most tellingly, the horse wouldn't be able to answer questions that the questioner couldn't.

Now, how does this relate to the wife in the next room? I had that experience myself, several times. When I would fiddle with some components or circuit parameters, and sat listening joyously to the results of my creative labors, my wife would often notice as well that my ministrations had been effective. Clearly, with this unbiased ear (she knew nothing whatever of electronics or acoustics) validating my impressions, I must be on the right track... or so I thought, until one evening, some doubts crept in. Thinking uncomfortably about a variable that I hadn't controlled, I changed nothing in my sound system, but managed to get a, "Did you change something? It sounds nicer," from the next room. A pin to my ballooned ego. How did I prompt this comment without changing anything in my system?

Simple. I played a cut from "Jazz at the Pawnshop" and a cut from "Kor," both very popular "audiophile" albums of that era, brilliantly recorded, but of somewhat limited musical interest. I had fallen into the habit of using these for evaluating my system, but wouldn't ever play these for the sheer joy of hearing boring music. Completely unconsciously, I was cuing my wife that Something Changed and that I was Seriously Evaluating. And being that she liked to say things that made me happy because of the positive feedback to her, her response to those two cuts was to say something nice about the sound. Nothing conscious on either of our parts, mind you, just a lovely *folie a deux* that happens far more often than many of us would be comfortable to admit.

The point of this is that, even when you've been careful to hide the obvious variables, there are ways of cueing others, even when they can't explicitly see what's being changed (5). Beware the unintended variable!

For this reason, a valid test will be double blind, that is, any persons in the presence of the listener need to also be unaware of what among the choices is being heard. The experimenter can easily cue the listener with neither of them being consciously aware. If components are manually switched in and out of a system, it has to be either done out of sight of the listener, or the listener has to exit the room while it's being done. Naturally, the person doing the switching will need to leave the room before the listener returns.

3c. Timing

When equipment is interchanged, time is of the essence. This has two meanings- first, the human auditory memory is rather short. If it takes 20 minutes of fiddling to change from one component to another, your memory of the first component will be quite imperfect. Your mood may subtly change,

the barometric pressure may change... it's important to try to keep switching time as fast as possible for any direct comparison testing.

The second meaning is a bit more subtle. Say I'm comparing component A to component B. For each trial, my assistant randomizes what I'm listening to. If it's truly random, half the time, the next presentation will be the same as the last, i.e., A will change to to A, half the time the next presentation will be different, i.e., A will change to B. If the assistant takes 10 seconds to determine that there's no change needed, but 2 minutes to change something, I can tell whether or not there's been a change from the time lag. This is a bit of an extreme case, but in order to prevent more subtle non-auditory cueing, the assistant should actually disconnect and re-connect A (or B) even when the next presentation is unchanged from the last. Besides eliminating the timing cue, the other salutary side effect of this procedure is to ensure that any switch contacts or jacks/plugs are continually exercised.

3d. Level

There are lots of ways to consciously or unconsciously bias a listening test. I've run across several of them... A favorite trick in hifi showrooms is level. Curiously, small differences in level (<1dB) are not generally perceived as such. Our ear/brain tells us that the slightly louder choice sounds "clearer," "more open," or a similar descriptor. It doesn't take much for sensitive listeners- some people can detect level changes as low as 0.1dB. So the salesman confidently offers the potential customer a switch-box and tells him to compare the cheap hifi component with the more expensive one (which the salesman has judged that this mark can afford). The level on the more expensive unit is just a wee bit higher. Aided by the salesman's encouragement, the more expensive unit DOES sound better and the checkbook is opened.

As designers and experimenters, we don't want that simple variable to interfere with what we're looking for. So it's best to match levels to the limits of what expert listeners can hear lest you fall for your own inadvertent sales pitch. It's fine to make comparisons where you can change the volume, but the volume of both components being compared for sound needs to be varied simultaneously and equally- no matter what the system volume, the volume of the two components be matched. The same goes for frequency response- often, this is an effect of component changes and should be measured before doing any listening tests. If the test is to determine audibility of something other than a frequency response or level change, these should be equalized before beginning the controlled subjective trials.

3e. Miscellaneous

A particularly amusing cue, which actually WAS sonic (though not as intended) was related by Professor Stanley Lipshitz (6). In this experiment, a first generation digital processor (Sony F1) was inserted into an audio circuit and compared to a bypass using a relay-driven switching box (7). The test listener, who was a prominent critic of digital audio (and just happened to be a manufacturer of turntables) couldn't hear the difference with the Sony in or out of the circuit. Lipshitz could, detect-

ing a small change in the background noise- and that's absolutely a valid and audible difference. Lip-shitz's colleague noticed one other thing, which in a sense was an auditory clue- the relays that switched between the Sony and the bypass were located in different positions on their chassis and thus made a slightly different sounding "click" when they opened and closed. He could then tell which unit was switched in when there was no music playing by switching back and forth and listening to the different tones of the clicks. Oops.

4. Test Formats

It is important to keep terminology straight- many audiophiles casually interchange terms like "dou-ble blind test," "objective evaluation," and "ABX" despite these terms having very different meaning. As we discussed above, any valid test of audibility (a subjective phenomenon) needs to be controlled for non-auditory cueing, and that generally means double blind. Double blind listening tests are both subjective and objective- if you can subjectively distinguish A from B ten times in a row, you have objectively demonstrated that they subjectively sound different (the converse is not true- can you see why?). Double blind tests can be done in many different formats, not just the well-known ABX- we will outline a few of them.

This would be an appropriate place to talk about statistics, but I won't. There are some excellent treat-ments of the basic statistics needed for test design in about a million textbooks. A particularly good online treatment applied to listening tests is given in Reference (4). In fact, the entire site is well worth reading. In a nutshell, a single positive result means very little, usually no more than a single coin flip. Two positive results means more, two hundred mean a LOT more. The choice of the number of repeated trials is a tradeoff between fatigue factor of the listener and the desired certainty. In most sensory work, the number of trials and required number of correct answers is chosen to give a 95% confidence that the results are not due to pure chance. For example, if the chances of a correct an-swer purely by chance are 50% for each trial (like coin flips), a set of 10 trials will require 8 correct to have a 95% chance of being other than random (actually, it's slightly less than 95%; 9 out of 10 cor-rect means that it's 99% likely that the results are not due to chance). An excellent set of calculators for a variety of test setups may be found at www.stattrek.com.

One side note: statistics of large groups mean that if you have 100 people making random guesses, the chances are good that at least one or two people will get 9 or 10 out of 10, even if there is no au-dible difference. Similarly, if listeners are biased to want to hear differences (very common among au-diophiles!), it is very important that the test statistics account for that fact if a test is structured for people to guess "same" or "different," they will prefer "different," even absent any differences. This is not a problem for other test configurations.

4a. ABX

In the ABX test format, the two different devices to be compared are labeled as A and B and con-nected to some sort of switch box. The listener is free to switch between A and B to get a handle on any sonic differences. The third switch position is X- randomly chosen to be either A or B. The job of

the listener is to determine whether X is A or B. The test can be structured in many ways- the listener should always have switching control, and can have control of volume, source material. There is no inherent reason why the listening and judgment need to be rapid- with proper controls in place, they can extend over days or weeks, if you desire.

There have been commercial hardware implementations of the ABX tests (7), which have been used to demonstrate high listener sensitivity to minor changes in level, frequency response, absolute polarity, and phase shift (6, 7). Although some have objected to the use of this particular hardware implementation, there has been no demonstration that their inability to distinguish particular electronics is due to a flaw in the Clark hardware rather than the possibility that they indeed cannot distinguish between the electronic devices under test. Nonetheless, if a particular hardware implementation of the ABX test is found wanting, it is not difficult to construct an ABX box with whatever switches or relays are deemed adequate for audiophile use. After all, the signal in an audio system has passed through many switch and/or relay contacts during recording and mastering, and most audio systems have source selector switches. More on this below.

An important point to note is that in each trial, the chances of correct identification even if the two choices are indistinguishable is 50%. Hence, multiple trials are needed to achieve any sort of significance. The more trials, the better for the statistics, but worse for the listener- once the interesting aspect of the listening test has passed, the test can easily become drudgery, and subjects get easily bored.

4b. Triangle
The triangle test is very commonly used in organoleptic (smell and taste) analysis and is nearly universal in wine evaluation. In a triangle test, the listener is presented with three choices, A, B, and C. Much like the old Sesame Street song, "One of These Things is Not Like the Others," two of the choices are the same, one is different. The listener must choose which of the choices is the odd man out. One advantage to this method is that it is statistically more powerful than ABX, that is, it takes fewer trials to establish significance. It should be used more in audio, but it isn't.

4c. Paired Forced Choice
The Forced Choice is a powerful and effective tool for determining thresholds of subjective perceptions by basing the next presentation on the outcome of the last one rather than randomizing. It typically requires a low number of trials to achieve significance, but does require some dedicated assistance- keeping in mind, of course, the need for double-blind (unless your name is Hans). It's best to use for situations where the test component is inexpensive or can be easily duplicated. It's the first choice if the sensory variable under test is amenable to software simulation (e.g., level, frequency response, distortion, compression). An example to illustrate the use of Paired Forced Choice is given below.

4d. Sorting

This is most useful for phenomena which can be captured on digital files or can be easily replicated. There is a population comprising two different sorts, A and B. The listener needs to separate the population into two piles. The number of A and B in any population needn't be equal. We show an example of how this is done below.

5. Hardware Solutions

5a. Case Study: Coupling Capacitors

The dielectric materials and construction of coupling caps gives audiophiles nightmares- or more cynically, a way of entertaining themselves for years. By and large, measurements have shown that one can measure differences between capacitor types in very particular applications, for example, high current or DC timing (8). How well do these measured differences translate into audible performance of coupling caps, where DC accuracy is not an issue and currents are low? Do hyper-expensive "audiophile" caps actually improve the sound? Can you even hear the difference between a super capacitor and a cheap piece of junk in that position?

This was a question on my mind and led to the construction of the Bastard Box, the schematic for which is shown in **Figure 1**. Basically, the Box is a method of doing a double blind comparison be-

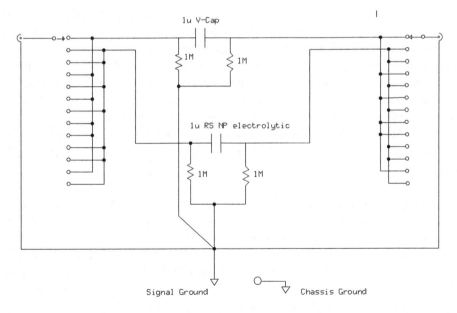

Figure 1. The Bastard Box. In this configuration, Position 1 is a V-Cap Teflon, Position 2 is a Radio Shack electrolytic, and positions 3 through 14 are randomized.

tween two types of capacitors without worrying about level matching, allowing the listener to choose source material, switching times, and can be easily inserted into nearly any sound system at line level. The Box comprises a pair of high pass filters with the same cutoff frequency allowing different capacitor types to be auditioned with a constant frequency response and level. To make the comparison as easy as possible, the two capacitor types being compared were a very high priced Teflon dielectric capacitor (V-Cap TFTF, about $300 each) and a cheap bipolar electrolytic (Radio Shack, about $1). The caps were confirmed to be within 5% of nominal value- matching COULD be tighter, but it's doubtful that the minor changes in frequency response at subsonic frequencies will be audible. The values given here are chosen to be compatible with my power amplifier's input impedance, 100k. With the values shown here, the 3dB down frequency is roughly 2 Hz, low enough to prevent excessive phase shift at the low frequency limits of my system (20 Hz).

The box is fitted with premium RCA plugs for input and output, is wired with audiophile-approved silver wire insulated with Teflon, and internal connections soldered using silver-bearing solder. The switch is a massive Cinema Engineering 14 position three pole rotary switch, with silver contacts and a leaf-spring washer. Overkill for sure, but you don't want to have poor quality switch contacts obscure the differences we want to listen for. The resistors diminish the tendency for clicks and pops to occur when switching and perhaps inadvertently cue the listener.

In this circuit, position 1 (A) corresponds to the V-Cap in series with the signal. Position 2 (B) corresponds to the cheap electrolytic in series with the signal. The next 12 positions of the switch (X) are randomized- I used coin flips to determine which of the two capacitors would be switched in-circuit for each switch position, then wired accordingly. The schematic as shown can be (and should be) modified to reflect whatever random sequence you come up with. Coin flips work well for this; an electronic version may be accessed at http://random.org/coins. Another way to get a random sequence for A and B of length n is to go to a table of the decimal places of pi (or some other transcendental number), pick a spot at random, then for the next n numbers, assign even to A and odd to B. Note that doing a randomization by arbitrarily picking "A" or "B" is not as good- humans feel that having too many As or Bs together spoils the randomness. Yet Nature is just as likely to pick an A following an A as it is to pick a B following an A.

If you're trying to test your own perception, have a Trusty Assistant connect the randomized positions in your absence and keep a key sheet. You now have all the time you like to try to determine the identity of each switch position. Record the guesses, then hand your score sheet to your Trusty Assistant. A little bit of statistical crunching and you'll soon know if you really could hear a difference. The test box can just as easily be configured for a triangle test by having positions 3, 4, and 5 be one triangle, 5, 6, and 7 be another, and so on. The box can also be used in a sorting mode where the listener groups the sonic impressions of the different switch positions.

Can the presence of the switchbox (switch contacts, extra interconnect, plugs and jacks) obscure the differences one is trying to hear? To determine this, before installing the capacitors, I wired several

of the positions directly with a short length of silver wire. This put all of the "extras" into the signal path, other than the capacitors. I manually connected and disconnected the box between my pre-amp and power amp. There was no difference that I could hear. If you do the same and think that connecting the switchbox is degrading the sound, this can be easily confirmed with the help of the Trusty Assistant. Arrange some sort of visual barrier so that you cannot see whether or not the switchbox is present. Leave the room. Have Trusty Assistant flip a coin- if it's heads, he should connect the box, if it's tails, he should bypass it. After a predetermined time (4 or 5 minutes is usually more than adequate), he should exit the room and you can return. Can you hear the degradation? Mark a scoresheet, then repeat the process several times. If indeed you can identify the presence of the box, you can try to determine where the malfunction is and correct it.

I spent a week playing with this setup comparing capacitors and marked my scoresheets. I scored 7 out of 12 correct identifications. I'll be interested to see if others can do better.

One interesting variation of this test involves only changing the variable in one channel of a stereo pair, leaving it fixed in the other. Our ear/brain is highly sensitive to localization (the direction the sabertooth tiger is coming from is important to know in order to prevent being eaten)- if two channels in a stereo setup are not perfectly symmetrical, the image or soundstage can be smeared from its intended position- in some cases, an instrument's location can seem to wander depending on the note being played. To look at this effect, the Bastard Box was wired to have just the V-Cap in one channel and switch between the V-Cap and the electrolytic in the other. My score was 8 out of 12- a little better than before, not quite at the point of significance, but close enough that I want to try this again. The use of switching presentations in one channel only to take advantage of localization abilities is another ripe area for designers and experimenters to play with.

5b. Paired Forced Choice Case Study: The Audibility of Op Amp Buffers
This case study illuminates an interesting technique in sensory analysis, the Paired Forced Choice.

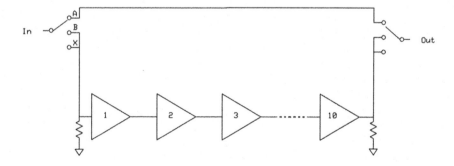

Figure 2. Buffer Test Circuit. Position A is a straight wire, Position B is a chain of up to ten buffers, and Position X is randomized. In the shown configuration, Position X selects the chain of buffers.

I was interested in using an IC op amp in unity gain mode as a buffer in a mike preamp that I was building. I admit to a bit of a bias against them- they're seemingly too perfect and definitely too easy. Would it foul the sound to my ears? I enlisted a Trusty Assistant and proceeded to find out. I put together a simple prototype circuit, then built nine more! Placing all ten in series between my preamp and power amp, I fed music into the input and listened to the output compared to a wire bypass around the chain of buffers - I was certain there was a difference! To confirm that I did, we wired up a three position switch as shown in **Figure 2**. As before, A was the chain of buffers, B was the straight wire bypass, and X was one of the two (I did not know which in advance). It was easy to identify X by ear.

Trusty Assistant then removed one buffer from the chain, leaving nine connected in series, then re-randomized X by a coin flip. Again, no problem identifying which was which by ear. Trusty Assistant then removed one more buffer, leaving eight. Harder this time, but I got the right answer. Trusty Assistant, not surprisingly, removed one more buffer, leaving seven. This time, I guessed wrong. Trusty Assistant added the last buffer back, bringing it back to eight. I guessed right. Back to seven, I guessed right, so we went back to six. I guessed right. Down to five. Wrong. Back to six, right. Down to five, right, down to four, wrong. Back to five wrong. Back to six, right. A diagram of these trials is shown in **Figure 3**.

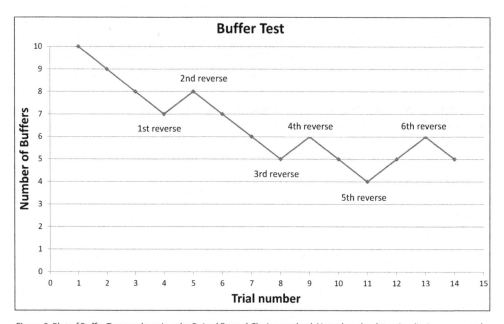

Figure 3. Plot of Buffer Test results using the Paired Forced Choice method. Note that the detection limit appears to be somewhere around 5 buffers in the chain.

I think you can see the pattern- every time I guessed right, the number of buffers was reduced, when I guessed wrong, the number was increased. By prior agreement, we decided to end the test when the direction of the addition/removal of the buffers changed six times or until we ran out of buffers to remove. So if, for example, I could reliably detect a single buffer, that would end the test. If I were able to reliably identify the presence of six buffers, but couldn't reliably identify five, my answers around five buffers would be random and thus frequently switch directions (analogous to a random walk!).

In this case, my threshold seemed to be somewhere around six buffers. So I felt pretty safe using just one in the signal path. As a reward for the first reader to guess what I heard and how I identified the buffers, I'm offering a free, autographed portrait of Joe M. Varilla.

This shows the usefulness of Forced Choice in getting information beyond "can/can't hear" with a relatively small number of tests.

5c. Listening Time Case Study: Preamplifiers

One commonly made assertion is that Technology X (fill in the blank with your favorite) reduces listener fatigue. The audiophile spends more time listening and is more relaxed. This is not something that will be captured in a relatively short conventional blind test. I had two line stages on hand which seemed like they would be good candidates for such a test- their measurements were excellent and in a short A/B sighted comparison, I couldn't tell them apart. I also had some surplus hour meters, similar to what one finds on industrial equipment to let the operator know how many hours the equipment had been in service (useful for periodic maintenance). At the start of every listening session, an electronic coin flipper (bought as a science fair kit) activated a relay which switched the signal through one or the other of the line stages- the volume control was common to both and under my control. Each linestage got its own hour meter to measure how long it was used.

I left this set up for about two months, then read the meters. One had about 15% greater elapsed time than the other. Is that significant? I don't think so, but this is a rich area for experimentation (several approaches to a hedonic measurement come to mind), and I would love to hear about your results if you try something like this.

5d. Sorting Case Study: Wire Directionality

This was quite a fun one, but with no resolution so far. Nonetheless, the test setup is instructive. A question arose about the audibility of the direction in which a standard coaxial interconnect was connected. Conventional engineering would have it that for audio signals, the interconnect "direction" should have no effect. Yet reports persist that this might not be the case. One person in particular was insistent that reversals of interconnects were clearly and ambiguously audible.

A reel of coaxial wire was obtained and ten interconnects were assembled using standard RCA connectors. The interconnects were labeled individually and the direction of the cable with respect to the winding direction of the reel was noted for each interconnect. One end of each interconnect was randomly marked and a key sheet was kept as to whether the mark was on the "leading" or "trailing"

end. The interconnects were then sent to the listener to sort. Unfortunately, the listener decided not to proceed with the test, so this one is still ripe. I can say that I can't hear any difference with wire or cable direction, but if someone can sort them in a test like this, it may well be an issue worth considering.

6.   Software Solutions

If the presentations are amenable to digitization (for example, the effects of EQ or compression), then .wav files can be conveniently compared in an ABX format using the foobar2000 media player (available for download at www.foobar2000.org). This is an amazingly convenient way to do double blind comparisons!

7. Wrap-Up

If you think you hear a difference between two things and want to KNOW that you or your audio buddies really are hearing something, and then use that knowledge to optimize the sonic aspect of your designs, controlled subjective testing lets you isolate the sonics. The oft-heard canards ("There's test pressure!" "The switchboxes are no good!" "The switching is too rapid!" "The reference systems suck!") which are used to object to trusting ones ears are easily accounted for- IF the designer or experimenter wants to. Doing a controlled subjective test is relatively simple, inexpensive, and usually needs no more than one Trusty Assistant. With only a moderate effort and expenditure, a designer can quickly get good actionable data.

References:

(1) Randi, James. 1982. "Flim-Flam" Prometheus Books.

(2) Proctor, Philip; Austin, Phil; Bergman, Peter and Ossman, Dave. 1970. "Don't Crush That Dwarf, Hand Me the Pliers," Columbia C 30102.

(3) Toole, Floyd. 2008. "Sound Reproduction: The Acoustics and Psychoacoustics of Loudspeakers and Rooms," Elsevier.

(4) Martin, Geoff. 2011. "Introduction to Sound Recording," available through www.tonmeister.ca; Lipshitz, Stanley and Vanderkooy, J. 1981. "The Great Debate: Subjective Evaluation", J. Audio Eng. Soc., Vol. 29 (July/Aug.), pp. 482-491.

(5) Rosenthal, Robert. 1998. "Covert Communication in Classrooms, Clinics, and Courtrooms," Eye on Psi Chi. Vol. 3, No. 1, pp. 18-22.

(6) Lipshitz, Stanley. 1984. "The Digital Challenge: A Report" BAS Speaker Aug.-Sept., available at http://www.bostonaudiosociety.org/bas_speaker/abx_testing2.htm.

(7) Clark, David. 1982. "High-Resolution Subjective Testing Using a Double-Blind Comparator", J. Audio Eng. Soc., Vol. 30 (May), pp. 330-338.

(8) See, for example, Grant, Doug and Wurcer, Scott. "Avoiding Passive Component Pitfalls," Analog Devices Application Note AN-348.

Book review - The design of Active Crossovers

Kendall Castor-Perry

The design of Active Crossovers – Douglas Self. Focal Press(Oxford, England, UK, www.elsevier.com), 2011. Paperback, 579 pages, ISBN 978-0-240-81738-5. $69.95

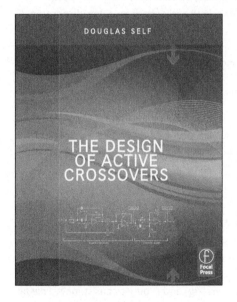

Until I heard of this volume, it had never occurred to me that until now, there's never been a book concentrating on active crossover design for loudspeakers. The discipline requires a combined understanding of loudspeaker principles, audio circuit design and filter theory. This book almost manages to combine all three; I'll explain the 'almost' later.

For busy executives who don't want to read to the end of the review, here's the summary right away. This substantial book is a significant and worthy addition to Doug Self's oeuvre (I'll refer to him henceforth as DS because 'Doug' is over-familiar and yet 'Self' seems too formal). It's an important contribution to the field of practical, very high performance analogue signal path design, and contains plenty of original observations. DS's dry wit carries the material along and fans of his previous work won't be disappointed. The occasional topical overlap with his other books is essential to get a good 'flow' in this one. Anyone whose job or passion involves making high quality audio, industrial or scientific signal-processing equipment with a deliberately non-flat frequency response should get a copy of this book. And if you don't know that much about loudspeaker principles, the early chapters of the book make a good introduction.

The book concentrates on active realizations of crossover filters. There isn't much here to help someone interested in either a wholly passive or a wholly digital solution. That's not a criticism of the book; DS's strength is in active analogue system design. The analogue approach shouldn't be dis-

missed as somehow outmoded by modern digital techniques. DS extracts such good signal path performance from his realizations that it will prove surprisingly non-trivial to replicate that quality in a digital system, whose performance can be limited not only by the converters but also by numerical issues in the digital filter clockwork itself. DS misses a minor opportunity here to blow the trumpet for the potential advantages of good active filter realizations over mediocre digital ones.

The book shows why, when compared to the prevailing passive approach, active filter techniques make it easier to distribute the audio signal between multiple loudspeaker drive units in a precise and well-defined way, accommodating myriad driver and diffraction response artefacts. The book seems to represent a personal voyage of discovery in a previously poorly-charted land, leading to a 'Holy Grail' of a high quality active crossover-plus-amplifier ecosystem for delivering super-high-quality home and pro audio. As those with long memories will recall, this idea has fired the imaginations of many, yet sadly has filled the cash registers of very few. One factor might be that the more complex forms of crossover, with careful equalization for tonal neutrality and monitor-standard accuracy, represent an approach to loudspeaker sound that hasn't been in the ascendant for a decade or more. If you're a loudspeaker builder of the persuasion that the pinnacle of speaker musicality is reached only when the crossover has been reduced to a single capacitor (or less), then you'll not find so much traction in the more sophisticated currents flowing in DS's book.

Most high performance active crossovers go into 'professional' applications, chiefly sound reinforcement. Engineers in companies responsible for such equipment will be much more familiar with the issues that DS systematically addresses and resolves throughout the book. In fact, they might be a bit miffed that reference-quality implementations (including a completely engineered design for a comprehensive 3-way crossover) are now available to all their peers and competitors. This book will certainly level the playing field amongst suppliers of high quality analogue crossover equipment.

DS points out that the book is not intended to be a filter design or theory textbook. I'd concur with this; think of it as a combination of best-practice circuit design handbook and filter 'cookbook', with recipes that you need only follow carefully, not understand in principle. DS applies his expertise in audio signal path design to the inevitable input, output and power issues faced when building active crossovers to the highest standards of headroom, linearity and product consistency. Like all good cookbooks, a lot of diligent experimentation went into it; true enthusiasts will find the plentiful Audio Precision plots just as mouthwatering as a picture of a nice pie. Though as a long-time filter designer, I'm a two-pie man myself...

Content-wise, there's a lot of material here, including some very welcome new work not reported before. The tables of designs for highpass and lowpass filters with practical component ratios are handy cookbook material. Responses from first order through to fourth order are covered systematically and comprehensively, for both common and unusual response alignments (including the effects of deliberate frequency misalignment). DS embraces the Sallen & Key architecture here, and

explores it in more pragmatic, user-oriented detail than you'll find anywhere else. Amplifier selection for low-gain non-inverting (especially unity-gain follower) applications, under high signal, heavy load applications is carefully scrutinized. The signal path performance of some less frequently used blocks such as allpass networks and biquad equalizers is also examined, and their use in correcting both frequency and time response artefacts due to driver placement and baffle design is outlined.

DS has been doing valuable work on passive component imperfections for some years now. Frequency-selective networks impose extra complexity here, and the investigation into filter distortion contribution from capacitor dielectrics is fresh and new, and relevant to equipment designers whether they use APs or ears to make their performance assessments.

I'll wind up with a handful of well-meant criticisms. Firstly, DS's determination not to sully the book with any significant amount of maths or filter theory robs the material of some of its deeper elegance and symmetry. I really do believe that understanding some simple manipulations of frequency response functions, with just enough complex arithmetic and algebra, elevates filter design from cookbook empiricism to a proper quantitative discipline. Without the math, the central section on filtering functions does lapse into a rather lengthy catalogue of simulation graphs and parameter tables indexed by the names of dead mathematicians. This material is still interesting and of practical value, but it's less conceptually manageable without some kind of analytical context. Just my personal view, of course. The literature on filters is ancient and obscure; I'll send DS some technical paper references that shine additional light on some of the questions he raises in the book.

Secondly, DS just occasionally lapses into handwaving – a habit he so rightly excoriates others for indulging in. One gets so used to him supporting his assertions rigorously, with simulation, measurement or both, that it sticks out when he leaves it at "X probably results in Y", without testing the assertion. I noticed it in the section on higher-order filters that use a single low-gain amplifier. The noise behaviour of these circuits has some non-intuitive aspects, and saving amplifiers this way can sometimes increase the total noise and distortion. Noise simulation of active filters in SPICE can quickly compare the different configurations, and I wondered why DS sometimes doesn't do it. So much simulation and measurement has gone into this book, though, that lack of time is a fine excuse for such small omissions. In the first edition, anyway.

Lastly, the material on statistical improvement of component tolerance is great, and novel as far as I'm aware. I'm a bit bothered about DS's use of the term 'accuracy' when what he really means is 'precision'; but I'm being picky. This is a diligent, useful and fascinating book, clearly a labour of love by DS, and it will advance the state of the art in active crossover implementation. And if it kick-starts a standardization revolution leading to multi-manufacturer compatibility for connectors and levels in active loudspeakers, we will all have some filtering and listening fun to look forward to!

Book review – Fundamental Amplifier Techniques with Electron Tubes

Guido Tent

Fundamental Amplifier Techniques with Electron Tubes - Rudolf Moers. Elektor International Media BV (Susteren, The Netherlands, www.elektor.com), 2010. Hardcover, 821 pages, ISBN 978-0-905705-93-4. £ 65.00

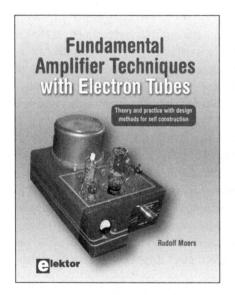

I discovered Rudolf's book about a year ago. I didn't know Rudolf personally but over 800 pages of valve technology sounded fascinating; who was this man who must have spent hundreds of evenings working on such a major undertaking?

Eventually we met at the European Triode Festival 2010, at Stella Plage, France. Rudolf presented a lecture about the ultra linear output stage, which came as a shock to some people at a Triode Fest, since such circuits are based on pentodes! Nevertheless he shared knowledge that was highly interesting, and new to me and many others in the audience.

Later, Rudolf and I got a beer and started to talk. Co-incidentally, he lives in the same town as I do, and, while bicycling to his work, passes the street where my lab is located. His regular job by the way is at chip machine maker ASML, where he leads an electronic development group. One of the members of that group is a good friend of mine; it is small world after all.....

So, what do you do when Jan (Didden) asks you to review an 800 pages thick book? It is exhausting and boring to do that page by page. Moreover, many topics covered by Rudolf are also addressed in other books, although often with a different approach. To start at the end: Moers' book is interesting and worthwhile and I'd recommend you buy it. It is not a beginner's book, and contains quite some

math. This math is not always required to obtain insight in most issues, but Rudolfs' approach is interesting, because he looks at issues in a different way than is usually done. He is an electronics engineer, not a tube dude. Rudolf often takes the hard route, which not always helps in keeping focus to the original problem. Nevertheless some of his results are fascinating, so do keep reading.

Moers starts in chapter 1 with an introduction, application areas and a short history of tubes. He discusses coding of European types and concludes that there is little logic in the American type numbering systems (the same, unfortunately, holds for American and Japanese transistors).

Chapter 2 describes principles of emission. Chapter 3 describes the diode, instructions on how to measure the characteristics and applications like rectifiers and filtering techniques for power supplies. It is quite impressive to note that all power supply filters described are supported by maths to carry out your own calculations. This may look a bit silly in the days of Spice or Duncan's PSUD, but the insight gained by calculating makes you understand what is going on (or what is wrong). An extensive setup with a very experimental power transformer enabled Moers to measure and verify all the maths.

Chapter 3 also describes heater, filament and negative bias supplies, and comes along with some practical hints for their use.

Next are triodes. Chapter 4 describes directly and indirectly heated types, their typical operation and discusses the Child-Langmuir equation. As you would expect, Moers shows a test circuit to obtain triode characteristics. He is very clear about the island effect, which is responsible for the triode cutting off later than expected. Thank you. After that, Mu, gm and Ri are introduced and explained. Then on to dynamic properties, with a resistor placed in series with the anode. Truly interesting are his "power analysis" methods, giving a clear insight in efficiency.

In chapter 4.5, Rudolf makes a side step and deals with the influence of the filament supply current on the anode current. I've published about this quite a while ago; this is the second publication on this subject I've seen. Also, his conclusions (feed filaments with a high impedance source) are the same: Chapeau!

Chapter 4 continues with most popular triode circuits, extensively I should say. As you may expect by now, Rudolf's maths keeps supporting all the circuits he discusses.

Now that all the basic circuits are understood, the various types of phase shifters follow next. He finishes this chapter discussing output stages and transformers. Getting close to the loudspeaker, so to speak, he touches on the damping factor, and this is one area where I do not agree with him.

Triode output stages are dealt with in a great extend. Over a 100 pages cover principles, calculations, measurements, handy examples and test circuits.

It is no surprise that chapter 5 discusses tetrodes.

Chapter 6 covers pentodes. To me, this is the most valueable part of the book. Over 200 pages are dedicated to this type of tube. He starts like any textbook, explains how pentodes work, and describes the functionallity of the grids, based on earlier explanations of triodes and tetrodes.

Then, he encourages the reader to measure the transfer characteristics of an EF86. To me this is excellent advice. I did so about 30 years ago when looking for curves for an ECC83. By assembling the curves yourself, you directly see the influence of the various grid voltages, affecting the anode- and G2 current.

Rudolf treats the mu stage in this chapter, likely because he uses pentodes for it. I do not agree with his conclusion about the performance of such stages and see that his implementation (figure 6.60) suffers from unneccesary loading of the output. A current source instead of R_{g2} would improve the circuit, but anyhow, cascoding as done using the upper EF86 is healthy.

Chapter 6.10 deals with the ultra linear amplifier. This analysis is *the* most interesting topic of the whole book. Look at the straight line in figure 6.114. I later learned that Rudolf will threat this subject in this issue of Linear Audio as well, and rightly so: this is serious and very enlightening stuff! (*See "The Ultra-Linear Power Amplifier - An adventure between triode and pentode" elsewhere in this issue – ed.*).

Chapter 7 describes the frequency depending behaviour of components and circuits. After a thorough introduction, passive components are measured, where I suspect a measurement error as I do not trust the measured results of inductive behaviour of resistors. As Morgan Jones put it: "you need an awfull lot of inductance to get a rising impedance from a 10k resistor" and he is right: at 20kHz, that is 70uH, say the equivalent of 70cm straight wire. Nevertheless the point is made: Passive components do have frequency dependant behaviour.

Non-linear distortion and noise are dealt with in chapter 8. His noise analysis is confusing, but the harmonic analysis of electron tubes is fine. In chapter 8.6.4 he shows that distortion depends on anode loading: it's a pity that his spectrum analyser was not running parallel to his thd meter while carrying out the measurement; figure 8.36 shows a near null for an EF86 loaded with 100k-ohm. That may be interesting as "the" operating point, but it is not in terms of harmonic spectra; at that point 2nd is nearly cancelled, but 3rd dominates. Some fine homework for the serious reader of this book: go for it as it explains a lot about the sound of such gain stages.

Chapter 9 describes negative feedback. In chapter 10, the reader is finally allowed to construct an amplifier ("the construction of electron tube amplifiers "). I have to say that this chapter is quite thin, compared to the others. One could conclude that it doesn't do the subtitle of this book "Theory and practice with design methods for self construction" enough justice.

In conclusion

I could be nitpicking on the use of the English language and some wording like *steepness* where *slope* should be used; and figures that are clearly from the previous century. Nevertheless, all can and will be forgiven as it does not diminish the importance and impact of this book. One should anyway leave room for improvement and extending chapter 10 may even bring the page count above 1000, which could be a real challenge for the next edition!

To me chapter 6 about the pentode and the analysis of its ultra-linear application are the most interesting parts of this book. Isn't it wonderful to see that the pentode (invented in our home town of Eindhoven) gets such attention after 90 years?

I own many of the books Moers refers to, especially the ones written by the old Philips engineers (Deketh cs). But Rudolf's book is a very worthwhile addition, and it will have a prominent place in my library. Recommended!

Made in the USA
Coppell, TX
28 February 2021